Transforming Community

Stories of Connection Through the Lens of Relational-Cultural Theory

Edited by
CONNIE GUNDERSON, PhD, LISW
DOROTHY GRAFF, PhD, LICSW
KAREN CRADDOCK, PhD, EdM

WholePerson
Mental Health & Wellness
publisher of therapy, counseling, and self-help resources

Duluth, Minnesota

publisher of therapy, counseling, and self-help resources

101 West 2nd Street, Suite 203
Duluth, MN 55802

800-247-6789

Books@WholePerson.com
WholePerson.com

Transforming Community
Stories of Connection Through the Lens of Relational-Cultural Theory

Printed in the United States of America

10 9 8 7 6 5 4 3 2 1

Editor: Peg Johnson
Art Director: Mathew Pawlak
Cover Artwork: Carl Gawboy

Library of Congress Control Number: 2017956355
ISBN:978-157025-355-3

Table of Contents

──────────── ···■■■··· ────────────

Table of Contents

———————— · · · ■ ■ ■ · · · ————————

Table of Contents

··· ■ ■ ■ ···

Table of Contents

—————————— ···■■■··· ——————————

About the Editors

--- • • • ■ ■ ■ • • • ---

Connie Gunderson, PhD, LISW, is an associate professor
at The College of St. Scholastica. Having completed her
undergraduate studies at The College of St. Scholastica, she
worked in Germany until 2012. She completed her MSW in
clinical social work practice at the Alice Salomon Hochschule
in Berlin, Germany and received her PhD from the University
of Bremen, in Bremen, Germany. She maintains advisory
partnerships with universities and colleges in Europe. Her
areas of scholarship and research include women, trauma
and addiction, human trafficking, intercultural education, and
international social work. In 2006 and 2008, she organized
international symposiums in Bremen and Berlin to address
gender responsive trauma and addiction recovery models. In
2012, she organized an international conference in Hildesheim,
Germany to address human trafficking from a Relational-
Cultural perspective. In 2016, in collaboration with The
College of St. Scholastica, the Jean Baker Miller Training
Institute and Wellesley Centers for Women, she coordinated
the Transforming Community: The Radical Reality of
Relationship Conference. Dr. Gunderson has edited and
published numerous books and articles to address social issues
including trauma and addiction, human trafficking, diversity,
and gender.

Dorothy Graff, PhD, LICSW, worked in New York for over 10
years as a clinical social worker with individuals, couples,
families, and groups whose ages ranged from young children
to seniors. She received her PhD in social work from the
University of Texas in Austin and has taught in social work
programs both in Texas and Minnesota for over 16 years.

Most recently she taught for 10 years at The College of St. Scholastica—initially in their BSW program and then helped to develop as well as teach in their new MSW program. She has presented her research in international, national, and local conferences and has been published in a variety of professional journals.

Karen T. Craddock PhD, EdM is an Applied Psychologist concentrating on the socio-cultural context and relational frameworks associated with human development, social capital, equity, and capacity building across sectors and specifically within racially and ethno-culturally diverse communities. Using the lens of psycho-social functioning and intersectionality, she explores resistance to marginalization, mothering/women studies, systems of care, social-emotional learning, trauma-healing paradigms, and the relational-neurophysiology of inclusion. She is the Director of Strategic Initiatives and Network Engagement at EmbraceRace and founder of KCollaborative Connections, a relationship-based consultation and coaching practice. She has led research, presenting nationally and internationally, held senior administrative roles at Harvard University and Education Development Center, lectured at Tufts University and is a lead scholar of Relational-Cultural Theory and Social Action at JBTI Center for Relational-Cultural Growth. Karen is an editor of the volume *Black Motherhood(s): Contours, Contexts and Considerations,* developer of the analytical framework "Profiles of Resistance to Marginalization" and co-lead of an action research team exploring optimal forms of resistance that build resilience and wellness, primarily for women of color. She earned her EdM in Human Development and Psychology from Harvard University and a PhD in Applied Developmental Psychology from Tufts University.

Acknowledgments

—————— · · · ■ ■ ■ · · · ——————

CONNIE GUNDERSON, PhD, LISW

As a Benedictine institution, The College of St. Scholastica strives to foster an environment that provides a strong sense of belonging and community where all persons feel welcomed, valued, and respected.

We would like to share our gratitude for the many volunteers who helped to create community during the conference. We express our sincere appreciation for the support of our conference sponsors: The College of St. Scholastica, including the Department of Social Work, and Well-U, the Jean Baker Miller Training Institute, Wellesley Centers for Women, The Irene Stiver Foundation, the Feminist Theologies Committee of The St. Scholastica Monastery, Essentia Health, The Duluth-Superior Area Community Foundation, Whole Person Associates, the Alworth Center for Peace and Justice, St. Louis County Public Health and Human Services, and private donors.

We would like to recognize the editorial support received from Judith Jordan, Amy Banks, Maureen Walker, and the RCT Writers' Group. Their recommendations and dialogue with the contributors and us have helped to shape this publication.

Thank you, all!

Forward

—————————— · · · ■ ■ ■ · · · ——————————

DOROTHY GRAFF, PhD, LICSW

The *Transforming Community: The Radical Reality of Relationship Conference* on June 9 – 12, 2016, brought together 172 people from 20 states, two provinces in Canada and two countries on other continents. They ranged in ages from teens to those in their 70s and represented a wide range from long-time Relational-Cultural practitioners to students and interested community members.

This book is designed to promote connection through the sharing of ideas in traditional research papers as well as thought provoking narratives, poems, and stories. Authors have also provided a brief personal statement at the beginning of each piece to provide context for their work. Some have provided email addresses to encourage communication with readers and continue the dialogue begun at the Conference.

As at the Conference, this book begins with Maureen Walker's keynote address and concludes with a summary of the dialogue group discussions with Taylor Gunderson's "Taking Action to Transform Community with the Radical Reality of Relationship". The four main sections of Neuroscience and Health Care, Education, Environment, and Social Justice are reflective of the discussion groups convened at the conference.

Introduction

——————————— • • • ■ ■ ■ • • • ———————————

JUDITH JORDAN, PhD

Relational-Cultural theory (RCT) posits that we grow through and toward relationships throughout our lives and that growth-fostering relationships are the source of meaning and empowerment. The Five Good Things (Miller & Stiver, 1997) characterize these "good relationships": (1) zest, (2) clarity, (3) sense if worth, (4) productivity, (5) a desire for more connection. We need connection the way we need air and water. Relationships are central to our lives, not secondary or peripheral. Self-interest is a social prescription rather than a biological imperative.

What has come to be known as Relational-Cultural theory was created in the late 1970s by a collaborative group of four women clinicians (Jean Baker Miller, Irene Stiver, Janet Surrey and myself). Foundational to the model was the work of Jean Baker Miller who wrote her best selling book *Toward a New Psychology of Women* in 1976. Seated in Jean's living room in Brookline, Massachusetts, beneath an antique quilt (undoubtedly the creation of several women from another era with a recognizable pleasure in creating something together) these four women came together to better understand clinical practice and the psychology of women. Jean Baker Miller could see the ways in which theories of personality and development, written by men (mostly white, well-educated, straight men), when applied to women, often led to distortions in understanding. Jean invited us to listen to women, to hear their stories, to understand their needs and motivations, to see strengths where others often saw weakness or deficiency. As we tried to represent women's voices we sought to understand the impact of race, culture, sexuality, and sociopolitical power issues. Thus began a re-working of the dominant psychological theories of the time. The journey would take us from a celebration of the Separate Self to an appreciation of the centrality of relationships in our lives. Much to our chagrin, critical feedback from marginalized people pointed to the irony that in trying to describe "woman's voice" we committed the very same hubristic error we had accused male theorists of. We presented our model as if there was one, homogenous voice of women. We have worked hard to listen to and represent the range of experience of women and to move beyond our own white privilege with its incumbent blind-spots (and other sources of unearned advantage such as class, sexual orientation, gender.) We have tried to represent many of the voices of women. We sought to "challenge assumptions of a powerful mythic norm that would define woman as a white, economically privileged, able-bodied, and heterosexual female. Unchallenged, this norm becomes a standard against which all women's existence is interpreted and evaluated" (Jordan, Walker & Hartling, 2004, p.3).

RCT examined the ways in which chronic disconnections from empathically failing and non-responsive relationships early in life get encoded as relational images which shape our expectations for current relationships. Acute disconnections offer opportunities for re-working earlier relational failures; in fact when we can represent our authentic feelings and find respect, responsiveness, and empathic attunement we build trust and a sense of relational competence. When, however, disconnections are disregarded and a person is treated as if he or she doesn't matter, she learns to twist herself to fit in to the relationships with powerful others in her life (e.g. parents for children; bosses for employees). The misunderstood individual becomes less and less authentic, mutuality ebbs, and the disconnection becomes chronic. In such situations we see depression, low energy, confusion, immobilization, isolating, self-blame; the opposite of The Five Good Things of zest, worth, clarity, productivity, and desire for more connection.

Traditional models of psychological growth at the time that we began our theory building (late 1970s) emphasized that humans move from dependence to independence; that the goal of healthy development is to be able to stand on your own two feet, to be independent, to be rational and autonomous. Unrealistic standards for adulthood left many people, both men and women, feeling inadequate and ashamed. In many ways, the restrictions placed on boys in terms of emotional vulnerability (necessary for the formation of mutual relationships) and demands for unattainable self-sufficiency (to encourage functioning in a hyper-individualistic society) are deeply destructive for boys (Stone, 2011).

In the last decade, modern neuroscience has validated almost all of the early tenets of Relational-Cultural theory: We need relationships like we need air and water; exclusion and isolation create real pain for people; the brain is wired to register the pain of exclusion in the same way it registers physical pain or absence of water and oxygen. We are simply hardwired to connect. We come into the world with the underpinnings of empathic ability (mirror neurons). Just as we need others for survival, we need to give to others and to participate in the growth of others. This model points to the mutuality of human growth. Our inevitable interdependence provides us with a sense of meaning and belonging. When society sets up expectations that are at odds or clash with our neurobiology, when a connection-seeking being is met with cultural conditioning that valorizes self-sufficiency and standing on your own two feet, emotional stress and physical ill health ensue. Chronic stress, resulting from this mismatch wreaks havoc with our overall well-being. We now know that exclusion and isolation cause pain... real, demonstrable neurobiological pain. We know that there is amazing plasticity in the human brain; we also have learned that empathic attunement alters brain function. We are born with an impulse to connect which is not based only on satisfaction of biological needs. We are hard-wired to connect. We need to engage in and participate in relationships that go beyond just needing others to take care of us or resonate with us. We have a need for mutual empathy, resonance; we need to contribute to others. And we need to build community together.

While this work was quite controversial in the late 1970s, modern neuroscience, with its revealing functional MRIs, has confirmed almost every position put forth regarding the power of connection in people's lives. Social Pain Overlap Theory (SPOT) has demonstrated that the pain of social exclusion (or even the anticipation of exclusion) travels the same neuronal pathways to the same brain area (the anterior cingulate) as physical pain (Eisenberger & Lieberman, 2004). This tells us that relationships are essential to our survival; physical injury and isolation are both wired to demand our attention, to send out survival alarms.

Although initially the model was widely accepted by many female therapists ("It's what I knew in my heart about therapy and people"), other traditional therapists at first overlooked it, then labeled it "dangerous", and later often concluded: "We knew it all along. Relationships heal." While RCT is a relative newcomer to the psychological community, it has gained widespread acceptance, and has engendered a significant amount of research (Jordan, 2010; Jordan, in press). The American Psychological Association invited RCT into its "Psychotherapy monographs series", noting it was one of the ten most important psychological theories in North America.

While originally anchored in the need to correctly represent the psychology of women and bring about changes in the practice of psychotherapy, RCT has been increasingly applied more widely. A small sampling of RCT research shows it has been used to better understand

- organizational dynamics (Fletcher, 1999)
- counseling theory and practice (Comstock, 2005)
- diversity and marginalization (Comstock et al, 2008; Frey, 2013)
- social justice (Gunderson, 2012; Gunderson, Mueller, & Teichert 2013)
- men (Englar-Carlson, Stevens & Scholtz, 2010; Lombardi, 2011)
- eating disorders (Tantillo & Sanftner, 2010)
- addiction, (Covington, 2008; Gahleitner & Gunderson, 2009; Gahleitner & Gunderson, 2007)

- mindfulness (Surrey, 2005; Surrey & Jordan, 2005)
- relational psychotherapy (Jordan, 2010; Walker & Rosen, 2004)
- education (Schwartz & Holloway, 2014)
- mentoring (Gunderson et al, 2015; Spencer, Jordan, & Sazama, 2004)
- empowerment of girls (Covington, 2008; Jordan, 2016)
- friendships (Miller & Stiver, 1997)
- neurobiology of relationship (Banks, 2016)
- couples (Jordan & Carlson, 2013)
- resilience in girls (Jordan, 2013)
- clinical outcome (Oakley et al, 2013)
- chapter representations in college psychology texts (Engler, 2003; Frager & Fadiman, 2012)
- summary of research on RCT's usefulness in the field of counseling (Comstock, 2008; Duffy & Trepal, 2016).

Many more references to RCT can be found in the forthcoming APA 2nd edition of *Relational–Cultural Therapy* (Jordan, in press).

In terms of power analyses, RCT suggests that power over models severely restrict the development of mutuality. When people exercise power over, they seek to maintain the status quo, the imbalance of power that affords them considerable privilege in a stratified society. "Power with" and "power for" models provide healthier social arrangements in which all people matter, all people contribute to one another and the relationship and all people grow as a result of their interactions. In empowerment, we participate and value the growth of the less powerful person. The goal is mutual benefit and movement toward a greater sense of the power of connection.

RCT views isolation as one of the core factors in psychological suffering and dysfunction. Re-establishing meaningful connection with others fuels healthy development. As the client experiences empathic responsiveness with the therapist, she feels understood and she also feels less alone. She begins to entertain the possibility of healing and feeling that she matters. Strategies of disconnection begin to shift and the client begins to take small, appropriate risks in bringing vulnerability to relationships. This vulnerability is essential to being open and affected by our relationships with others and hence being able to grow in connection.

This book addresses many of RCT's newest applications. It is a compilation of writings by people who attended the conference *Transforming Community: The Radical Reality of Relationships* co-sponsored by The College of St. Scholastica, the Wellesley Centers for Women, and the Jean Baker Miller Training Institute at Wellesley College from June 9-12 in Duluth, Minnesota. This conference represented a wide array of approaches, interests, and practitioners. The ideas and feeling-thoughts were carefully listened to; some of the presentations brought tears; some invoked such intense listening that an immense silence embraced the listeners. Some who were new to the model felt tentative; some who were old hands also found new insights, stirring up old, settled ideas. There was laughter. There was inspiration. There was the good fatigue of really grappling with things that are challenging. There was Minnesota nice and east coast uptight (There's a lot to be said for Minnesota nice!). There was compelling drumming and singing. There were s'mores and bonfires and wonderful posters. The rise in energy in the course of our time together was palpable. There were those who wanted something slightly different, some who missed the midnight swims at Wellesley. And those who hoped this conference would be repeated exactly as it was every year from now on. There was recognition of Connie Gunderson and her mother, Lois Gunderson, for all they have given to RCT. We feel deep gratitude to The College of St. Scholastica for welcoming us so warmly and for sharing so many values and goals. It was a great partnership in those few days; a partnership we want to build on.

This book is part of an effort to capture the spirit of those days in Duluth in June 2016. While nothing can quite capture the spirit and excitement generated at this conference, we hope that the reader will resonate with these works. Jean Baker Miller focused on the destructive consequences of domination and subordination and her belief that women's truths were not being represented. She articulated her strong belief that to put relationships at the center of human development "changes everything". With this book's emphasis on mutuality and power dynamics, it provides a useful lens for looking at social responsibility. We hope readers will be inspired to expand the model and bring it to more and more people. A sampling of the chapters reveals an application of RCT to education, race, white privilege, the neurobiology of connection, resistance to marginalization, LBGTQI issues, mentorship, girl-centered practice, intellectual mattering, disruptive empathy, the radical reality of relationships, integrating critical race and relational cultural theories, our intrinsic relationship with the environment, relational advocacy, and the C.A.R.E. program. Some of it is written in the cogent, tight language of science and research, other chapters are the result of collaborative musings. Some come from seasoned clinicians or educators, others come from young people, interested in a developing a different world view from the one our culture has bestowed on them. Two are given with the gift of poetry.

It is hoped, more than anything, that this book inspires some of you (all of you?) to keep on the path of developing the practice and the understanding of the power of connection and the possibility of building more empathic community. We hope this will reveal the destructiveness of a model of human nature that says self-interest is a biological imperative and that the height of development is autonomy and separation. The old model overlooks the intrinsic need for connection throughout the lifespan. We hope people will re-read Darwin and see that cooperation and collaboration are better avenues to species survival than competitive, aggressive, cut-throat functioning. It is hoped that the small light of RCT will illuminate some aspect of your work or your life, bringing about increased empathy and compassion. We hope you will find RCT useful in working with clients and institutions. We hope it will bring forth bright new energy that you can bring to loved ones and others. And we hope that you will join us in honoring what many

of us have known, deep in our hearts for a long, long time: We
need connection and we thrive in growth-fostering relationships.
We grow through and toward connection throughout our lives. We
need to align cultural messages of what constitutes growth and
well-being so that they support our compelling, deeply connecting
neurobiology. We need to do this with others, in groups, and
communities that care for the well-being of all their members.
With this paradigm shift, *from the separate self to relational being,*
we can hope to transform communities in such a way that safety
and creative connection emerge as the bedrock of our policies
and practices at an individual and collective level. Transformation
through connection is not only a viable, but a necessary next
step for us in our effort to heal one another and to honor our
forgiving planet. Mutual empathy is essential to our individual and
collective survival.

References

Banks, A. (2016). *Wired to connect*. New York: Tarcher/Penguin.

Comstock, D. L., Hammer, T. R., Strentzsch, J., Cannon, K., Parsons, J., & Salazar II, G. (2008). Relational-Cultural theory: A framework for bridging relational, multicultural and social justice competencies. *Journal of Counseling and Development* 86(3), 279-287.

Comstock, D. (Ed.). (2005). *Diversity and development: Critical contexts that shape our lives and relationships*. Belmont, CA: Brooks/Cole.

Covington, S. (2008). Women and addiction: A trauma informed approach. *Journal of Psychoactive Drugs*, 5(3), 377- 385.

Duffey, T., & Haberstroh, S. (2014). Developmental relational counseling: Applications for counseling men. *Journal of Counseling and Development*, 92(1), 104-113.

Duffy, T., & Trepal, H. (2016). Introduction to the special section on Relational-Cultural theory. *Journal of Counseling and Development*. 94, 379-382.

Eisenberger, N., & Lieberman, M. (2004). Why rejection hurts: A common neural alarm system for physical and social pain. *Trends in Cognitive Sciences*. 8, 294-300.

Englar-Carlson, M., Stevens, M., & Scholtz, R. (2010). *Psychotherapy with men*. New York: Springer.

Engler, B. (2003). *Personality theories: An introduction (6th ed)*. Boston: Houghton Mifflin.

Fedele, N. (2004). Relationships in groups: Connection, resonance and paradox. In J Jordan, M Walker &L Hartling (Eds.), *The complexity of connection: Writings from the Stone Center's Jean Baker Miller Training Institute* (pp. 194-219) New York: Guilford Press.

Fletcher, J. (1999). *Disappearing acts: Gender, power and relational practice at work*. Cambridge, MA: MIT Press.

Frager, R., & Fadiman, J. (Eds.). (2012). *Personality and personal growth*. New York: Addison Wesley Longman.

Frey, M. (2013). Relational-Cultural therapy: Theory, research and application to counseling competencies. *Professional Psychology Research and Practice*. 44(3), 177-185.

Gahleitner, S., & Gunderson, C. (Eds.). (2009). *Gender, Trauma und Sucht: Neues aus Forschung, Diagnostik und Praxis*. Kröning: Asanger Verlag.

Gahleitner, S., & Gunderson, C. (Eds.), (2007). *Frauen, Trauma, Sucht: Neue Forschungsergebnisse und Praxiserfahrungen*. Kröning: Asanger Verlag.

Gunderson, C. (2012). *Human trafficking: The trafficking of women in Northern Germany for the purpose of sexual exploitation. A systemic overview of community based responses and challenges*. Münster, Germany: LIT Verlag

Gunderson, C., Müller, A., & Teichert, G. (2013). *Zwangsprostitution und Menschenhandel/Sex slavery and human trafficking*. Münster, Germany: LIT Verlag

Jordan, J. (in press). *Relational-Cultural therapy*. (2nd ed.) Washington DC: American Psychological Association.

Jordan, J. (2013). Relational resilience in girls. In S. Goldstein and R. Brooks (Eds.), *Handbook of resilience in children* (2nd ed.) pp. 73-86. New York: Springer Science and Business Medico.

Jordan, J. (2010). *Relational-Cultural Therapy*. Washington, DC: American Psychological Association.

Jordan, J., Kaplan, A., Miller, J., Stiver, I., & Surrey, J. (1991). *Women's growth in connection*. New York: Guilford.

Jordan, J., Walker, M., & Hartling, L. (Eds.). (2004). *The complexity of connection*. New York: Guilford.

Lombardi, K. (2011). The *mama's boy myth*. New York: Penguin.

Miller, J. (1976). Toward a new psychology of women. Boston: Beacon Press.

Miller, J., & Stiver, I. (1997). *The healing connection: How women form relationships in therapy and in life*. Boston: Beacon Press.

Norcross, J. (Ed.). (2002). *Psychotherapy relationships that work: Therapist contributions and responsiveness to patient*. New York: Oxford University Press.

Oakley, A., Addison, S.C., Piran, N., Johnston, G., Damianakis, M., Curry, J., ...(2013). Outcome study of brief relational-cultural therapy in a women's mental health center. *Psychotherapy Research*, 23(2), 137-151.

Schwartz, H. (2014). " I become part of the learning process": Mentoring episodes and individualized attention in graduate education. *Mentoring and Tutoring: Partnership in Learning,* 22(1), 3855.

Sparks, E. (1999). Against the odds: Resistance and resilience in African American welfare mothers. *Work in Progress, No 81.* Wellesley, MA: Stone Center Working Paper Series.

Spencer, R., Jordan, J., & Sazama, J. (2004). Growth –promoting relationships between youth and adults: A focus group study. *Families in Society,* 7(3), 354-363.

Surrey, J. (2005). Relational psychotherapy, relational mindfulness. In C. Germer, R. Siegel, & P. Fulton (Eds.), *Mindfulness and psychotherapy,* (pp. 91-110). New York: Guilford Press.

Surrey, J., & Jordan, J. (2013). The wisdom of connection. In C. Germer, R. Siegel (Eds.), Wisdom and compassion in psychotherapy: *Deepening mindfulness in clinical practice.* (pp. 163-175). New York: Guilford Press.

Tantillo, M., & Sanftner, J. (2010). Measuring perceived mutuality in women with eating disorders: The development of the Connection-disconnection scale. *Journal of Nursing Measurement,* 18(2), 100-119.

Walker, M., & Rosen, W. (Eds.). (2004). *How connections heal: Stories from Relational-Cultural therapy.* New York: Guilford Press.

Keynote Address: Transforming Community Through Disruptive Empathy

— · · · ■ ■ ■ · · · —

MAUREEN WALKER, PhD

As the Director of Program Development at the Jean Baker Miller Training Institute of the Stone Center at Wellesley College, Dr. Maureen Walker explores the linkages between social-cultural identities and relational development, as well as the impact of power arrangements on mental health. Through her publications and her work as an educator and licensed psychologist, she often uses Relational-Cultural theory as the lens to illustrate the interface between spiritual practice and social justice. In addition to journal articles and several papers in the Stone Center Works in Progress Series, she is the co-editor of two books which convey her strong interest in disruptive empathy as an essential practice for all who are engaged in the work of transforming community. Dr. Maureen Walker can be contacted at maureen@maureenwalker.com.

Here we are at a Kairos moment. We have the gift of this time to contemplate, collaborate, and challenge each other as we engage a very special project: transforming community. When we talk about community, we often do so in ways that take for granted a level of shared assumptions and expectations. We come with our shared assumptions, hopes, and expectations, but we each come with our particular claims on community: claims that may be at once aspirational, insistent, and conflictual. The radical reality of our relationships is that we ourselves are in the throes of transformation. And who are we?

Four decades ago, our "we" was self-described as "five, white, well-educated women" who found a community of place at Wellesley College, specifically the Stone Center. Who are "we" now—this motley collection of us—gathered here in 2106? And more pertinent to our purposes over the next four days, who do we hope to become?

When Connie Gunderson and I first talked about the theme of this talk, I have to say I was completely undaunted and completely in love with the title: Transforming Community through Disruptive Empathy. All of the right words were put together in one evocative phrase. But then the inevitable happened; the more I reflected on the title the more aware I became that I really didn't know what it meant. And that was okay. Because the more I participate in these kinds of gatherings, the more I make peace with the reality that my starting place is often in a state of profound befuddlement—which is also okay particularly since I'm never content to stay in that place alone. I invite other people into it with me. So I started asking: What comes to mind when you hear the word community? What makes community different from an organization, or working group, or network? It's probably not surprising that the first associations that came to mind were words like trust, like-mindedness, nurture, commitment, and belonging. And just to make sure our thoughts were not overly lofty, we threw in reminiscences of the Cheers Bar, the setting of a popular 1990s sitcom. Community, according to the promotional jingle, is a place "where everybody knows your name, and they're oh so glad you came"—even if they give you a hard time once you get there. In other words, community is a place where we can be known; people miss us when we don't show up; and, perhaps, someone even cares.

We are social beings—born to thrive in connection with each other—so it is no surprise that we find the life blood of our dreams, our values, and our expectations in community. We feel more alive when we are bound together by captivating ideas; we feel that we matter when we are in pursuit of compelling goals. Right here, right now, we are enlivened as we gather around this evolving body of work that we call Relational-Cultural theory.

Right here, right now we are enlivened as we gather to insist on our right to forge a narrative of human possibility to heal the suffering in the world as we know it now. We are here—right now—to press our righteous claim and lay the groundwork for future we want to call into being. And somewhere, perhaps not too far away, so is the Ku Klux Klan. They too are enlivened by their connection to a communal narrative, perhaps one that promises to restore America to its greatness. Like us, they are captivated by a vision of possibility. The content of that vision may be different from ours; but, *like us,* they derive meaning from their connection to a narrative grounded in an **imagination** of justice, fairness, and the right order of relationships. We learn every day about young people who are drawn into terrorist activities—whether it is the terrorism of ISIS or the terrorism that led Dylan Roof to murder nine people in a house of worship. They too have an **audacious** vision of possibility and a yearning to belong. So right here, right now, a question worth asking ourselves is: **What makes our claim on community different from theirs?**

They have a compelling mission – just as we do.

They have powerful rituals – just as we do.

They believe they are right – just as we do.

Let me be very, very clear. I am not in any way suggesting some kind of moral equivalence between the mission of KKK and of this assembly gathered here tonight. What we share in common, however, is the fact that we come together to forge a narrative about power—the power of belonging. Relationship, like any currency of power can be used to dominate and exclude; to determine who is in; who is out; who can never belong; and, in the extreme, who must be destroyed. When we talk about our own beloved community, we often speak of Ubuntu as a relational ideal: that cultural ethos of "I am because we are". What I am saying tonight is that as much as we might aspire to build our communities around that narrative, we cannot take refuge in linguistic niceties. "I am because we are" speaks to relationship as a currency of power. And unless we are mindful of how we *do* that power, "I am because we are" can quite easily devolve into "I am because we are" and "<u>we</u> *are* because <u>you</u> *are not*". We all know that it can happen: that there can be a "disconnect" between our explicit narratives—who we <u>say</u> we are in relationship—and, our implicit, sometimes largely unconscious narratives—how we actually *do* our relationships. We all know that as much as we might like to associate the dogma of disconnection with corporate board rooms and the global political stage, an implicit narrative of disconnection can play out in our class rooms, clinics, and churches—presumptive spaces of health, hope, and healing. It's a fair guess that we all have known the heartbreak of good work gone bad—when we embarked on some noble mission, with righteous ideas and fierce resolve and noble intentions, only to find that our good intentions are not enough. Unless we are mindful of how we do the politics of belonging, we too are susceptible to the same faults we so readily recognize in others.

And speaking of the others, who do we think they are? Two great thinkers, Albert Einstein and Jean Baker Miller, have given us our theoretical foundation to start answering that question. If we truly believe *as we say we do* that separation is an illusion, then we are free to embrace disruption. If we truly believe that we grow **through** relationship for the purpose of relationship, we can free ourselves from the constrictions of the ego—those boundaries ostensibly built to protect us—to ensure our survival against those pesky intruders who are trying to invade our borders. We are also freed from constricted notions of community that are defined by ego boundaries. "We are" because "you are not" is simply a variation on a very old theme that we must use our boundaries to protect us from each other. Indeed, we may be tempted to follow the advice of no less a personage as Freud and use our boundaries to protect us from what we perceive to be intrusive stimuli.

At core of our communal narrative as Relational-Cultural practitioners is the notion of boundaries of spaces of meeting and transformation. Jean Baker Miller (1976) put it this way: the essence of life is movement and change. She went on to say that we become more fully human by engaging difference — not just theoretical difference — by engaging real bodies whom we perceive to be other, opposite, and even enemy. So who do we think we are? And who do we think the others are? If we truly believe that as we say we do, then we are challenged to continually interrogate our notions of self and other. *[Frankly, that scares me! I don't want to be Donald Trump...which is not too much of a problem because I'm pretty sure Donald Trump doesn't want to be me either.]*

But isn't that the very fear that causes us to misuse the power of belonging? Isn't that the very fear that can cause us to weaponize our relationships — to use our relationships as fortified boundaries against engagement and inclusion? We do that not because we are bad people, but because we want to protect that which we know to be good. When we narrate our history and our hopes, we talk about growth through authentic connection.

And the radical reality of that narrative is that it calls us to transformation. The radical reality is that the power of belonging can support and propel us toward ever more expansive enactments of our humanity.

Or... we can ignore the call to transformation. We can say what we have is so good and so never want it to change. But to do so is to become reduced to a smaller and smaller version of what we call community.

So what are we to do? How can we use our powers of belonging — our powers of relationship — to foster hope and healing? It is important for us to start by *asking* the question "who are we" to develop an explicit, well-articulated narrative. But it is equally important for us to notice how we live the question: to embrace community as process, community as movement, and as evolving narratives of co-creation and human possibility.

I propose that we start with disruptive empathy. Disruption and empathy: I know—the words don't seem to go together. But it captures the paradox of relationship, and what Keltner (2016) calls the paradox of power. And actually if we refer back to the foundational tenets of Relational-Cultural theory, the pairing of these two words may not be as peculiar as it might initially seem. When Judy Jordan defined empathy about three decades ago, she described it as a process of thinking and feeling, of joining with clarity and awareness (Jordan, Surrey & Kaplan, 1983). In other words, empathy requires engagement with paradox. Disruptive empathy both anchors and overturns.

It leads us to *challenge* our most *sacrosanct notions* of community while grounding us in the shared power of belonging.

Just a few days ago, I witnessed this shared power of belonging enacted on the sidewalks of lower east side Manhattan. There were two gentlemen in conversation, one of whom definitely appeared to be homeless, and the other, who if not currently homeless appeared to be quite familiar with that condition. The latter gentleman was explaining to his companion how to obtain services, what would happen on certain days in one agency or another, how to avoid getting caught up in a bureaucratic tangle when searching for shelter. And I thought: now that is power. Jean Baker Miller (1976) defined power as the capacity to induce responsiveness—a relational energy. Similarly, Keltner (2016) defines power as the capacity to make a difference, particularly through connections with others. In other words, power is not the exclusive province of the rich and the famous—as the burgeoning growth of reality TV would have it—the rich and the infamous.

And here's the paradox. Power is also intoxicating. Keltner (2016) describes it as a dopamine high. We are not much soothed and made to feel calm by it, as we are made to feel more confident, more competent, and more deserving of whatever it is that we want. We now have tons of research showing that feeling powerful makes us—all of us—more likely to use others to our own advantage: whether that's cutting in line or taking up more space than we need, or consuming more goods than we need, or taking candy from a baby. *[Literally, not metaphorically.]* In other words, the paradox is that this same power that can be used for good can foster a sense of entitlement and exceptionalism. Of course, we can see how this plays out in the world of national and global politics, but it happens in small ways as well. Let me give an example. I spend way too much time in my favorite grocery store in Wellesley, MA. It's a very special store and all of us who feel like very special people like to shop there. I can't count the number of times I have seen loving, suburban mothers trying to shop with their children in tow—all the while grabbing fruit for their children to eat while they shop. What I'm saying is that they haven't paid for it. And I'm thinking: why isn't this called shoplifting? I don't see any signs that say "this is free; you can take it". Yet they feel entitled to appropriate someone else's property for own use. *[A client of mine once told me that's the key to all successful shoplifting: you just have to believe it's already rightfully yours.]* I'm fairly certain the store owners calculate theft into the cost of goods sold; so, in fact, we're all paying for that bunch of grapes. I'm also fairly certain that the shoplifters are upstanding, law-abiding, good-hearted mothers who are just doing the best they can to mollify cranky toddlers. I'm not saying they are bad people. I am saying they are people who are so comfortable—and confident about their status in this specific culture of shoppers that they feel entitled to exercise power without question. Whether it's in a grocery store or a community of scholars and practitioners, disruptive empathy counters this sense of exceptionalism by anchoring us in awareness. It focuses our attention on the text of our narratives, as well as the context and the subtext. I think of it as relational corrective. To the extent that we are prone to deny our power—or to use it without regard to its impact on others, it prompts us toward mindful appreciation of what is real, what is present, and what is emerging in relationship. In our communities, disruptive empathy helps us to see what we prefer not to see; it helps us face down our implicit narratives that define who can be one of us—and who cannot. Disruptive empathy gives us the courage to name reality as we see it—to tell our multiple and conflictual truths—the cliques, the secrets, the taken-for-granted understandings that build impenetrable boundaries that may belie any explicit story we might tell about ourselves. It helps us to speak the unspeakable with humility and compassion and an occasional dose of good humor.

There is something that is core to our humanity that impels us toward authenticity. We want to be real; we want to be known. Yet we know that the central paradox of relationship is that we are often afraid of being known. We are drawn to community because of our deep yearning to be known and connected. Ironically, our fear of being known sometimes results in an implicit narrative framed around isolation and subterfuge. Not because we want to lie, but because community brings us face to face with what Audre Lorde (1984) called our fear and loathing of difference. This is the same fear and loathing that might deceive us into believing that we can use the master's tools to dismantle the master's house. This is the same fear and loathing that would cause us to shirk away from good conflict. Again, the explicit narrative of relational-cultural community is that conflict is both inevitable and necessary for growth. And growth means change—transformation. You simply can't grow and keep the same boundaries. That brings us again to the heart of disruptive empathy—respect for otherness. We don't have to settle for pseudo-empathy or sentimentality. I find that absolutely liberating, because it means that we don't have to always pretend to like each other all of the time. The good news here is that disruptive empathy is not about mutual attraction. I should be clear: I think mutual attraction is a good thing, but we don't always have to go along to get along. There is no way that strong-willed, creative, and passionate people will avoid going into conflict with each other. We do have to enter conflict with respect, curiosity, and openness to the possibility that we just might learn something.

You also have to care enough to go into conflict. I say that as a personal confession: I know that one of my preferred strategies of disconnection is being nice. I know that because my family has told me so—many times. It often sounds something like: "Okay – sure. Peace out". Let me say that there may be times when that strategy is absolutely appropriate. It may be all the relationship can bear—at the moment. But let us also be clear: a lot of exclusion and relational violence happens under the guise of being nice. Being nice—pseudo-empathy—is the antithesis of authentic engagement; it fortifies our boundaries against the other; it is refusal to invest the time and energy required to sustain relationship. Pseudo-empathy is a refusal to relinquish our attachment to the relational images we have stored in our brains about how our relationships should work. Disruptive empathy, on the other hand, reminds me of a quote by the 13th century poet Rumi: "Out beyond ideas of wrongdoing and rightdoing, there is a field. I'll meet you there." (Moyne & Bark, 1999, p. 8).

What happens in that field between rightdoing and wrong-doing? For one thing, anxiety happens. No one wants to feel anxious. Interestingly, the poet W.H. Auden (2009) encourages us to seek truth in the kingdom of anxiety...to go into the land of "unlikeness"...to stay in the here and now...to encounter rare beasts (the other)...to have unique adventures in the world of the flesh.

Jean Baker Miller (1976) was slightly less poetic, but just as clear—that we become more fully human through embodied engagement with difference. Becoming more fully human requires a little bit more of us than an eloquent theory or good intentions.

Let me give a quick example. One of our traditions at Harvard Business School—probably much like other schools—is that very senior administrators or faculty will hold informal lunches with small groups of students. This is a favorite ritual: the students get to feel good about themselves and the hosting faculty or administrator can feel good as well. At one of these lunches hosted by a senior faculty, an African American male student recounted his recent encounter with campus security. He had been detained, had a flashlight shone into his face, and had been required to produce his student identification because someone fitting his description had committed a robbery in a nearby neighborhood. He was hurt and angry—and actually reeling in disbelief that all of his accomplishments (which included a law degree from Yale) did not protect him from the indignity of racialized bias. When he told his story, his listeners were appropriately horrified; and the hosting faculty, a white male, suggested that he report the incident to another high-level white female administrator. So far, so good: Everyone is acting with the best of intentions. Later that month I was inadvertently included on part of an email trail. A part of the trail was meant for me; the other part was a private debriefing conversation between the two higher-level administrators—clearly not my business, but of course I read it! And the conversation went something like:

Female: "He certainly had very strong emotions".

Male: "Oh my, I hope he spoke to you respectfully".

Female: "It wasn't too bad. I just hope he will channel his anger appropriately".

I later met with the student, and his mirror neurons were fully functional. He knew what had happened in the field. People, who might have exercised their power to facilitate change and cultural healing, used it instead to curate his narrative of heartbreak. We have a choice when we enter into the field between rightdoing and wrongdoing: we can wrap ourselves in our protective boundaries, or we can shed the mantle of entitlement and become open to the possibility of learning something—maybe even becoming something new.

Our beloved scholar Irene Stiver (1997) taught us that when we enter that field of anxiety, between right-doing and wrong-doing, we must move out of the protective boundaries of image and authority and orthodoxy and toward relationship.

It is in this field of anxiety — between right-doing and wrong-doing — that we might exercise our power to say just one true thing. The poet Mary Oliver (2006) remarks on the important of silence.

To create a silence in which another voice may speak is at the heart of community transformation. It doesn't sound that hard; in fact, it sounds like just the kind of thing we say we want to do. But we would do well to recognize from the outset that making a space for other voices is in fact a disruptive process. It may quite literally take us out of our communal skin. Fifteen years ago we probably couldn't have imagined that our skin/our boundaries stretch from Waban Pond to the shores of Lake Superior. But here we are tonight, making a space into which other voices may emerge and speak to our communal narrative.

When I was very young, my primary babysitter was my great-grandmother. I was about four years old and I thought she was about 217; and, frankly, we did not get along. I don't know what I could have done at four years old to cause her to characterize me in this way, but she would complain to my mother that I was "mouthy" and "brazen". To her enduring consternation (and mine) she would complain that I, "Always wanted to have the last word." I confess that I still struggle with that, and *sometimes* as a community, so do we.

We have struggled long and hard to speak our truths to a power-over culture that did not always care to listen. And we have become quite good at it; we have filled vast spaces with our spoken word. And we have defined ourselves with our spoken word. This year 2016 is the 49th anniversary of the publication of Jean's book, *Toward a New Psychology of Women*. After 40 years, we might say that we have established ourselves as members of the pantheon of thinkers and theorists who are trying to tell the story of what it means to be fully human.

Now, right here, we are gathered as a community because it is equally radical to listen: to embrace the reality that the practice of empathy may just disrupt who we think we are. Listening leads to transformation and what makes this radical is that we live in a culture that posits impermeability as a measure of strength. In fact, we are taught to fear that if we listen too well—if we allow ourselves to be influenced by others—we may lose our selves. Perhaps that is precisely what community calls us to do: to loosen our death grip on this construction of images, expectations, and entitlements that we call self. The paradox of listening to another voice is that we may come to more deeply appreciate who we truly are and who we may truly become.

In Relational-Cultural practice, we have a narrative about the transformative power of mutuality—of being influenced by voices of others. To listen to the voices of others is an act of courage; it is to open ourselves to disruption and to risk knowing that which we thought was the final has dissolved. The final word has not been spoken, and that, perhaps, it is not for us to speak. By no means am I talking about moral relativism. I am talking about moral humility. I am talking about the courage to stand for what we believe is right, without being self-righteous. This is the space where courage and compassion grow precisely because we encounter our indivisibility—our common humanity. This is the space where we lay down our sword and shield, and study war no more.

I can think of a no more beautiful example of the practice of disruptive empathy than the story told of C. P. Ellis and Ann Atwater in Davidson's (2007), a book that I highly recommend: *The Best of Enemies*. Ellis and Atwater both grew up in Durham, North Carolina, in a culture where deeply entrenched racial segregation was the way of life. Segregation by race and class defined the narratives of identity and possibility: this is who you are and this is all you can become (Davidson, 2007). C. P. Ellis grew up as a poor white boy, who regularly witnessed his father's humiliation when he had to step off the sidewalk, so that the "big white men"—men with money—could pass (Davidson, 2007). He grew up hiding under stairwells, so that his school mates wouldn't see that all he had to eat for lunch was a lard sandwich, but he became a "somebody" (Davidson, 2007). He, like his father before him, was eventually inducted into the Ku Klux Klan, and he rose to leadership as the Exalted Cyclops (Davidson, 2007). Ann Atwater grew up poor and Black and female in this same culture (Davidson, 2007). She was deeply intimate with the indignities of being poor and Black and female—all of which according to the cultural narrative would relegate her to a status of nobody-ness; but she too became "somebody" (Davidson, 2007). She became one of Durham's most audacious and outspoken advocates for civil rights; she was a single mother, and housing activist who could not be silenced (Davidson, 2007). During the 70s, in the midst of the cataclysm of racial violence sparked by school desegregation, Atwater and Ellis were brought together in a series of meetings called a *charrette,* where they were to tell their truths and listen to the truths of the other (Davidson, 2007). As C. P. Ellis described it:

> Here we are, two people from the far end of the fence, having identical problems, except her being Black and me being White…The amazing thing about it, her and I, up to that point, [had] cussed each other, bawled each other, we hated each other. Up to that point, we didn't know each other. We didn't know we had things in common. (Atwater, 2016, para. 13)

When C. P. Ellis died in 2005, Ann Atwater took her rightful place seated with the family; and when questioned, she said, "CP was my brother" (Davidson, 2007, p. 6).

By practicing disruptive empathy, Atwater and Ellis learned how to tell their own truths and how to listen to the truths of the other. They never backed down, but they created a pause—a silence into which another voice could speak. The poet Paul Williams puts to words so well the truths that I needed to learn as a "mouthy and brazen" little girl; the truths that every community needs to learn, that Ellis needed to learn, that Atwater needed to learn; and it is this:

34

When you just have to talk,
Try being silent.
When you feel reluctant to say anything
Make the effort
To put what you're feeling into words...
Look and see
if you're willing to trust
yourselves
to misunderstand each other
and go from there...
Listen as if.
Listen as if you can't always tell
what the truth is
Listen as if you might be wrong,
Especially when you know you're right.
Listen as if
you were willing to take the risk
of growing beyond
your righteousness
Listen as if
love mattered.

And at the end of our days, isn't love what community is all about?

References

Atwater, A. |Web page]. (2016). Retrieved from http://en.wikipedia.org/ wiki/Ann_Atwater

Auden, W. H. (2009). For the time being: Xmas Oratorio. In R. Housden (Ed.), *For lovers of God everywhere: Poems of the Christian mystics*. US: Hay House Inc.

Davidson, O. G. (2007). *The best of enemies: Race and redemption in the new south*. Chapel Hill, North Carolina: University of North Carolina Press.

Jordan, J. V., Surrey, J. L. & Kaplan, A. G.(1983). *Women and empathy*. Wellesley, MA: Stone Center Working Paper Series.

Keltner, D. (2016) *The power paradox: How we gain and lose influence*. NY: Penguin Press.

Lorde, A. (1984). *Sister outsider*. CA: Crossing Press.

Miller, J. B. (1976). *Toward a new psychology of women*. Boston: Beacon Press.

Moyne, J. & Bark, C. (1999). *Open secret: Versions of Rumi*. Boston: Shamble Publications.

Oliver, M. (2006). Praying. *Thirst*. Boston: Beacon Press.

Stiver, I. (1997). A relational approach to therapeutic impasses. In J. V. Jordan (Ed.), *Women's growth in diversity: More writings from the Stone Center*. NY: Guilford Press.

Williams, P. (1990). How to tell the truth. *Nation of Lawyers*. Used with permission by Cindy Lee Berryhill.

Part I

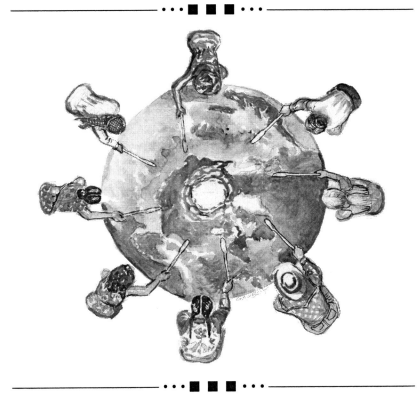

Transforming Community: Relational Neuroscience and Healthcare

Stopping the Pain of Social Exclusion: Using Relational Neuroscience as an Approach for Social Action

• • • ■ ■ ■ • • •

KAREN CRADDOCK, PhD, EdM, and AMY BANKS, MD

The role of relationship and the cultural context have always been a central part of my scholarship and practice. Therefore when I learned about Relational-Cultural theory (RCT) there was an abiding resonance that stimulated further inquiry and interest. My explorations included comparisons and correlations to my research on strategies of psychological resistance to marginalization and multiple forms of resilience, both of which involved relational dynamics that pointed to more adaptive social-emotional functioning and wellness. Soon after there was palpable synergy with Amy Banks' relational neuroscience work, and since I continue to find exciting and innovative areas to blend the work in ways to both extend and deepen the correlative connections and applications of RCT. This essay explores the pain of social exclusion using relational neuroscience with optimal resistance to marginalization theory, and the development of our STOP model is an example of how I seek to illustrate and integrate theoretical constructs to effect social action and transformative change. Karen T Craddock may be contacted at karen_craddock@post.harvard.edu.

Three years ago Karen Craddock and I met during the Jean Baker Miller Summer Training Institute at Wellesley College and it was immediately clear that we had work to do together. I was

41

teaching about the neuroscience of human relationship and the neural correlates that help explain how painful and deadly social exclusion is. Karen was working on social exclusion from the perspective of resilience and what strategies people develop to cope with being marginalized. We hit it off right away and could see the power of joining our two perspectives into a new approach to helping people on all sides of social exclusion understand what's happening and how to STOP it. Our contribution is a summary of that new model with a reflection from Karen of how she saw people using it at the Transforming Community Conference. Amy Banks, M.D. may be contacted atabanks14@gmail.com.

Human beings are built to function physically, emotionally, and spiritually in supportive groups. This simple fact has recently been supported by neuroscience research and helps explain why individuals and groups of people that are marginalized or socially excluded often suffer from higher levels of chronic health problems and shorter life expectancy.

SPOT – Social Pain Overlap Theory: How and Why Social Exclusion Hurts

Being part of a group is so critical to humans that our nervous system literally uses the same alarm (the dorsal anterior cingulate cortex) to register the danger and distress of physical pain or injury AND social exclusion (Eisenberger & Leiberman, 2005). This neuroscience finding requires that we stop bifurcating pain into physical and emotional and start realizing that pain is pain and that social exclusion and marginalization are forms of violence that impact individuals and whole groups of people.

Social Pain Forms – Covert and Overt

Social pain occurs in a number of different forms, some obvious, some not so obvious. The not so obvious may be hard to see, they are insidious like the background noise or the air we breathe. They are chronic assumptions about who we are and what our interests, strengths, and weaknesses might be. They are assumed by others and attached to our identities such as race, ethnicity, sexual orientation, and gender.

These subtle daily attacks or microaggressions, generally described as denigrating messages that occur on a regular basis to certain individuals because of their group membership, can have devastating short and long term impact (Paludi, 2012; Pierce, 1974; Sue, 2010). Dr. Chester Pierce, Harvard psychiatrist and originator of the term microaggression, reinforced "…the subtle, cumulative mini-assault is the substance of today's racism" (Pierce, 1974, p. 516). For example, Indigenous or Native Americans constantly have to combat broad assumptions about cultural sacred practices, misuse of regalia, offensive displays of imagery in athletic team mascots, or even the ongoing challenge to defend one's very existence in the face of a society that can often relegate an entire people to mythical caricatures or historical figures.

The overt forms of social pain are glaringly obvious, often flagrant and extreme. Black men and women being stopped by police, detained or harassed, and imprisoned at sweepingly disproportionate rates compared to white people; too often resulting in violence and even murder.

Both the subtle and blatant forms of social pain emerge together and take place across a range of areas including reliable public safety, access to and quality of healthcare, education and jobs, affordable sustainable housing, and more. Institutional and personal marginalization can lead to layers of social pain.

Psychological Resistance to Marginalization

We know that people who are being marginalized have always pushed back in some way. Emerging ideas and theories about how and why to resist are being explored and developed. Psychological

Resistance Theory is a central construct and reference point based on research about women of color who must confront marginalization and the ensuing social pain associated with both race and gender (Robinson & Ward, 1991).

Research on Psychological Resistance Theory outlines optimal and suboptimal ways of resisting marginalization, and in fact, they often co-occur. Further exploration revealed that both optimal and suboptimal resistance strategies are used together and in patterned ways that have implications for how we manage marginalization and social pain. These patterned responses include affective, behavioral, and cognitive strategies—the ABC Framework of Resistance (Robinson-Wood, 2017) in specific optimal and suboptimal paired forms known as Profiles of Resistance (Craddock, 2007, 2015). For example, a "purposeful resister" may use optimal cognitive coping in their clear awareness of the marginalizing stressors, yet may also engage in suboptimal affect, which can give way to feelings of hopelessness and despair about long-term change over time. It is as if they cannot get up to go on another day under the weight of awareness about exclusionary worldviews and practices around them (Craddock, 2007, 2015).

The more we know about how we push back against being excluded, left out, or disregarded, the more we can understand the impact of social pain on our neurological, social, and emotional health and find effective solutions to address it.

Social Pain is Everywhere

Social pain occurs in layers depending on who and where you are. It can be experienced in your family, at work, in your community, and often in more than one place. It is always embedded in our daily lives.

It is time to STOP the pain of social exclusion and STOP SPOT is one model we have created to help people take action to stop the pain of social exclusion wherever they may experience it, feel it, or participate in it. Because whether the initiator, the targeted, or the bystander, we are all capable of inflicting it and all are vulnerable to the effects of it.

STOP SPOT!

Each activity to counter social pain is a multi-sensory experience incorporating your mind, your body, and your soul. When you STOP the pain of social exclusion and marginalization you are literally changing your own neurophysiology, as well as the neurophysiology of those around you. These activities can be used in daily human interactions wherever we see social exclusion arising.

To STOP SPOT:

S – See Stratification

Use your eyes, mind, and body to discern what's happening to you and around you. Being aware is the first step to combatting any damaging circumstance or issue. Social pain is embedded across the many layers of our lives and it is often so densely intertwined with everyday life that we do not see it or we ignore it. The "it" could be the casual bigoted comment or a gender stereotype reflected in media. It can also be race or ethnicity based assumptions made about someone's capability in the workplace or classroom. We must begin by seeing the stratification that we are perpetrating, experiencing, or witnessing.

Through the lens of Relational Neuroscience...

Seeing stratifications and value judgments toward you or others helps you to locate the problem outside of yourself, which in turn helps to lessen the shame and pain that accompanies the exclusion. Shame stimulates the parasympathetic nervous system often leading to a decrease in energy, motivation, and a withdrawal from human contact. In addition, the distress pain of social exclusion or marginalization may stimulate the sympathetic nervous system's fight or flight response leading to chronic stress, which ultimately impairs the immune system. When this occurs often enough, the third pathway of the autonomic nervous system (the smart vagus) is not getting a regular workout from healthy relationships. The smart vagus nerve fires when a person is in a safe relationship and inhibits the sympathetic nervous system. When it is weak it is more difficult to find calming comfort from close connections (Banks & Hirschman, 2015).

T – Talk and Tell

Use your voice, mind, and body to describe, express, and share what you see and feel. It is often said that there is power in the spoken word and when we talk through what we experience and witness it can lead to transformation and healing. Storytelling is a powerful change agent and we know that personal narrative is a central way humans make meaning of life. Therefore talking and telling are essential components of claiming power, especially in the midst of social pain. Telling one's story can create a path of understanding and an avenue for others to understand and join you.

Through the lens of Relational Neuroscience...

When you talk and tell others about the experience of the social exclusion, you are using the muscles of facial expression as well as the muscles in your throat and larynx. As you communicate the experience you may listen more intently to the person you are sharing with. All of these actions stimulate the smart vagus nerve, which in turn will inhibit your sympathetic nervous system lowering the distress of being marginalized, witnessing, or causing marginalization.

O – Open Outreach

Use your heart, mind, and body to deconstruct the hurtful impact of what is occurring and replace it with healing interactions. This may be the most challenging step in the process of stopping social pain. However, being open and vulnerable in acknowledging how you have either been hurt by, caused, or witnessed social pain is key to transformation. Being open and reaching out allows us to get in touch with our humanity and commonality, which is where all great change begins. It is core to human connection.

Through the lens of Relational Neuroscience ...

It is biologically difficult to remain open and vulnerable when you are feeling threatened by social exclusion. Truth is, your sympathetic nervous system is usually running the show at this point and the message it is sending is to either flee from the situation or gear up to attack back. When you have participated in or witnessed social exclusion, your sympathetic nervous system is also in charge. Regardless of where you are in the scenario your frontal lobe can be a huge help. With a little or a lot of help from this thinking part of your brain, energy can be channeled towards an outreach to others who have your back and want to comfort and support you. This connection in a place of vulnerability and pain can be transformative. It reconnects you with a larger experience of wholeness or oneness within community and this bigger belonging helps to sooth the pain pathways that are activated by social exclusion. And healthy connection with others helps you to act in relationship and to use your hurt, anger, or guilt for social change.

P – Partnered Protest and Production

Use your networks, mind, and body to develop action that counters the social exclusion and pain that is happening, and create a new reality. Building alliances within group, across group, peer to peer, with many voices using multiple actions, we can forge connection and leverage our power to effect change exponentially.

Through the lens of Relational Neuroscience...

Partnered Protest amplifies the message of change and transformation. How does this happen? As a group moves into the physiology of healthy relationship, the level of pain they are experiencing or causing from being isolated, marginalized, or disconnected through power over others lessens. Biological resonance through the mirror neuron system transforms individual voices into echoed support. Dopamine will flow freely as people interact in safety with one another and in a common purpose of social change. Dopamine provides focus, attention, and energy to act within the hurtful settings to change them. The smart vagus nerve will be engaged in these interactions adding a steady "de-stressing" message to the rest of the autonomic nervous system. Ultimately, lasting strength and staying power for social change comes from being centered and held within healthy relationship!

ABC's of Optimal Resistance to STOP SPOT

The STOP model fits well into the Affect, Behavior, and Cognitive (ABC) Framework of Resistance Theory. Research shows that internal and external success or wellness is seen in resisters who incorporate connection and relationship building into their strategies to counter social exclusion and marginalization. Marginalized individuals who valued and sought connection with others using each of the Affect, Behavior, and Cognition resistance strategies had achieved higher levels of psychological well-being and concrete supports and outcomes such as achievement in education, work, and financial stability (Craddock, 2007, 2015).

Ultimately it comes down to our Partnered Protest and Production. When we are able to come together to collectively resist exclusion, we can come together to create new realities in an integrated fashion. It is at this step that we can begin to truly generate transformative change and overall wellness.

STOP as a Model of Optimal Resistance

The STOP model operationalizes the core Optimal Resistance ABC framework (Affect, Behavior, Cognition) and maps onto core neurophysiological properties that can enhance connection and healing.

SEE – using COGNITIVE capacities to discern the situation
TALK – using BEHAVIORAL functions to express how and what occurred
OPEN – using AFFECTIVE means to engage the experience and others
PARTNER – using AFFECTIVE, BEHAVIORAL and COGNITIVE strategies to build RELATIONAL connections

Through the lens of Relational Neuroscience...

Relational and individual neural integration and collective social action lead to optimal health and wellness for all. Integration should not be confused with assimilation or colorblindness. An essential component of STOP is to (SEE) your role in the circumstance and to take action with an awareness of the part you may play by omission or commission. Those holding race/gender/ socioeconomic status privilege need to accept how they benefit from systemic social exclusion and enact STOP activities in their spheres of influence. This can begin by acknowledging how they may be immune to or blindly conspire with social exclusive activities. It is also necessary for those who are being marginalized to SEE the specifics of their marginalization while being careful not to subsume or minimize the marginalized pain of others. While resisting marginalization broadly, we must also resist the impulse to equate all social exclusionary realities and thereby reify systems of oppression within marginalized groups.

The upshot is that this notion of integration emphasizes honoring the distinct realities and experiences of marginalization that are socially constructed and operated in varying forms of hierarchy and intensity, and then come together as a strong force to counter the layers of social exclusion.

Taking Social Action to STOP SPOT

Because social pain in all of its forms occurs across multiple strata of our society, it is imperative that we take action to STOP SPOT at all levels. This includes changing perspectives, practices and policy. This change must be done in interpersonal and systemic ways by integrating resistance strategies and healthy neuronal activity within us, in our relationships and across our institutions.

STOP in Action: A Reflective Commentary by Karen Craddock

The steps of the STOP model are timely, and can be further discussed in light of our current national climate, specifically around issues of race, ethnicity, gender, immigration and the disturbingly growing xenophobic and violent attitudes and actions surrounding these factors. The intersecting dynamics of these social contingencies that are connected to identities deemed "less than" by societal norms amplify the pain of marginalization. The impact is a pernicious and painful attack on our collective being and psyche as a result of these direct and indirect messages that exclude and ultimately convey, "you don't matter." The social-justice resistance movements, bystander/upstander strategy interventions, and creative engagement initiatives to cultivate resiliency that counter this onslaught of attack and exclusion are examples of how and where the STOP model can be used. Even among like-minded and relationally aware individuals and groups the steps of the STOP model are useful for raising awareness and catalyzing opportunities to examine less apparent forms of exclusion.

Such was the case while processing STOP model itself during the 2016 Transforming Community conference in Duluth, Minnesota, discussing the media example that we used to illustrate the need for understanding the widespread reach of marginalizing images rampant globally and even among ethno-culturally diverse communities each of whom have been targets of stereotypes and aggressive forms of exclusion. In this case, a popular international Asian television commercial depicts the demeaning and destructive image of a Black male entering a washing machine and remerging as a "clean" pale skin Asian male. This was meant to be a humorous ploy to sell laundry detergent. Conference participants of Asian descent expressed discomfort in seeing the commercial and an urgency to convey to peer group members that these were not ideologies they subscribed to or adopted. Further sharing of this experience to the larger group evoked sentiments of compassion and support. Additionally, participants of African descent shared with the larger group the pain that they experienced while watching the clip and cautioned against silencing or muting discussion of how these illustrations reinforce stratification and perpetrations of violence regardless of source. These comments came amidst the relentless murders of black men and women sweeping the United States at the time, and thus were all the more potent.

A broader discussion allowed us to return to the root of our presentation—that systems of power and privilege actively subordinate and exclude certain members of society which reflects the longstanding and embedded hierarchal framework of oppression where the narrative of race and racism ranks highest and bears down and across communities worldwide. Every level and layer of our group dialogue and processing exemplified the STOP model in action. In these conversations Seeing stratification of experiences within and across the intersecting identities of our conference community, Talking candidly about our impressions and impact, Opening up to embrace one another in vulnerability and strength, and Partnering to protest or redress what felt uncomfortable and together produce a new reality that allowed for all to be heard and that stimulated increased learning. Putting the model's steps into action will be vital in our ongoing journey to transform community in ways that will confront and dismantle the structural and interpersonal racism and inequalities at the center of social exclusion.

Everyone needs the pain to stop, everyone needs to stop the pain. Together we can. Together we must.

References

Banks, A., & Hirschman, L. A. (2015). *Four ways to click: Rewire your brain for stronger, more rewarding relationships*. New York: Penguin.

Craddock, K. (2007). *Mother to mother: Profiles of psychological resistance in young Black mothers and models of mother involvement in relationship with their mothers* (Unpublished doctoral dissertation). Tufts University, Medford, MA.

Craddock, K. (2015). Pushing back with our souls intact: Young Black mother's resistance to marginalization. In K. Craddock (Ed.), *Black motherhood(s): Contours, contexts and considerations*. California: Brunswick Press.

Eisenberger, N. I. & Lieberman, M. (2005). Why it hurts to be left out: The neurocognitive overlap between physical and social pain. In K.D. Williams, J. P. Forgas, and W. von Hippel (Eds.), *The social outcast: Ostracism, social exclusion, Rejection and bullying* (109-27). New York: Cambridge University Press.

Paludi, M. A. (2012). *Managing diversity in today's workplace: Strategies for employees and employers*. New York: Praeger.

Pierce, C. (1974). Psychiatric problems of the Black minority. In S. Arieti (Ed.), *American handbook of psychiatry* (512-523). New York: Basic Books.

Robinson, T. (2000). *The convergence of race, ethnicity, and gender: Multiple identities in counseling*. Thousand Oaks, CA: SAGE Publications.

Robinson, T. & Ward, J. V. (1991). A belief in self far greater than anyone's disbelief: Cultivating resistance among African American female adolescents. *Women & Therapy*, 11(3-4), 87-103.

Robinson-Wood, T. (2017). *The convergence of race, ethnicity, and gender: Multiple identities in counseling* (5th ed.). Thousand Oaks, CA: SAGE Publications.

Sue, D. W. (2010). *Microaggressions in everyday life: Race, gender, and sexual orientation*. Hoboken, NJ: John Wiley & Sons.

Combining the Neurobiology of Relational-Cultural Theory and Clinical Practice

···■ ■ ■ ···

ELIZABETH (LIBBY)
MARLATT-MURDOCH, LPCA, LCAS-A, CTRTC, CCTP

Since learning about Relational-Cultural theory (RCT) and relational neuroscience, they have become key components of my approach to mental health and substance abuse treatment with my clients. Using relational neuroscience in my work has been a particularly useful tool for depathologizing clients' experiences and helping them to understand that we are hard-wired for connection with others. Elizabeth (Libby) Marlatt-Murdoch may be contacted at libbymarlatt@yahoo.com.

Your brain is shaped by your mind—including your conscious and unconscious experiences, your body, the natural world, human culture and relationships (Hanson & Mendius, 2009). Relational-Cultural theory (RCT) is a psychological theory that acknowledges the radical power of relationship. RCT posits that throughout the lifespan, individuals grow through and toward relationship, and that culture has a profound impact on these relationships (Jordan, 2010). Relational neuroscience provides evidence that the brain is designed for connection and that without connection we cannot thrive (Banks, 2015). The neuroscience of Relational-Cultural theory offers a window into the mind and calls attention to the need to address not only an individual's relationships in therapy, but also the social context in which they exist (Banks, 2015). Based on experience as a clinician, Relational-Cultural theory and relational neuroscience can positively impact individual outcomes in healthcare and psychotherapy as well as improve relationships and quality of life by providing a way to depathologize individual's experiences. Sharing an understanding of relational neuroscience as it relates to RCT can be essential in promoting mutuality and growth in relationships in many areas. Multidimensional models for psychoeducation can provide key elements in accomplishing this.

Considerations and Connections

Sharing information on relational neuroscience with others can be powerful. Education is one way to begin this process. More specifically, psychoeducation, which is defined as information that is presented to individuals with a mental health condition and their families to help empower them to manage their condition in an optimal way (Bauml, 2006). So providing psychoeducation to clients about how the brain is hardwired for connection, and cannot thrive without healthy mutual connections, empowers individuals to push back against the hyperindividualistic social pressures that can undermine their health and well-being (Banks, 2015). In treatment, this knowledge can inform the process between client and clinician as they collaborate to come up with a plan to assess and improve the individual's relational skills and to discover how previous relationships have impacted the client's welfare. Outside of treatment, this same information may encourage individuals to evaluate their current relationships for mutuality, and provide the catalyst they need to seek more mutual relationships in an effort to improve their quality of life. The feelings of empowerment that come from this psychoeducation process can cultivate hope.

Relational neuroscience also has the power to depathologize an individual's experience for them. In a culture that sees development as a means to independence and ignores the devastating impacts of social pain, having knowledge to educate individuals about connection as a basic need can normalize an individual's experience of pain as it relates to social exclusion can be powerful (Banks, 2015). At the 2016 Transforming Community conference, Banks and Craddock presented their STOP SPOT model for empowering individuals to identify and address the pain of social exclusion. Social Pain Overlap Theory (SPOT) proposes that social pain which is the result of damaged or lost relationships, and physical pain which is the result of physical injury are experienced in the same part of the brain (Eisenberger & Lieberman, 2005). In the STOP SPOT model that Banks and Craddock presented at the conference, an individual must first See Stratification, then Talk and Tell their individual story related to the stratification or exclusion. The next steps they proposed are Open Outreach and finally Partnered Protest and Production.

Based on clinical experience, the ability to teach someone that his or her brain is working and responding in the way that it was designed to often results in the client or individual feeling validated. Instead of experiencing the shame or embarrassment of feeling like they are broken or their brain is broken, the client experiences a sense of safety and compassion from the therapist. This safety and compassion are necessary for the client to heal from the damage that may have resulted from relationships that are not mutual, are chronically disconnected, or in other ways are experienced as traumatic. Relational neuroscience empowers individuals by depathologizing her/his experience. This often results in increased self-compassion.

According to Walker at the Transforming Community conference, compassion is bearing witness without judgment. She also described in her ARC3 Model of Empathy that Awareness, Receptiveness, Curiosity and Courage, plus Compassion are all necessary ingredients for empathy. According to her model, Awareness is being mindful of "what is"; Receptiveness is being open to innovative and possibly conflicting knowledge; Curiosity and Courage are about embracing constructive ambiguity, vulnerability, and limitations. Relational neuroscience has the potential to depathologize a persons' sense of self leading to less shame, which in turn opens that person up for more vulnerable relational skills of compassion and empathy. In the words of Alamaas (2016) "it is only when compassion is present that people will allow themselves to see the truth" (para. 1). The feelings of empathy and compassion that are created through the psychoeducation process can be essential for clients in working through difficult experiences and for cultivating healing and hope.

Understanding of Neuroscience in RCT

To understand the neurobiological roots of interdependence we must start with understanding the brain. The reptilian brain, also known as the brain stem, is designed for regulation of the most basic functions such as heart rate and respiration, and is also involved in rapid mobilization of the brain and body for survival (Hanson & Mendius, 2009; Siegel, 2010). The paleo-mammalian brain, also known as the limbic system, works closely with the reptilian brain stem and is designed for creating our basic drives, emotions, memory, and is essential in establishing relationships and forming emotional attachments to others (Hanson & Mendius, 2009; Siegel, 2010). And finally, the neo-mammalian brain, also known as the cortex, "represents the three-dimensional world beyond the bodily functions and survival reactions mediated by the lower, subcortical regions," is involved in creating ideas and concepts (Siegel, 2010, p. 19). According to Banks and Craddock (2016) "being a part of a group is so critical to humans that our nervous system literally uses the same alarm (the dorsal anterior cingulate cortex) to register the distress of physical pain or injury AND social exclusion" (para. 3). Additional evidence for this concept is provided in studies that show the link between connection and survival. Research has shown that the human brain responds in a similar way to both food and connection, that the brains of neglected orphans from World War II did not have enough neural activity to support life, and that relational trauma impacts our mental and physical health and well-being long term (Bowlby, 1969; Center for Disease Control and Prevention, 2016; Hanson & Mendius, 2009). By looking at the different levels of the brain, we can begin to gather insight into how the basic need for survival led to the development of connection as a basic need in mammals.

Relational neuroscience has the power to shed even more light on love and belonging as a basic need. In fact, the research has shown that "lasting strength comes from being centered, and held within healthy relationships" (Banks & Craddock, 2016, para. 21). Banks' (2015) C.A.R.E. program was designed to illustrate how individuals can strengthen the neural pathways in their brains to encourage closeness and connection. In Bank's C.A.R.E. acronym, each letter represents a quality of a healthy relationship dictated by the functioning of one of four neural pathways of connection. In this model, she describes C is for Calm which represents the feeling that you get when you have a well-toned smart vagus nerve. She also explains that when we encounter potential danger, or when we are feeling stressed, the subcortical regions (primitive brain) becomes active and helps prepare the person to deal with the threat. According to Banks (2015), this primitive brain often makes decisions that negatively impact our relationships. She indicates having robust relationships helps to keep a person's smart vagus nerve well-toned, which in turn makes our relationships calmer. She describes how having a well-toned vagus nerve will allow us to mediate the primitive brain's response and prevent it from taking over; and, as a result, we are healthier and have greater mental clarity. In the C.A.R.E. model, Banks (2015) describes A is for Accepted, and represents the sense of belonging that comes when your dorsal anterior cingulate cortex (dACC) is functioning properly. This part of the brain is described by Eisenberger & Lieberman (2005) in their ground breaking work, Social Pain Overlap Theory (SPOT). Banks (2015) explains the dACC acts as an alarm for social exclusion; being chronically excluded or isolated can result in an over-reactive dACC, which means the alarm can go off even when others are welcoming. She describes R as Resonance you feel in healthy relationships, which is facilitated by the action of the mirror neuron system. She further states that when an individual's mirroring system is healthy the individual is able to understand other's experiences, actions and feelings by creating an internal neurological template of the same experience, action or feeling (ex. noticing you are crying while watching a movie where the characters are sad and crying). She clarifies that if the mirroring system is unhealthy, it results in the individual having difficulty understanding others and can cause difficulty for others in understanding the experience of the individual. She describes E as Energy which represents the feeling of euphoria and zest we get in healthy relationships if our brain's dopamine reward system remains closely attached to connection. She further relates the purpose of the dopamine system is to reward the brain and body for activities that promote survival—including approach behaviors, such as mating.

Unfortunately, when individuals do not get enough dopamine from healthy relationships, they may turn to unhealthy alternatives or addictive behaviors such as using drugs, gambling, or compulsive shopping (Banks, 2015). In this case the individual is rewiring their dopamine pathway away from connection and relationships, so that even when they are in relatively healthy relationships they may not derive energy and motivation from them (Banks, 2015). In summary, the C.A.R.E. acronym combined with describing how the qualities of a healthy relationship reflect the functioning of the four pathways for connection provides a solid, basic understanding of relational neuroscience.

Models

Banks (2015) cautions that concepts of neuroscience often appear more clear than they actually are and we must always respect the complexity of the central nervous system and what we have yet to discover. When starting the process of psychoeducation as it relates to the brain, it can be helpful to begin with some basic information about the brain. For example, the brain weighs approximately three pounds and is comprised of 100 billion neurons (Hanson & Mendius, 2009). Neurons connect via synapses and get their signals from other neurons through these receiving synapses and the signal is usually a burst of chemicals called neurotransmitters (Hanson & Mendius, 2009). Neural signals represent a piece of information according to Hanson &

Mendius (2009), and the mind can be defined in a broad sense as the totality of those pieces of information. It is important to recognize that no single area of the brain is exclusively responsible for regulating relationship, which means creating healthy relationships is an easier task if your central nervous system is integrated, balanced, and flexible (Banks, 2015). Every interaction an individual has with the world changes the brain in some way, and individuals are capable of neurogenesis (creating new connections in the brain) as well as neuroplasticity (altering existing connections in the brain throughout their lives) (Banks, 2015; Siegel, 2010).

Visual aids for use in psychoeducation, such as Siegel's hand brain (2012) or van Eys' felt brain (personal communication, July 7, 2016), allow individuals to see how the brain works so they can change what the brain does. Siegel's hand brain (2012) provides a portable and accessible brain model for neurologists and clients alike. His model is quite simple to create: take your thumb and fold it in towards your palm, then put your fingers over the top. He describes how the wrist represents the spinal cord, the palm represents the brain stem, the thumb folded inward onto the palm represents the limbic system, and the fingers covering the thumb represent the cortex.

To understand how the brain works, it is helpful to differentiate between parts of the brain that we have conscious control of from those we do not. In Siegel's hand brain model (2012), if you raise your four fingers then you separate these two areas. He describes the four raised fingers as representing the cortex which is the part you have conscious control over. He elaborates that the thumb folded over the palm represents the subcortical regions that are beyond our direct conscious control. The importance of this distinction can be further emphasized by pointing out that the fear activation response takes 50 milliseconds, which is about 1/20 of a second, whereas conscious thought takes 500-600 milliseconds, or half a second (Cozolino, 2010).

Using Siegel's hand brain model (2012), you can get a visual understanding of the first component of the C.A.R.E. program— Calm. He illustrates the process of "flipping our lids" by unfolding the fingers that were covering the thumb and palm to expose the rest of the hand which represents the limbic system and brain stem. When a person is triggered, the individual's primitive brain is responding without the protective inhibition of the cortex— the logical/rational part of the brain (Banks, 2015). When this happens, Banks (2015) indicates the individual's brain is not experiencing the feeling of calm that results when the individual can use their well-toned smart vagus nerve to mediate the response of the primitive brain. The Siegel hand brain model (2012) can be taken one step further by showing clients the location of the vagus nerve which runs between the right hemisphere (right two fingers) and left hemisphere (left two fingers) of the brain down through the limbic system and (via the parasympathetic nerve) into the brain stem and the rest of the body. Providing a visual representation of the location of the vagus nerve can increase understanding for the client about the role a well-toned smart vagus nerve has in calming both the brain and the body. In simple terms, when an individual has good smart vagal tone, they are able to accurately read a situation or person as safe and respond with engagement behaviors that result in enhanced connections and mutuality in relationships (Banks, 2015).

The second component of Banks' C.A.R.E. program (2015), Accepted, involves the dorsal anterior cingulate cortex which is located deep in the frontal cortex, and can be illustrated using the hand brain model by showing the underside of the two middle fingers (Siegel, 2012). In Siegel's hand brain model (2012), the two middle fingers represent the middle prefrontal cortex, which includes the dACC. It is important to emphasize that the dACC is part of an alarm system that responds to physical pain and injury as well as social exclusion, both of which are dangerous if left unaddressed (Banks, 2015). Both individual relationships and culture can impact our dACC explains Banks (2015). Developmental models that focus on independence and promote interpersonal competition often stratify and judge human differences creating an over reactive dACC, and consequently reactive pain pathways (Banks, 2015; Banks & Craddock, 2015).

The third component of Banks' C.A.R.E. program (2015), Resonance, reflects the functioning of the mirror neuron system which is located in the parietal, frontal, and temporal lobes. In Siegel's hand brain model (2012), the four fingers represent the cortical areas of the frontal and parietal lobes while the thumb represents the temporal lobe where the amygdala is located. It can be helpful to explain that the area of the cortex (four fingers) that is activated depends on the particular behavior or feeling that is being mirrored (Banks, 2015). In the hand brain model, Siegel (2012) indicates that the fingers overlap the thumb and palm illustrating how mirrored messages are created in the cortical areas and then transferred downward into the limbic system, then into the brain stem, and on into the body. He clarifies that these messages are transferred via the insula, also known as the "information superhighway" between the mirror neurons areas and the subcortical regions of the brain. The existence of the mirror neuron system is further evidence that we are biologically hardwired and evolutionarily designed to be interconnected (Banks, 2015). In fact, individuals understand what others are thinking and feeling by imitating them internally (Banks, 2015).

The final component of Banks' C.A.R.E. program (2015), Energy, involves the social motivation system/dopamine reward system. This is located in the mesolimbic dopamine pathway, which travels from the brainstem through the limbic system, into the anterior cingulate gyrus and orbitomedial prefrontal cortex (Banks, 2015). This pathway can be identified on Siegel's hand brain model (2012) by placing the pointer finger of your free hand on the palm of the hand brain model, moving it up to and through the thumb and ending at the fingers that represent the cortex.

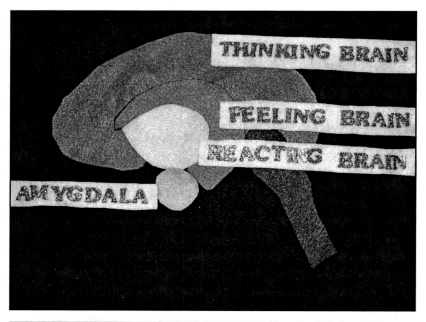

Figure 1:Van Eys' Felt Brain or Brain Puzzle

Another model or visual aid for making Relational Neuroscience accessible to clinicians and clients is the van Eys' felt brain (personal communication, July 7, 2016), also referred to as the Brain Puzzle (see Figure 1). She indicated that this model was designed to create a basic understanding of the brain and its functions and to illustrate and facilitate an understanding of the body's alarm system response. She described the felt brain as made of several pieces of felt: a large blue piece of felt shaped like the cortex labeled "thinking brain"; a pink piece of felt shaped like the brain stem added to the bottom right of the cortex; pieces of green felt and orange felt labeled "feeling brain" and representing the limbic system placed directly under the cortex and in front of the brain stem; a light orange almond shaped piece of felt represents the amygdala which together with the limbic system and brain stem is labeled "reacting brain". She indicated that a felt star is used as a visual representation of a trigger and is placed over the top of the amygdala. She further explained that after the star has been placed over the amygdala a black piece of felt shaped like the cortex is placed over the top of the cortex to represent the idea that the cortex is not online during an amygdala highjack. This model, much like Siegel's hand brain (2012), can be used to communicate a wealth of information about neuroscience, including RCT's relational neuroscience. The felt brain model can be used to communicate the elements of the C.A.R.E. program in much the same way that the hand brain model was adapted.

Both of these models can be used in an interactive way. Clinicians can ask their clients to mirror the movements of the hand brain and/or work with their client to assemble the Brain puzzle. The felt brain model described by van Eys (personal communication, July 7, 2016) was created by van Eys and Tisthammer in 2015 and also includes a script containing informal language interspersed with scientific terms that makes the script easy to read and easy to follow. Their script even includes opportunities for discussion, encourages the user to change it in any way that makes sense for the audience, and even explains an amygdala highjack—which is the same principle discussed in the first component of Banks' C.A.R.E. program (2015), Calm. This script by van Eys and Tisthammer (personal communication, July 7, 2016) states in part:

> Now, the limbic system cannot think...it can only feel and react. Only the blue part, the thinking brain, can think. Sometimes, the limbic system gets a danger signal and it gets afraid. It feels and reacts. So the brain's alarm goes off because the reacting brain recognizes danger. So, let's put this red star on the amygdala to show that the brain got that kind of danger signal. Let's call this the "amygdala alarm."
>
> When the alarm goes off, the brain sends out chemicals that give our body energy to cope with danger (or "to handle the danger in order to get safe"). Our hearts beat faster, we breathe more rapidly, there is more energy sent to our muscles so that we can fight or run away from the danger. Or sometimes, we freeze or hide so that the danger won't come to us.
>
> Here's an important thing: only the parts of our brain that help us survive are working when the amygdala alarm goes off. The other parts of the brain shut off until we have learned that we are safe; we will talk later about how we can recognize "triggers" so that we can quickly know that we are safe and turn the alarm off. The thinking part of the brain isn't working because it isn't needed at this time. (p. 7-8)

There are a number of things that may be taken from these two multidimensional models that can make relational neuroscience more accessible to practitioners.

- First, simplify the concepts of neuroscience appropriately in order to more effectively educate others.
- Second, build a foundation for understanding by introducing the intended audience to fundamental facts about the brain by using basic language to convey the message.
- Third, think outside the box and adapt existing visual aids or models to work for a new objective — in much the same way that the hand brain and felt brain models have been adapted to provide psychoeducation on relational neuroscience.
- Fourth, promote understanding by asking open-ended questions, gathering feedback, and experimenting with interactive methods instead of just using the model as a visual aid.
- Finally, use caution in deciding when it is appropriate to use relational neuroscience with clients or other individuals; this comes from experience and the ability to be attuned to those we serve.

The importance of sharing relational neuroscience with our clients has been supported by a number of considerations based on the tenets of Relational-Cultural theory. Psychoeducation on relational neuroscience has the ability to empower the individual to make changes in addition to depathologizing and validating the individual's experience. This can often result in increased levels of compassion and empathy necessary to be with the pain that can result from relational trauma, loss, exclusion and/or isolation. Learning and sharing relational neuroscience represents a practical opportunity to enhance well-being, develop compassion, and reduce suffering through cultivating healing and hope.

References

Alamaas, A. H. *(2016) Compassion leads to the truth*. Retrieved from: http://www.ahalmaas.com/glossary/compassion

Banks, A. (2015). *Wired to connect: The surprising link between brain science and strong, healthy relationships*. New York: Penguin.

Banks, A., & Craddock, K. (2016). *Stopping the pain of social exclusion*. Retrieved from: https://www.wcwonline.org/News-Events-Extra-Information/full-article-stopping-%09the-pain-of-social-exclusion-full-blog-article

Bauml, J. (2006). Psychoeducation: A basic psychotherapeutic intervention for patients with schizophrenia and their families. *Schizophrenia Bulletin*, (32)1.

Bowlby, J. (1969). *Attachment and loss* (Vol. 1). New York: Basic Books.

Center for Disease Control and Prevention. (2016). About adverse childhood experiences. Retrieved from:https://www.cdc.gov/violenceprevention/acestudy/about_ace.html

Cozolino, L. (2010). *The neuroscience of psychotherapy: Healing the social brain* (2nd ed.). New York: W.W. Norton & Co.

Eisenberger, N.I. & Lieberman, M.D. (2005). Why it hurts to be left out: The neurocognitive overlap between physical and social pain. In K. D. Williams, J. P. Forgas, & W. von Hippel (Eds.), *The social outcast: Ostracism, social exclusion, rejection, and bullying* (pp. 109-127). New York: Cambridge University Press.

Hanson, R., & Mendius, R. (2009). *Buddha's brain: The practical neuroscience of happiness, love & wisdom*. Oakland, CA: New Harbinger Publications.

Jordan, J. V. (2010). *Relational cultural therapy* (1st ed.). Washington, DC: American Psychological Association.

Siegel, D. (2012). Dr. Daniel Siegel presenting a Hand Model of the Brain. Retrieved from https://www.youtube.com/watch?v=gm9CIJ74Oxw

Siegel, D. J. (2010). *Mindsight: The new science of personal transformation*. New York: Bantam Books.

See the Girl: Transforming Community Through Girl-Centered Practice

———————— • • • ■ ■ ■ • • • ————————

INDERJIT (VICKY) BASRA, LMSW
NATALIE ARCE INDELICATO, PhD
VANESSA PATINO LYDIA, MPA
LAWANDA RAVOIRA, PhD

This paper is a collaborative effort between three staff members at the Delores Barr Weaver Policy Center and a faculty member at the University of North Florida after discussing our collective desire to share the work the Policy Center is doing to engage communities, organizations and individuals through quality research, community organizing, advocacy, training and model programming to advance the rights of girls and young women, especially those in the justice system. Our personal and professional identities are tied to partnership and mutuality with girls and young women. We value their lived experiences, knowledge, culture, ethnicity, and language, which also aligns with the tenants of Relational-Cultural theory. With this paper, we hope to highlight the need for comprehensive, girl-centered practice to transform communities, share the girl-centered practice model of the Policy Center, and clarify how the constructs of Relational-Cultural theory are used to "See the Girl". Inderjit Vicky Basra, LMSW, at vbasra@seethegirl.org. Dr. Natalie Arce Indelicato may be contacted at n.indelicato@unf.edu. Vanessa Patino Lydia, MPA may be contacted at vpatinolydia@seethegirl.org. Dr. Lawanda Ravoira may be contacted at lravoira@seethegirl.org.

Over the past two decades, efforts have been made to increase gender-specific services and understand gendered pathways for girls involved in, or at risk for entering into, the juvenile justice system; however, there is still significant opportunity for reform. Radical transformation of community and public resources, attitudes, and responses to address the unique psychosocial and educational issues of girls are needed (American Bar Association & National Bar Association, 2001; Bloom & Covington, 2001; Sharp & Simon, 2004; Sherman, 2005). In addition, comprehensive girl-centered practice models grounded in Relational-Cultural theory (RCT) should be adopted. Those place growth fostering relationships and the lived experiences of girls at the center of decision making and advocacy, and offer girls many points of access to needed services along the continuum of involvement with the justice system. In this paper, we discuss why comprehensive girl-centered practice models are critical to continued reform, offer an example of a girl-centered practice model grounded in RCT, and illustrate, through sharing several stories, how we are creating growth fostering relationships to transform community as we "See the Girl".

Why Comprehensive Girl-Centered Practice Models are Needed

Researchers, practitioners, and policy makers have begun to acknowledge gender bias within the juvenile justice system and have started to examine the unique needs of girls. Resulting gender specific programming and service delivery models have included acknowledging the unique needs of women and girls, their perspectives, development, and the biased attitudes that prevent or discourage young women from recognizing their potential (Belknap et al., 1997).

While these contributions have significantly advanced the dialogue regarding system reforms, they typically have been translated into single policy or intervention programs, which have not addressed the overarching system practices within or across programs at local and state levels (Ravoira & Patino Lydia, 2013). For example, a policy change may focus on a school suspension, a specific charge, or a dependency issue, rather than seeing the interconnectedness among all aspects of girls' lived experiences. Ravoira and Patino Lydia (2013) note that this "piecemeal response can result in compartmentalizing the lives of girls with little or no interfacing among the systems charged with providing services and interventions" (p. 300). Another consequence of this approach is that it tends to minimize the importance of mutuality, or connectedness, which is at the core of growth in relationships, particularly for girls and women (Miller, 1997). Without continuity and coordination among multiple points of care, relationships are often short-term interactions with providers rather than the deeper, mutually empowering and growth-fostering relationships that girls need to overcome the disconnections they have faced and continue to face as they navigate multiple systems (Covington, 2007). Additionally, it is important to note that most gender responsive treatment programs or policies do not include the girls or families in the development of the programs and policies that are provided for them, which inevitably leaves them feeling more disconnected and increases the risk for revictimization by the system.

Contextual and sociocultural challenges for girls who are involved in the justice system frequently include poverty, addiction, history of family violence, housing instability, sexual and/or physical abuse, caregivers' physical and mental health problems, caregivers' incarceration, and educational failures (Acoca & Dedel, 1998; Patino, Ravoira & Wolf, 2006; Watson & Edelman, 2012; Zahn, Hawkins, Chiancone & Whitworth, 2008). These relational disconnections and violations happen early and often for most girls. Kaplan (1986) discussed the consequences of these types of chronic disconnection including feelings of loss, inhibition to take action, internalized anger, and low self-esteem. Miller and Stiver (1997) also named the consequences of chronic disconnection as the central relational paradox. They wrote:

> In the face of repeated experiences of disconnection,
> we believe people yearn even more for relationships
> to help with the confused mixture of painful feelings.
> However, they also become so afraid of engaging with
> others about their experience that they keep important
> parts of themselves out of the relationship and develop
> techniques for staying out of connection. (p. 2)

Not being able to represent oneself authentically can lead
to psychological distress, inauthentic expressions of self, and
lack of connection with others (Miller & Stiver, 1997). This is
similar to situations Gilligan (1982) described for adolescent girls
who, when they perceive the threat of loss of connection, lose
theoretical "voice" by keeping important thoughts and feelings,
either verbally or non-verbally, out of relationships in order to
save the relationship. Chronic disconnection can lead to decreased
energy, disempowerment, confusion, diminished worth, and
turning away from relationships (Jordan & Dooley, 2000). Turning
away from relationships can result in feelings of isolation, which
has been described as the source of most suffering (Jordan &
Hartling, 2002). Further, these disconnections occur in the context
of individual, family, and sociocultural experiences (Jordan &
Hartling, 2002), which calls for comprehensive intervention at all
levels, as well as models of care that allow girls and young women
to enter at multiple points along a continuum - from prevention
to intervention to system advocacy - in order to have support to
navigate the various connections and disconnections in their lives.

Relational-Cultural theory gives a theoretical underpinning
for why comprehensive, girl-centered models are needed for
continued system reform because it argues that systemic change,
along with relationally focused individual intervention, is needed
to move girls out of condemned isolation to connection and
empowerment. Comstock and colleagues (2008) noted:

> RCT complements the multicultural/social justice
> movement by (a) identifying how contextual

and sociocultural challenges impede individuals' ability to create, sustain, and participate in growth-fostering relationships in therapy and life and (b) illuminating the complexities of human development by offering an expansive examination of the development of relational competencies over the life span. (p.279)

Although chronic disconnections can lead to psychological distress, researchers have consistently found that connected relationships predict health and well-being (Meyers, 2000; VanderVoort, 1999). People who have supportive, close relationships with friends, family, and support networks are less vulnerable to negative life events and some physical illnesses than those who have few social ties (Meyers, 2000). Relationships provide the opportunity to develop a positive sense of identity through constructive feedback, meaningful connections, and other people with whom one can work through problems (VanderVoort, 1999). Relationships promote positive and creative growth in addition to protecting us from stress (Jordan, 1992). Relational Cultural theorists argue that growth-fostering relationships, characterized by movement toward mutuality, mutual empathy, and mutual empowerment, are essential for lifelong resilience (Jordan & Hartling, 2002). Hartling (2005) defined resilience as relational rather than a unique, internal quality that is the ability to be tough or resistant to difficult challenges. Therefore, from an RCT perspective, resilience can be nurtured through developing and maintaining growth-fostering relationships. This is a critical perspective when engaging and reengaging with girls who are marginalized.

Delores Barr Weaver Policy Center
Girl-Centered Practice Model

Several years ago, I, Lawanda, was to give testimony before the Florida legislature about urgently needed changes in the justice system. On my way to the session, I stopped at a lock up facility to talk with the girls about what they felt needed to change. We sat on gray metal chairs in a small circle. I shared with the girls why I was there and asked each girl what message they would like me to share with members of the Florida House and Senate who had the power to change how girls are treated in the justice system. Maria, an intelligent, thoughtful girl who had spent most of her adolescence locked up simply said:

> Ask the adults to be there for us, to do what our parents couldn't do, be somebody we didn't have. Be a friend. We don't have anyone to really talk to. That's where you can start to help us. Whether we are good or bad, I have no one. And I really try to be good, but I always mess up. See me for who I am, not who you think I am. See me for who I can become.

"Seeing the Girl" is the mission of the Delores Barr Weaver Policy Center. Utilizing Relational-Cultural theory as a framework, along with decades of knowledge and efforts toward advancing the rights of girls involved in, or at risk for entering into, the juvenile justice system, the Policy Center has created a comprehensive, girl-centered practice model to "See the Girl". We do this by creating and maintaining mutual, growth-fostering relationships with girls, among staff and trainees, and within the community. The Policy Center is unique. The model is grounded in and driven by the voices and lived experiences of girls. All aspects of the Policy Center's work, from research, service delivery, and training to advocacy efforts to reform the system, is informed by girls and their families, who are considered partners in the work. This is how the Policy Center operationalizes the concept of mutuality and challenges systems to move toward a "power with" versus a "power over" paradigm with regard to girls in the community. Transforming community requires a mutual understanding among all those who are involved in girls' lives, including families, schools, mental health and medical providers, and the court system.

History and Approach of the Policy Center

The Policy Center is an outgrowth of the Justice for Girls movement that began in Florida in the late 1990s. In response to the need for reform, the Justice for Girls: Blueprint for Action (Ravoira & Miller, 2007) called for comprehensive reform in how Florida responded to girls in the juvenile justice system. The Blueprint stated that girls have a fundamental right to fair and equitable treatment, to freedom from violence and exploitation, to be valued and respected by those who interact with them, to be able to trust the system, and to have a system advocate. It is through these rights, coupled with the RCT framework, that new training and community awareness initiatives, service delivery modalities, changes in public and organizational policy and practices, individual and system level advocacy, and research were initiated. The work is about operationalizing girl-centered principles (see Table 1) that guide our mission and addressing issues that violate girls' rights. We provide access to a continuum of services and support for girls and young women—starting from prevention through intervention —such as skills-building in elementary schools, girls' groups in alternative schools and detention, individual counseling, comprehensive care management, and transition services. Although each component of the Policy Center's girl-centered practice model is outlined separately in Table 2, it is critical to note that, in practice, the programs are interconnected and are continually being informed and updated through feedback from girls engaged with the Policy Center and in response to policies that either support or violate rights of girls within the community and nationally. The model demonstrates the need for comprehensive services to address the fragmented and disconnected experiences girls are facing.

The programming and services at the Policy Center are based on understanding the trends of the local community in incarcerating girls and the needs of girls. We develop an understanding of girls' needs through listening sessions where we provide space to listen to girls and ask them for their recommendations and what they want others to know. This information is used in our advocacy agenda to educate the community about what girls are experiencing. We partner with girls in every aspect of our work because we believe they are the experts of their life stories and should be partners in making recommendations for system reform, program development, and advocacy efforts. Additionally, we use relational, reflective research practices that include vetting assessments and measures to ensure they are appropriate, strengths-based, and help to build connection and relationship with the girls. For example, we measure the strength of the therapeutic relationship, but would not use assessments that include questions that are blaming or do not provide context to understand her experiences.

The girl-centered practice model components have been developed based on the information and insights girls and families share with staff at multiple points along development, implementation and evaluation of services. For example, girls in the Girl Matters: It's Elementary program to reduce suspensions and increase social supports share that the most impactful part of their involvement is the relationships they build with the interns. The interns share the great experiences they have working with girls from a girl-centered lens.

When using a therapeutic alliance measure with girls involved in the justice system, preliminary data shows that although there is not always agreement about what needs to be done to improve a situation, the girls report when having a voice in their goals and plans that they feel appreciated and heard. Ninety percent of the girls reported that something had changed in their lives that they feel good about. At the beginning of counseling, girls noted changes in family relationships. As girls continued to attend sessions, they identified positive school related outcomes. With time they named examples of changes about how they saw themselves. Programming staff attributes this emerging pattern to how the therapeutic goals emerge. Initially, meet girls where they are—which is often starting in crisis—and then working to stabilize basic needs and family relationships before moving towards addressing school and other goals. As Basra explained, "We see the therapeutic process at work when the work deepens and the girls' understanding of who they are shift, as other people reflect back to them their value and worth, even when they make mistakes" (Patino Lydia & Zayets, 2016).

Our qualitative research with girls confirms that they have experienced relational disconnection from individuals and institutional systems. The research also indicated many points of intervention where connections could be strengthened (Patino & Moore, 2015). This information affirms our comprehensive services at multiple points along the system that are grounded in mutual empathy and mutual empowerment, the building blocks for growth fostering relationships (Jordan et al., 1991). Research has shown the mental health benefits of situations where individuals receive support from others as well as situations where benefit is derived from ongoing exchanges of supportive behaviors (Cutrona, 1996). These exchanges are the cornerstone of mutuality in relationships with girls and their families, as well as among staff, at the Policy Center.

Building Internal Staff Supports and Community Partnerships

Among Policy Center staff, mutuality is nurtured through the multidisciplinary team approach to staffing and supervision. Everyone is invested in relational growth with the girls and with one another. Communication about clients and their needs happens daily, and we value the different perspectives that all team members bring. We have found this to be very helpful in growing our collective and individual knowledge base. One of our newest staff members shared that she loves the "we environment" of the Policy Center. In prior work environments, she stated that she felt like she was always on her own and at the Policy Center she feels like she has a whole team supporting her and everyone is invested in the girls' successes.

The Policy Center recognizes that a key component to implementing the girl-centered principles in practice depends on hiring staff that understands the importance of the Center's values and their roles in shifting the culture. Our hiring process focuses on connecting with the core values of the staff along with recognizing the skills they bring. Through the questions asked during the interview process, we hope to better understand how a candidate would make choices aligned with the organization's values. Individuals applying for a position at the Policy Center meet with the hiring supervisor, the CEO/President, the team they will be working with, and with anyone else at the Policy Center who is interested in participating in the interview process. The extended interview process also allows for a relationship to be built and for the individual to better understand the culture of the Policy Center and what it offers the community. In this way, the Policy Center team and the interviewee can see if the Policy Center is the right environment to work together to address the needs of girls.

The Policy Center recognizes that the development of girl-centered tools and ongoing training are critical components to effectively meeting the needs of girls and young women, families and the community. Ongoing training and professional development is provided for the community, Policy Center staff, and student interns. This helps providers interact with girls in a girl-centered manner, allowing our community to see the girl, not just the behavior. This is especially important when interacting with girls who have often experienced trauma. Experiencing trauma can affect the way a girl or young woman perceives and responds to the world, yet staff members are, at times, ill-equipped to respond in an effective manner. We make significant effort to ensure that our language, trainings, and curriculum do not result in victim blaming. As a way of creating mutuality and shared power, we invite girls to co-facilitate trainings and presentations with us. Many times, presentations are designed with the girls and the girls decide what they would like to present.

Through training undergraduate and graduate interns, we have opportunities to develop mutuality in our relationships, as well as help them build the skills to develop mutual relationships with the girls. Many interns share that they initially work with the girls in elementary school assuming the girls would learn so much from them. In the end, interns share that they learn just as much from the girls as the girls learn from them, which underscores the RCT concept of mutuality in growth fostering relationships.

Addressing Multiple Levels of Advocacy

Relational-Cultural theory acknowledges that chronic disconnection occurs on an individual level, and also, simultaneously, on a cultural and institutional level. Racism, sexism, classism, and heterosexism create social and cultural disconnections and have a direct impact on an individual's sense of connection and disconnection. Jordan (1997) wrote, "Due to our culture's handling of difference, through a system of hierarchy and dismissal, major, chronic, and painful disconnections occur around diversity; racism, sexism, heterosexism, classism, and ageism all become forces in creating disconnection rather than connection" (p. 3). Jordan goes on to say that these forces create deeper isolation, withdrawal, fear, and shame. Ultimately, especially for marginalized groups, this leads to chronic disconnection. At the same time, "empathy across difference", can serve as a catalyst for growth and validation in relationships (Jordan, 1997).

Since chronic disconnection can occur at the cultural and institutional level, the Policy Center is actively engaged in public policy changes that impact the advancement of girls' rights. Advocacy is provided at the individual, community and systemic level. On the individual level, advocacy for each girl is provided during participation in multidisciplinary staffing, in court, in school, and during counseling sessions with girls and families/caregivers. Through advocacy we are able to identify the services that are needed and also identify points along the continuum where the system(s) failed to meet girls' needs. Many of our girls have experienced acute disconnections and advocacy helps them to engage in the systems to rework the acute disconnections and develop more positive relationships. Through all of the work, we bring authenticity with other staff members and with the girls.

On a community level, the care manager advocates on behalf of the girl with juvenile probation officers, the State Attorney's Office, the Public Defender's Office, the judge, and community partners to ensure the voices of girls and their families/caregivers are heard in the judicial system. The care manager helps the girls and families navigate the complex legal system and processes, which includes arranging pro-bono legal services when indicated. The care manager also works with community partners to build a network of care for each girl based on her complex individual needs. Many times these care plans can serve as alternatives to locking girls up as it gives judges other options and a better understanding of the true needs of the girls.

Finally, what we learn from the girls directs the advocacy platform at the local, state, and national level used to develop better public policies, processes and practices informed by the lived experiences of the girls. For example, when girls were being transported within the residential facility, they told us that they had to walk with their hands behind their backs. The young women told us that this was re-traumatizing for them, given the trauma they had experienced in their lives, and that walking with their hands behind their backs increased their feelings of agitation, stress, and hyperawareness. After hearing from the young women, the Policy Center staff shared the concerns with the administrators at the residential facility and, ultimately, the young women were allowed to walk with their hands by their sides. Administrators reported fewer fighting incidents with guards and other residents due to this change in policy.

From development to evaluation, the Policy Center model is centered on our relationship with girls, their voices, and the research that comes from listening to girls and their families.

The goal is to "See the Girl" within the context of her family, community and lived experiences.

What it Means to "See the Girl"

From the relational exchange described earlier between Lawanda and Maria, along with the theoretical foundation of RCT, the girl-centered practice of "See the Girl," seeing the context of girls' lived experiences, has emerged. It guides the mission to advance the rights of girls in or at risk of juvenile justice system involvement by engaging others as partners in the movement. It requires staying in relationship through various individual and system level disconnections. In Maria's case, "seeing" her meant looking beyond her behavior to understanding the historical trauma that was part of her unresolved family and personal history. "Seeing the Girl" meant understanding the acute and chronic relational disconnections Maria faced as she navigated unstable living situations, the responsibility of care-taking for her siblings, and addiction. By age fourteen, Maria started selling drugs to get money for places to stay. She was arrested for drug paraphernalia, and while on probation she ran away and received a violation of probation and began the cycle in and out of locked facilities. Maria's story is the narrative of most of the girls trapped in the justice system. The Policy Center's research found that at the epicenter of the girls' stories are the shared experiences of grief, loss, and trauma as well as resilience and longing for connection (Patino Lydia & Moore, 2015).

Tina's Story

Like Maria, Tina's story also helps illustrate the multiple points at which girls can access and receive services. The first time the Policy Center staff met Tina and her mother was during a juvenile justice staffing where her support team was trying to put together an alternative plan so she would not be sent to a commitment program. The Policy Center had no prior connection with Tina but was invited to participate in the meeting as a

81

possible resource for her and her family. The group was made up of juvenile justice staff, including her probation officer, a representative of the school board, her attorney, a case manager, a therapist, and others who had been referred to Tina and her family.

The group started by reviewing Tina's file and sharing why they were there. When the group facilitator started reviewing Tina's past traumas and exposure to violence, the facilitator became very detailed in his questions and comments of her lived experience. The level of details that were shared made everyone in the meeting, including Tina and her mother, uncomfortable. Even though this was our first interaction with Tina and we were not very familiar with her story, the Policy Center staff chose to speak up and ask the purpose of going into such detail in the meeting. The staff member reminded everyone that this could re-traumatize Tina. The meeting facilitator shared that this was how these meetings were conducted, with the intent that everyone would know the details and have better options for Tina. Staff commented that they understood this, but did not understand the benefit of going into that level of detail with everyone. After the Policy Center staff member spoke up, the meeting facilitator became less detailed in his descriptions and shifted the way he addressed Tina.

Tina made eye contact with the staff member, her body language shifted, and she seemed more relaxed. Later, when Tina agreed to work with the Policy Center, she shared that she was grateful that we had attended the meeting and that, although she felt herself getting angry, she did not know how to stop the facilitator from continuing to ask intrusive and traumatizing questions.

The Policy Center provided Tina and her family with therapeutic and care management services. The therapist and care manager met with her and her family in their home and at the Policy Center depending on what was most convenient for Tina. The Policy Center staff attended court dates with her and continued to advocate with her, and at times, supported her basic needs such as helping her to purchase clothing, toiletries and other items for her home. After a year of services, Tina decided she no longer wanted to participate in services with the Policy Center.

We did not hear from her for over a year until a staff member received a collect call from Tina from the local jail. She had been arrested and was being held until her next court date. She was now eighteen and being held in the adult system. The Policy Center staff was present in the courtroom for her next court date. Since she was not presently receiving services, we were not able to approach the judge and advocate for her best interests; however, we were present and let Tina know that the relationship was still available to her. Tina made eye contact with staff when she was brought in front of the judge. Staff listened and, once the judge moved on to the next case, turned around, held Tina's mother's hand, gave her a business card, and told her to have Tina contact her if she needed support. The family later shared that based on their interactions with Policy Center staff; they trusted the authenticity of the relationship.

All of the choices the Policy Center makes are focused on keeping the relationship with the girl at the center because no matter what we do, if the girl does not trust us, there will not be growth. As illustrated in Tina's case, our work always includes her family and her community because they are important to her. By creating a model that focuses on the continuity of care for the girl and her family, we continue to enhance our relationships with Tina and her family. The goal is to be present and continue to build the relationship through the inevitable connections and disconnections that occur. The relationship continues to grow because the same people continue to support her regardless of where she is in the system. This is different from other experiences Tina has had, where her juvenile probation officer and/or case manager changed at different points.

Regardless of the program girls participate in or what point along the continuum of services they enter into, we recognize the importance of relational connection in girls' lives as we coordinate services within multiple systems. We make efforts to divert girls from incarceration, and identify appropriate, girl-centered interventions. The importance of growth fostering relationships to mental well-being is central to the interactions Policy Center staff have with girls and each other. Knowing that disconnection is the source of psychological suffering, Policy Center staff are able to understand and "See the Girl" through the disconnections she has experienced and connections she is driven to establish (Jordan, 1997). Jordan (1991) pointed out that even in relationships that are mutual overall, not every specific interaction is mutual. Therefore, even the most connected relationships will inevitably experience disconnection. Policy Center staff recognizes this inevitability, and contends that disconnections in relationships can serve, depending on the response of both parties, as opportunities for further growth. Policy Center staff recognizes that strategies of disconnection can be authentic experiences and someone can be disconnected from therapy but not from an authentic relationship (e.g., calling therapist while on the run). It takes energy to be connected. From an RCT perspective, if the hurt person is not able to express her feelings or is met with apathy, or disregard of her experience, she will begin to distort herself in order to keep the relationship. In our experience, most girls feel less powerful in most of their relationships; therefore, much of the service delivery component of our work involves establishing mutually empowering relationships, respect, and acknowledging relational disconnections. Counseling and care management focus on discovering and addressing the relational disconnections that often manifest as depression, anxiety, and/or externalizing behaviors such as substance abuse, running away, and aggression. Girls are an integral part of their care planning which focuses on the ability of girls to learn and employ healthy coping mechanisms and skills.

The approach to working with girls and families is relational and contextual, and the benefits of the continuity of care management and therapeutic services can follow a girl regardless of her point of entry. This type of intervention creates incredible opportunities for better understanding of girls' perceptions about their relationships and how their connections, disconnections, and sense of supports may shift over time.

Ann's Story

Ann's story is an example of how relationship building happens over time and occurs in the context of providing comprehensive support and care management. Ann was 16 years old and referred to the Policy Center by her mother and an investigator working with the family. She was very hesitant to reach out and connect with the Policy Center. Ann's mother was incarcerated, she did not have a relationship with her father, and she did not feel comfortable coming to the Policy Center on her own. Although many appointments were scheduled with the counselor, Ann continued to make excuses for why she could not meet with our staff. The counselor told Ann that she would meet wherever Ann wanted to meet and would support her in any way she needed, including providing bus passes. One day, the counselor received a text from Ann asking, "Do you think you could bring me a bus pass? I have a class at 6:00 pm today and I have no way of getting there. I also tried looking up different bus schedules and different buses, and I am not sure which one to take." The counselor immediately reached out to her supervisor and shared the text she received. They agreed that providing Ann with bus passes was an important part of building an authentic, trusting relationship. The counselor replied to Ann's text message by saying that she was in a meeting, but as soon as the meeting was over she would meet Ann and bring a bus pass. Once the counselor arrived at Ann's house with bus pass and the bus schedule, they sat down and reviewed the possible bus routes. Ann shared that tonight was her first college class and she was very nervous. The counselor explored with her what was making her nervous and they set up a plan to help her through the evening, which included being able to text the counselor when and if things became too overwhelming. The counselor also told Ann that if she did not hear from her that evening, she would check in with her the next day. From that moment on, Ann has been regularly attending her meetings with the counselor and feels supported.

The Policy Center recognizes that relationships are not only built during the counseling session, but by being present when someone needs you the most. Many times we lose clients even before we ever start working with them because we are never able to build mutuality in the relationship. Our clients need to know that they matter to us and that their well-being matters to us. By dropping off the bus pass and spending time to listen to Ann's concerns, the counselor was able to build a relationship that showed Ann that she mattered. Mutuality is the ability to step outside of the therapeutic "expert" role into the authentic trust building moments of connection. It is the ability to create a work space that gives permission for staff to build a relationship with the girls based on the needs of the girls in that present moment, allowing the girls to be the lead on how fast and when the therapeutic relationship will develop.

Conclusion

There are many girls and families hurting in our communities. The way a community and service providers respond is a critical piece to transformation. When we "See the Girl" as part of the community fabric, it has a lasting impact. Communities are transformed through mutual empathy, as it decreases the experience of isolation and increases the capacity for connectedness (Miller & Stiver, 1997).

Creating and participating in growth-fostering relationships are not only critical to individuals' psychological well-being and development (Comstock, Hammer, Strentzsch, Cannon, Parsons, & Salazar, 2008), they are essential to creating vital and responsive communities. Growth-fostering relationships are the central building blocks for both individuals and the communities in which they live. Service providers can contribute to community transformation by developing comprehensive care models grounded in Relational-Cultural theory. The Delores

Barr Weaver Policy Center has developed a girl-centered model, informed by Relational-Cultural theory. Together, we are creating system reform and transformation in our community through a comprehensive approach to service delivery, research, advocacy, and training for girls who are involved in, or at risk of entering into, the juvenile justice system.

Ultimately, "Seeing the Girl" transforms the community by reducing the number of girls involved in the juvenile justice system, keeping more girls connected to their communities through engagement in social services instead of locking them up, and sending a clear message to girls that they are valued, have power, and play significant roles in our communities. Communities are transformed by the healing power of mutual relationships.

Delores Barr Weaver Policy Center Girl-Centered Principles

Our mission is guided by girl-centered principles:
- Acknowledges girls as experts of their lives and relationships.
- Embraces sitting where the girls sit and seeing what they see.
- Honors and values girls' lived experiences, knowledge, culture, ethnicity, and language.
- Understands health as more than and different from the absence of illness.
- Emphasizes the importance of girls' connections (family, friends, schools, and others).
- Recognizes the dynamic community in which girls live, play, and learn.
- Focuses on the intersectionality of gender, race/ethnicity, sexual orientation, nationality, age, ability, and education.
- Uses reflective practice and listening without judging.
- Ensures that programs are guided by gender relevant theories.
- Promotes activism and informed advocacy.

Note: Developed with Dr. Barbara Guthrie, RN, PhD, FAAN

Delores Barr Weaver Policy Center Girl-Centered Practice Model		
Community Need	**Policy Center Response**	**Description**
Service Delivery (Prevention)	Girl Matters: It's Elementary School-based Interventions	Services provided in schools to interrupt school disconnection include individual care management and referrals to appropriate resources, groups for girls, mentoring and skill building, and or advocacy within the school system regarding academic and disciplinary matters.
Service Delivery (Prevention)	Girls Leadership Council	The Council is open to girls, age 12-21, and provides a bi-monthly meeting to promote confidence, leadership, knowledge and safety.
Service delivery (Intervention)	SAVVY Sister Groups for Girls	Groups for girls are intended to increase girls' knowledge and coping skills to address girls' pathways into the juvenile justice system. Each topic addresses safety with self, with others in the program and in the community. Girls explore both their personal and societal values. Additionally, they learn and practice important skills including communication, building relationships, activism, and team building.
Service Delivery (Intervention)	Care Management	Care management includes crisis intervention, individual level advocacy to have access to appropriate resources, monitoring of the quality of services, mentoring, transitional and re-entry services, housing, employment support, school connectedness and re-engagement, and advocacy at multi-disciplinary team (MDT) meetings. This includes helping girls as they transition back to the community and their families. Care managers also help girls and families navigate the legal process, which can include arranging pro-bono legal services when warranted.

Service Delivery (Intervention)	Girl-Centered Counseling and Telemental Health	Individual and family counseling is provided with girls who are referred due to their juvenile justice involvement (e.g. probation) or risk of involvement. Sessions focus on discovering and dealing with the relational disconnections driving her behavior, which creates difficulties for the girl (internalizing and externalizing behaviors). Girls are part of care planning, which focuses on the ability of girls to articulate coping mechanisms, learn, and employ healthy coping skills.
Research	Girl Centered Inquiry	Ongoing inclusion of girls' experiences, recommendations through listening sessions, assessments, and surveys, which inform service delivery, continued research, and advocacy for shifts in public policy.
Training	Community-based Training	Based on research, information shared by girls and community needs, trainings are developed or experts are brought in to train professionals in our community.
Training/ Advocacy	Girl Centered Practice	The Policy Center is one of the first organizations to collaborate with a local university to develop a continuing education curriculum focused on Girl Centered Practice and Development of Advocacy skills.
Advocacy	System Level Advocacy	Work with local, state, and national lawmakers and lobbyists to develop policies that advance the rights of girls.
Advocacy	Community Level Advocacy	Care managers advocate on behalf of the girls with probation officers, the State Attorney's Office, the Public Defender's Office by increasing awareness of Policy Center practice model and developing a contextual understanding of girls' behaviors.
Advocacy	Individual Level Advocacy	Advocacy for girls provided during multidisciplinary staffing, in court, in school, and with families/caregivers. Care managers also help girls and their families navigate the complex legal system.

References

Acoca, L. & Dedel, K. (1998). *No place to hide: Understanding and meeting the needs of girls in the California Juvenile Justice System.* San Francisco: National Council on Crime and Delinquency.

American Bar Association & National Bar Association. (2001). *Justice by gender: The lack of appropriate prevention, diversion, and treatment alternatives for girls in the justice system.* Retrieved from http://www.americanbar.org/content/dam/aba/publishing/criminal_ justice_section_newsletter/crimjust_juvjus_justicebygenderweb. authcheckdam.pdf

Belknap, J., Dunn, M., & Holsinger, K. (1997). *Moving toward juvenile justice and youth-serving systems that address the distinct experience of the adolescent female.* A Report to the Governor. Office of Criminal Justice Services, Columbus, OH.

Bloom, B.E. & Covington, S. (2001, November). *Effective gender-responsive interventions in juvenile justice: Addressing the lives of delinquent girls.* Paper presented at the Annual Meeting of the American Society of Criminology, Atlanta, GA. Retrieved from http://www.centerforgenderandjustice.org/assets/files/7.pdf

Comstock, D. L., Hammer, T. R., Strentzsch, J., Cannon, K., Parsons, J., & Salazar II, G. (2008). Relational-Cultural theory: A framework for bridging relational, multicultural, and social justice competencies. *Journal of Counseling & Development,* 86(3), 279-287.

Covington, S. (2007). *The relational theory of women's psychological development: Implications for the criminal justice system.* In Ruth T. Zaplin (Ed.), Female offenders: Critical perspectives and effective interventions (2nd ed.). Sudbury, MA: Jones & Bartlett.

Cutrona, C.E. (1996). *Social support in couples: Marriage as a resource in times of stress.* Thousand Oaks, CA: Sage Publications.

Gilligan, C. (1982). In a different voice. Cambridge, MA: Harvard University Press.

Hartling, L.M. (2005). *Fostering resilience throughout our lives: New relational possibilities.* In D. Comstock (Ed.), Diversity and development: Critical contexts that shape our lives and relationships (pp. 337-354). Belmont, CA: Thomson Brooks/Cole.

Jordan, J.V. (1992). *Relational resilience.* Work in Progress, No. 57. Wellesley, MA: Stone Center for Developmental Services and Studies.

Jordan, J.V. (Ed.). (1997). *Women's growth in diversity.* New York: The Guilford Press.

Jordan, J.V., & Dooley, C. (2000). *Relational practice in action: A group manual.* Wellesley, MA: Stone Center Publications.

Jordan, J. V. & Hartling, L.M. (2002). *New developments in Relational-Cultural theory.* In M. Ballou & L.S. Brown (Eds.), Rethinking mental health and disorder: Feminist perspectives (pp. 48-70). New York: The Guilford Press.

Kaplan, A. (1986). The "self-in-relation": Implications for depression in women. *Psychotherapy: Theory, research, and practice, 23,* 234-241.

Kaplan, J.B. Miller, I.P. Stiver, & J.L. Surrey (Eds.). *Women's growth in connection: Writings from the Stone Center.* New York: Guilford Press.

Meyers, D.G. (2000). The funds, friends, and faith of happy people. *American Psychologist,* 55(1), 56-67.

Miller, J.B. (1997). *The development of women's sense of self.* In J.V. Jordan, A.G.

Miller, J.B. & Stiver, I.P. (Eds.). The healing connection: How women form relationships in therapy and in life. Boston: Beacon Press.

Patino Lydia, V., & Moore, A. (2015). *Breaking new ground on the First Coast: Examining girls' pathways into the juvenile justice system.* Jacksonville, FL: Delores Barr Weaver Policy Center.

Patino, V., Ravoira, L. & Wolf, A. (2006). *A rallying cry for change: Charting a new direction in the state of Florida's response to girls.* Oakland, CA: National Council on Crime and Delinquency.

Patino Lydia, V., & Zayets, B. (2016). *Continuity of care model demonstration period outcomes report.* Jacksonville, FL: Delores Barr Weaver Policy Center.

Ravoira, L. & Miller, R. (2007). *Justice for girls: Blueprint for action.* Tallahassee, FL: Children's Campaign, Inc.

Ravoira, L. & Patino Lydia, V. (2013). Strategic training and technical assistance: A framework for reforming the juvenile justice system's treatment of girls and young women. *Georgetown Journal of Poverty Law & Policy,* xx(2), 297-319.

Sharp, C. & Simon, J. (2004). *Girls in the juvenile justice system: the need for more gender-responsive services*. Washington, DC: Child Welfare League of America.

Sherman, F.T. (2005). *Pathways to juvenile detention reform: Detention reform and girls, challenges and solutions*. Baltimore, MD: Annie E. Casey Foundation. Retrieved from http://www.pretrial. org/download/juvenile-pretrial/JDAI%20Pathway%2013%20 Detention%20Reform%20and%20Girls%20Challenges%20and%20 Solutions.pdf

VanderVoort, D. (1999). Quality of social support in mental and physical health. *Current Psychology,* 18(2), 205-222.

Watson, L. & Edelman, P. (2012). *Improving the juvenile justice system for girls: Lessons from the states*. Washington, DC: Georgetown Center on Poverty, Inequality and Public Policy.

Zahn, M.A., Hawkins, S.R., Chiancone, J. & Whitworth, A. (2008). *The girls study group: Charting the way to delinquency prevention for girls*. Washington, DC: US Department of Justice, Office of Justice Programs, Office of Juvenile Justice and Delinquency Prevention.

Gay Fathers of Intentional Families and Relational-Cultural Theory

····■ ■ ■ ····

MATTHEW RIDER BARCLAY

Matthew Rider Barclay, a licensed clinical counselor for over twenty years, works with couples and families as they seek connection to each other and heal their relational wounds. As a PhD student in Transformative Studies at the California Institute of Integral Studies, he is currently researching the lived experiences of gay male couples at the intersection of marriage equality and intentional fatherhood as they negotiate sociocultural identities and seek growth-fostering relationships with the larger gay male subculture, other gay fathers, and the heterosexual majority culture. Matthew Rider Barclay may be contacted at matt.rider.barclay@gmail.com.

Gay fatherhood challenges the cultural mores of both the larger gay male subculture and the dominant heterosexual majority culture, contributing to chronic disconnection from both cultures. Relational-Cultural theory (RCT) posits that humans are hardwired for connection, and that chronic disconnection results in isolation and developmental stagnation (Jordan, 2010). RCT provides a powerful theoretical framework for understanding gay fathers of intentional families and their need to connect with other gay dads. Social media, nonprofits, and other groups provide platforms for connection, empathic support, and mutual empowerment, which RCT emphasizes, are crucial for growth fostering relationships to develop between individuals and their culture (Jordan, 2010).

What are gay intentional families and how do they differ from other LGBT families? How can the RCT concepts of mutual empathy, growth fostering relationships, relational authenticity, and mutual empowerment support intentional families parented by gay fathers? This article describes how the key concepts of RCT can be applied to fathers of gay intentional families as they negotiate connection and disconnection with the larger gay male subculture, the dominant heterosexual majority culture, and other gay fathers.

Gay Intentional Families

Moore and Stambolis-Ruhstorfer's (2013) definition of gay intentional families is any family created within the context of a committed same-sex relationship as a gay intentional family. The literature on gay fatherhood makes a distinction between the families created by gay men who entered fatherhood within the context of a heterosexual relationship, and those created by gay men that chose to become fathers after having come out (Berkowitz, 2007; Berkowitz & Marsiglio, 2007; Lewin, 2009; Mallon, 2004). The research suggests that these two kinds of gay-parented families are structured differently, due mostly to the timing and identity formation involved in both paths (Dempsey & Hewitt, 2012; Tornello & Patterson, 2012). The type of social support sought and received varies along this line of distinction (Tornello & Patterson, 2012). It is important to note that while gay fathers of intentional families represent the fastest growing group among LGBT-parented families in the United States (Gates, 2012, 2013), they are the least represented in the literature on LGBT-parented families.

RCT uses the term connection to mean movement toward and through growth fostering relationships that emphasize reciprocity of respect and support (Walker & Rosen, 2004). Walker and Rosen (2004) state: "Connection involves the respectful negotiation of difference that facilitates growth and the emergence of something new" (p. 9). Connection does not protect people from conflict;

indeed, conflict often results in a strengthening of relational ties (Jordan & Hartling, 2002). Growth-fostering connection does, however, protect the individual from humiliation and shame by the nature of reciprocal respect (Jordan, Kaplan, Miller, Stiver, & Surrey, 1991). Jordan (2010) writes that disconnection describes movement away from mutually enriching relationships; and Jordan and Carlson (2013) further state that while being a part of normal human relationships, relational disconnection hurts. Relational movement—the process by which people in relationship alternately move toward and away from relationship—is considered a normal aspect of all healthy relationships (Jordan, 2010; Jordan & Carlson, 2013). Understanding connection and disconnection in this context is foundational to understanding the theory and its relevance to the topic of gay fatherhood.

Gay Fatherhood in Context

The rite of marriage and the act of family-building, which often go hand-in-hand, have traditionally been privileged developmental milestones and societal expectations exclusive to heterosexual men and women in American society (Lewin, 2009; Mallon, 2004). Legal and societal barriers have historically prevented gays and lesbians from accessing and participating in these privileged rites of passage with controlling images depicting gay men as perverts, ill-suited to raise children (Hicks, 2006). Within the last few decades, however, gay men and lesbians have been challenging the heterosexually-defined social constructs of family building and marriage by creating families via combinations of domestic partnerships, civil unions, adoption, in vitro fertilization, and other nontraditional avenues (Baca Zinn, Eitzen, & Wells, 2015; Gates, 2013; Hicks, 2006).

Statistics about the number of children being raised in same-sex households can be confusing. Compiling data from multiple sources including U.S. Census reports, the Williams Institute looked at the demographics of households that self-identified as being parented by gay fathers (Gates, 2012). While the overall number of households reported being parented by gay or lesbian couples has declined since 2006, the number of lesbian and gay couples creating families through adoption has doubled from 2000 to 2009, from 10 percent to 19 percent (Gates, 2012). Gates (2012) argues that society's attitudes about being lesbian, gay, or bisexual have become far more liberal since 2006, allowing young lesbian, gay, and bisexual (LGB) individuals to live authentic lives and avoid hiding in the closet by getting married to an opposite-sex spouse and having children. Regardless of the absence of an explanation for the trend, what remains clear is that of all households parented by LGB parents, families created by openly gay men and lesbians, are increasing in numbers. Lesbians have been able to enter into parenthood in larger numbers than gay men due to biological and sociological advantages (Macomber, Gates, Badgett, & Chambers, 2007; Rosenblum, 1991; Tasker & Patterson, 2007). Consequently, of all families parented by LGB couples, those created by openly gay male couples represent the smallest number, but the tide is showing signs of change (Gates, 2013). Openly gay men are creating families through foster and kinship care, adoption, and surrogacy at increasing numbers (Macomber, et al., 2007). As more LGB couples create intentional families, the portrait of the American nuclear family is being transformed.

As the direct result of activism on the part of the lesbian, gay, bisexual, transgender, and queer community and its allies from 2004 to 2013, American gay and lesbian couples were increasingly granted the legal right to marry in a growing number of states; culminating in June 2015 when same-sex couples were granted the legal right to marry in all 50 states (ProCon.org, 2015).

A growing backlash emerged in response to advances in gay civil rights by conservatives and Christian evangelicals (Adam, 2003; Becker, 2014; Linneman, 2004; Redding, 2008; Rimmerman & Wilcox, 2007; Savage, 2013; Schacter, 2009). While laws preventing gay couples from marrying have been abolished, new state legislation and organizational policies that discriminate against gay couples and the families they create continue to be proposed (Family Equality Council, 2015; National Conference of State Legislators, 2015; Savage, 2013). The struggle for equity in family building is far from over in the United States. With the right to legally marry and growing access to alternative ways of having children, gay-parented families are increasingly moving from the margins of society toward the mainstream, reconstructing and transforming the American nuclear family (Benson, Silverstein, & Auerbach, 2005).

Historically, most fathers who identify as gay or same-sex attracted have entered parenthood at relatively young ages within the context of heterosexual relationships, usually through heterosexual marriage (Bigner & Bozett, 1989; Bigner & Jacobsen, 1989a; Bigner & Jacobsen, 1989b; Bozett, 1989; Gates, 2012; Goldberg, 2010; Mallon, 2004). Some same-sex attracted fathers choose to remain married while others choose to end their marriages in order to live authentically as out gay men (Tasker, 2013; Tornello & Patterson, 2012). Recently, however, a generational shift in how gay men enter into fatherhood is taking place in western culture in which younger gay men are increasingly becoming fathers outside of heterosexual relationships forming gay intentional families (Berkowitz, 2007; Berkowitz & Marsiglio, 2007; Gates, 2013; Lewin, 2009; Patterson & Riskind, 2010).

Gay fatherhood as a life experience encompasses far more than simply the process by which a gay man becomes aware of his procreative consciousness (Marsiglio, 1991) and begins his journey into fatherhood (Caldwell & White, 2006; Sansiriphun, Kantaruksa, Klunklin, Baosuang, & Liamtrirat, 2015). However, the research on gay fatherhood has almost exclusively focused on that entry point into fatherhood (Bergman, Rubio, Green, & Padron, 2010; Dempsey, 2012; Mallon, 2004; Patterson, 1995). Researchers have begun to explore discrimination experienced by gay men as they attempt to have children through fostering (Mallon, 2004; Prince-Sayward, 2014), adoption (Wells, 2011), and surrogacy (Bergman et al., 2010; Berkowitz, 2013). To date, only two studies in the literature that address the marginalization experienced by gay coupled fathers after having had their children argue that marginalization and discrimination continue to affect the lives of gay fathers long after they have finished creating their families (Tuazon-McCheyne, 2010; Wells, 2011). While researchers are amassing a body of scholarly work on gay intentional families created outside of the institution of marriage, no studies as of this writing were found to have explored the lived experiences of gay men who became fathers within the context of a same-sex marriage. The impact that lifelong disenfranchisement, marginalization, and discrimination have on the families of intentional gay fathers remains poorly understood.

Relational-Cultural Theory

Relational-Cultural theory began as an alternative approach to the psychotherapy of women in the late 1970s by four feminist psychologists from the Stone Center in Boston, Massachusetts (Jordan, 2010). RCT deviated from the conventional paradigm of psychodynamic counseling that endorsed a maturational model that moved from dependence to independence (Jordan, 2010). Contrary to the prevailing Western model of development that stressed an autonomous self, RCT offered a developmental model that suggested that people, throughout the life span, grow through and toward meaningful relationships (Jordan, 2010). RCT has since expanded to become a robust theoretical model of relational development, well suited for framing discussions of relational connection in LGB families (Shrewsbury, 2015).

RCT embodies four main concepts that are interrelated, comprising a dynamic process of relational movement (Comstock et al., 2008). These four concepts, described below, richly describe the relational movement of gay fathers within the context of the relationships between the larger LGBTQ community and the dominant heterosexual culture.

Growth-Fostering Relationships

RCT presumes that the maturational process of most people is toward interdependence in mutually enriching relationships, with the most significant personal growth originating in relationships with others (Jordan, 2010). RCT suggests that acute disconnection—those moments in relationships when disappointment leads to conflict and withdrawal—is normal to the relational process and often results in breakthroughs of understanding and increased empathy (Jordan, 2000; Walker, 2005; Walker & Rosen, 2004). Chronic disconnection—the ever-widening separation between individuals and/or groups—is the challenge that RCT seeks to overcome (Jordan, 2010). Disconnection hurts (Jordan & Carlson, 2013). Divorce, death, separation, relocation, and even simple arguments with loved ones all result in psychological distress. Disconnection that results from power disparities evident in the relationship between the individual and culture are common and present opportunities for relational transformation (Comstock et al., 2008).

Relationships are entrenched in culture with shared experiences, similar worldviews and values, and common traditions (Jordan, 2010). "Culture is viewed as an active agent in relational processes that shape human possibility" (Walker, 2005, p. 48). Jordan (2010) argues that "understanding culture and its distortions is essential to understand the individual who lives within or on the periphery of that culture" (p. 6).

Gay fathers of intentional families experience chronic disconnection from the dominant heterosexual culture in the form of widespread marginalization and discrimination (Savage, 2013). Albeit to a lesser extent, gay fathers of intentional families also experience disconnection from the largely childfree gay male subculture in the form of disenfranchisement and marginalization (Bozett, 1987; Strah & Margolis, 2004). An emergent community of gay fathers provides its members with the opportunity to connect with other gay fathers who share their experiences, values, and

99

aspirations. The number of social media sites connecting gay fathers online continues to increase annually with the number of Facebook sites targeting families parented by gay men or LGBT families reaching into the hundreds as of this writing. The four social media groups with the largest membership as of this writing are *Gay Fathers (4,475 members), LGBT Parents Unite (3,607 members), Gay Dads (2,979 members), and Gay Fathers (1,223 members). Dozens of local Facebook groups have been formed in recent years in cities like Atlanta, Washington, D.C., and Houston, connecting gay fathers in local communities, and their membership continues to grow. Older LGBT adults who are coupled and/or raising children engage with regularity in LGBT social media sites specifically designed to cater to their community-seeking needs with other LGBT parents (Erosheva, Kim, Emlet, & Fredriksen-Goldsen, 2015). Gay fathers of intentional families report feeling less connected with their previous gay male friends and finding the most social support and empathy for their role as fathers from other gay fathers and heterosexual parents (Strah & Margolis, 2004).

Mutual Empathy

At the most basic level, mutual empathy occurs between two people who connect in mutuality and shared experience (Jordan, 2010). Mirror neurons allow mutual empathy to also occur between groups of people on much larger scales (Vittorio, 2005). The groundswell of support for the marriage equality movement on the part of heterosexual allies resulting in its eventual success is evidence of the human capacity to experience mutual empathy with strangers, even those whose lives are considerably different

---

*Gay Fathers Facebook group site created in 2013. Retrieved from:
    https://www.facebook.com/groups/gayfathers2/?ref=br_rs
LGBT Parents Unite Facebook group site created in 2014. Retrieved from:
    https://www.facebook.com/LGBTparentsUNITE/
Gay Dads Facebook group site created in 2008. Retrieved from:
    https://www.facebook.com/groups/7181147876/?ref=br_rs
Gay Fathers Facebook group site created in 2009. Retrieved from:
    https://www.facebook.com/groups/15368945293/?ref=br_rs

from our own (Becker, 2014; Brooks, 2015; Solomon, 2014). Movement toward mutuality rather than separation characterizes mature functioning (Jordan, 2000). Mutual empathy is a critical element of growth-fostering relationships and requires that each person feel, see, and know the responsiveness of the other person (Miller, 1986). Mutual empathy and empowerment heals old relational wounds and shifts relational expectations formed from earlier empathic failures (Hartling, Rosen, Walker, & Jordan, 2000). Altering expectations about relationships and learning new patterns of relating through mutual empathy results in relational competence and relational resilience (Jordan, 2010).

Gay fathers of intentional families who connect with other such fathers may be able to draw upon mutual empathy to heal relational wounds caused by disenfranchisement, marginalization, and discrimination. While it is not impossible for others outside of this community to empathize with experiences of marginalization such as having a birth mother decide not to place her child with a same-sex couple, or being unable to list both fathers' names on a birth certificate of a child born through a surrogate, mutual empathy may be more profound as Jordan (2010) indicates when the emotional pain of these scenarios is a shared experience. The co-creation of a community of gay fathers may increase the capacity for mutual empathy, relational resilience, and mutual empowerment among these men, ultimately contributing to relational transformation within the community and within its relationship to the larger dominant culture.

Relational Authenticity

A key component of growth-fostering relationships is the capacity for relational authenticity (Jordan, 2000). In order to be authentic in relationships, one must be able to depend upon a certain degree of safety in order to be vulnerable (Jordan, 2008, 2010). The moment-to-moment empathic responsiveness is the most important aspect of relational authenticity (Miller et al., 2004). Walker and Rosen (2004) describe relational authenticity as "an increasing capacity for representing oneself more fully in the relationship. It signals respect for the complexity of each person, acknowledges the importance of embodied difference, and invites expression of that difference in relationship" (p. 11). Jordan (2010) adds, "[Relational authenticity] does not give license to total reactivity (what we might call amygdala authenticity). Authenticity does not involve telling the 'whole truth' but rather sharing the 'one true thing' that will move the [relationship] in some positive way" (p. 102). Comstock et al. (2008) explain that in relating to others more authentically and empathically, "individuals are able to gain a clearer understanding of themselves, others, and the relational challenges they face within the unique cultural contexts in which they are situated" (p. 284).

Gay fathers of intentional families redefine gender roles to emphasize relational and nurturing aspects of the masculine self (Armesto & Shapiro, 2011). In their social media and organizational events, these fathers are able to seek support and advice, celebrate their families in a safe space, take risks with each other, and share truths with other gay fathers who offer a greater likelihood of empathizing with them. This ability to share truths in mutuality is a key aspect of the growth-fostering relationships and presents increased opportunities for gay fathers of intentional families to build community.

Mutual Empowerment

Social justice issues are central to RCT with scholars attempting to mitigate the impact of dominance and subordination on groups and individuals—particularly but not exclusively on women—since the 1970s (Jordan, 2010). The dominant culture tends to distort images of the self, others, and relational possibilities in ways that diminish and even preclude mutuality (Walker, 1999). A key focus of RCT is to resist and eradicate the sociopolitical factors that function as catalysts for relational disconnection among members of marginalized groups (Comstock et al., 2008).

Gay men who create intentional families continue to experience disenfranchisement, marginalization, and discrimination long after their children have come into their lives (Tuazon-McCheyne, 2010; Wells, 2011). Gay men who become fathers after having come out publicly as gay challenge powerful social mores, thereby becoming targets of religious and political conservatives (Dowd, 2000; Netwon Webb & Chonody, 2014). By creating a community that mutually empowers themselves, they are able to name their own reality and authentically express their thoughts and feelings (Comstock et al., 2008). The emergent community of intentional families parented by gay fathers can create a safe place for them to resist and ultimately transform the sociopolitical factors that foster cultural shame (Shannon, 2013). They are able to provide support for themselves in their individual and collective struggles for equality, and in so doing, they empower their own community to shed internalized homophobia and negative relational images of oppression, radically transforming their relational connections to the dominant culture (Shannon, 2013).

Conclusion

Today's political climate of ideological differences rooted in opposing core values has brought the United States back to a place of stark division on many issues; same-sex marriage and LGB parenting are certainly on this list. Mutuality, which includes mutual empathy and mutual empowerment, can offer hope of bringing opposing forces into alignment.

Relational authenticity holds space for these differences in ideology and creates a measure of safety for difficult dialogue to take place by requiring all parties to honor their own truths. Relational authenticity could allow gay men who are marrying and having children, and those who are opposed to same-sex marriage and/or gay intentional fatherhood, to name their own personal truths while seeking a way to meet as equals, admitting our ignorance, and being open to learn about the other so productive dialogue can take place in safety and respect.

Growth fostering relationships are inherently inclusive and thrive in relational movement with conflict and disconnection creating opportunities for stronger connection (Jordan, 1995). Gay men who practice heteronormative family building by getting married and having children often find themselves connecting more with heterosexual parents than with their own LGBTQ community who do not have children (Strah & Margolis, 2004). On the surface this can easily be misconstrued as selling out to the hegemony to gain privilege, but employing the concept of mutual empathy can reframe these connections by explaining that same-sex couples who are raising children are able to connect with heterosexual parents through the shared experience of parenthood, even when ideological differences are present between them. Mutual empathy and relational authenticity create space for transformative growth-fostering relationships (Jordan, 1995, 2000).

The modern LGBT civil rights movement in the United States appears to be following suit. Gay fathers of intentional families represent perhaps the smallest demographic among nontraditional families in the United States and are arguably the least understood. Positive depictions of families parented by gay fathers are finding their way into mainstream consciousness in everyday magazines, newspapers, commercials and TV shows, in our communities, our schools, and our churches, inspiring younger gay men to consider intentional fatherhood (Riggs, 2011). These positive depictions of gay intentional families in the media appear to promote mutual empathy between gay fathers and the dominant heterosexual culture, contributing to relational healing (Jordan, 2001; Walker & Rosen, 2004). Maureen Walker in the Transforming Community conference keynote speech described how a radical form of empathy, what she termed as "disruptive empathy," provides possibility for healing connection across stark ideological divides. RCT offers a strong theoretical framework for bridging social and ideological divides between this emergent community of gay fathers, the larger LGBTQ community, and the dominant heterosexual majority culture.

Anti-LGBT laws can and will change with enough persistence, but the radical power of mutual empathy can effect change in the hearts people from all sides of the LGBT civil rights debate and effectively transform communities.

References

Adam, B. D. (2003). The defense of marriage act and American exceptionalism: The "gay marriage" panic in the United States. *Journal of the History of Sexuality,* 12(2), 259-276.

Armesto, J. C., & Shapiro, E. R. (2011). Adoptive gay fathers: Transformations of the masculine homosexual self. *Journal of GLBT Family Studies,* 7(1-2), 72-92.

Baca Zinn, M., Eitzen, D. S., & Wells, B. (2015). *Diversity in families.* (10th, ed.) New York: Pearson.

Becker, J. (2014). *Forcing the spring: Inside the fight for marriage equality.* New York: Penguin.

Benson, A. L., Silverstein, L. B., & Auerbach, C. F. (2005). From the margins to the center: Gay fathers reconstruct the fathering role. *Journal of GLBT Family Studies,* 1(3), 1-29.

Bergman, K., Rubio, R. J., Green, R.-J., & Padron, E. (2010). Gay men who become fathers via surrogacy: The transition to parenthood. *Journal of GLBT Family Studies,* 6(2), 111-141.

Berkowitz, D. (2007). A sociohistorical analysis of gay men's procreative consciousness. *Journal of GLBT Family Studies,* 3(2/3), 157-190.

Berkowitz, D. (2013). Gay men and surrogacy. In *LGBT-parent families: Innovations in research and implications for practice.* New York: Springer.

Berkowitz, D., & Marsiglio, W. (2007). Gay men: Negotiating procreative, father, and family identities. *Journal of Marriage & Family Studies,* 69(2), 366-381.

Bigner, J. J., & Bozett, F. W. (1989). Parenting by gay fathers. *Marriage & Family Review,* 14(3/4), 155-175.

Bigner, J. J., & Jacobsen, R. B. (1989a). The value of children to gay and heterosexual fathers. *Journal of Homosexuality,* 18(1/2), 163-172.

Bigner, J. J., & Jacobsen, R. B. (1989b). Parenting behaviors of homosexual and heterosexual fathers. *Journal of Homosexuality,* 18(1/2), 173-186.

Bozett, F. W. (1987). *Gay and lesbian parents.* New York: Praeger.

Bozett, F. W. (1989). Gay fathers: A review of the literature. *Journal of Homosexuality,* 18(1/2), 137-162.

Brooks, A. (2015). *The right side of history: 100 years of LGBTQI activism.* New York: Cleis Press.

Caldwell, L. D., & White, J. L. (2006). Generative fathering: Challenges to Black masculine identity. In M. E. Conner, & J. White (Eds.), *Black fathers: An invisible presence in America* (pp. 53-69). Mahwah, NJ: Lawrence Erlbaum Associates.

Comstock, D. L., Hammer, T. R., Strentzsch, J., Cannon, K., Parsons, J., & Salazar II, G. (2008). Relational-Cultural theory: A framework for bridging relational, multicultural, and social justice competencies. *Journal of Counseling & Development,* 86(3), 279-287.

Dempsey, D. (2012). More like a donor or more like a father? Gay men's concepts of relatedness to children. *Sexualities,* 15(2), 156-174.

Dempsey, D., & Hewitt, B. (2012). Fatherhood in the 21st century. *Journal of Family Studies,* 18(2-3), 98-102.

Dowd, N. E. (2000). *Redefining fatherhood.* New York: New York University Press.

Erosheva, E. A., Kim, H. J., Emlet, C., & Fredriksen-Goldsen, K. I. (2015). Social networks of lesbian, gay, bisexual, and transgender older adults. *Research on Aging,* 38(1), 98-123.

Family Equality Council. (2016, Dec 04). *Equality Maps.* Retrieved Aug 15, 2016, from Family Equality Council: http://www.familyequality.org/get_informed/equality_maps/

Gates, G. (2012). Family formation and raising children among same-sex couples. (R. M. Sabetelli, Ed.) *National Council of Family Relations,* FF51(1), 1-4.

Gates, G. (2013, Feb). *LGBT Parenting in the United States.* Retrieved Nov 29, 2015, from UCLA: The Williams Institute: http://escholarship.org/uc/item/9xs6g8xx#

Goldberg, A. E. (2010). *Lesbian and gay parents and their children: Research on the family lifecycle.* Washington, DC: American Psychological Association.

Hartling, L., Rosen, W., Walker, M., & Jordan, J. V. (2000). Shame and humiliation: *From isolation to relational transformation* (Vols. Work in Progress, No. 88). Wellesley, MA: Stone Center, Wellesley College.

Hicks, S. (2006). Maternal men--perverts and deviants? Making sense of gay men as foster carers and adopters. *Journal of GLBT Family Studies,* 2(1), 93-114.

Jordan, J. V. (1995). Relational awareness: *Transforming disconnection.* Wellesley, MA: Stone Center: Wellesley College.

Jordan, J. V. (2000). The role of mutual empathy in Relational/Cultural Therapy. *Journal of Clinical Psychology,* 56(8), 1005-1016.

Jordan, J. V. (2001). A relational-cultural model: Healing through mutual empathy. *Bulletin of the Menninger Clinic,* 65(1), 92-103.

Jordan, J. V. (2008). Valuing vulnerability: New definitions of courage. *Women & Therapy,* 31(2-4), 209-233.

Jordan, J. V. (2010). *Relational-Cultural therapy.* Washington, DC: American Psychological Association.

Jordan, J. V., & Carlson, J. (2013). The pain of disconnection, the power of connection. In J. V. Jordan, & J. Carlson (Eds.), *Creating connection: A relational-cultural approach with couples.* New York: Routledge.

Jordan, J. V., & Hartling, L. M. (2002). New developments in Relational-Cultural theory. In M. Ballou, & L. S. Brown (Eds.), *Rethinking mental health and disorder: Feminist perspectives* (pp. 48-70). New York: Guilford Press.

Jordan, J., Kaplan, A., Miller, J., Stiver, I., & Surrey, J. (1991). *Women's Growth in Connection: Writings from the Stone Center.* Cambridge, MA: Harvard University Press.

Lewin, E. (2009). *Gay fatherhood: Narratives of family and citizenship in America.* Chicago, IL: University of Chicago Press.

Linneman, T. J. (2004). Homophobia and hostility: Christian conservative reactions to the political and cultural progress of lesbians and gay men. *Journal of the National Sexuality Research Center,* 1(2), 56-76.

Macomber, J. E., Gates, G. J., Badgett, M. L., & Chambers, K. (2007). *Adoption and foster care by gay and lesbian parents in the United States.* Los Angeles, CA: The Williams Institute, UCLA School of Law. Washington, DC: The Urban Institute.

Mallon, G. P. (2004). *Gay men choosing parenthood.* New York: Columbia University Press.

Marsiglio, W. (1991). Male procreative consciousness and responsibility: A conceptual analysis and research agenda. *Journal of Family Issues,* 12(3), 268-290.

Miller, J. B. (1986). *What do we mean by relationships?* (Vols. Work in Progress, No. 22). Wellesley, MA: Stone Center for Developmental Services and Studies, Wellesley College.

Miller, J. B., Jordan, J. V., Stiver, I. P., Walker, M., Surrey, J. L., & Eldridge, N. S. (2004). Therapists' Authenticity. In J. V. Jordan, L. M. Hartling, & M. Walker (Eds.), The complexity of connection: *Writings from the Stone Center's Jean Baker Miller Institute* (pp. 64-89). New York: Guilford Press.

Moore, M. R., & Stambolis-Ruhstorfer, M. (2013). LGBT sexuality and families at the start of the twenty-first century. *Annual Review of Sociology,* 39, 491-507.

National Conference of State Legislators. (2015, Sep 3). *2015 State religious freedom restoration legislation.* Retrieved Nov 29, 2015, from ncsl.org: http://www.ncsl.org/research/civil-and-criminal-justice/2015-state-rfra-legislation.aspx

Netwon Webb, S., & Chonody, J. (2014). Heterosexual attitudes toward same-sex marriage: The influence of attitudes toward same-sex parenting. *Journal of GLBT Studies,* 10(4), 404-421.

Patterson, C. J. (1995). Lesbian mothers, gay fathers, and their children. In A. R. D'Augelli, & C. J. Patterson (Eds.), *Lesbian, gay, and bisexual identities over the lifespan: Psychological perspectives* (pp. 269-290). New York: Oxford University Press.

Patterson, C. J., & Riskind, R. G. (2010). To be a parent: Issues in family formation among gay and lesbian adults. *Journal of GLBT Family Studies,* 6(3), 326-340.

Prince-Sayward, B. (2014, Nov/Dec). Therapeutic parenting of six children with special needs: One gay father's experience adopting from the foster care system. *Gay Parent Magazine,* 17(97), pp. 36-42.

ProCon.org. (2015, July 1). *50 States with legal gay marriage.* Retrieved Nov 29, 2015, from ProCon.org: http://gaymarriage.procon.org/view.resource.php?resourceID=004857

Redding, R. E. (2008). It's really about sex: Same-sex marriage, lesbigay parenting, and the psychology of disgust. *Duke Journal of Gender Law & Policy,* 18, 101-167.

Riggs, D. W. (2011). Let's go to the movies: Filmic representations of gay foster and adoptive parents. *Journal of GLBT Family Studies,* 7(3), 297-312.

Rimmerman, C., & Wilcox, C. (2007). *The politics of marriage.* Chicago, IL: University of Chicago Press.

Rosenblum, D. M. (1991). Custody rights of gay and lesbian parents. *Villanova Law Review,* 36(6), 1665-1696.

Sansiriphun, N., Kantaruksa, K., Klunklin, A., Baosuang, C., & Liamtrirat, S. (2015). The journey into fatherhood: A grounded theory study. *Nursing & Health Sciences,* 17(4), 460-466.

Savage, D. (2013). *American savage: Insights, slights, and fights on faith, sex, love, and politics.* New York: Penguin.

Schacter, J. S. (2009). Courts and the politics of backlash: Marriage equality litigation, then and now. *Southern California Law Review,* 82(6), 2009.

Shannon, D. M. (2013). Gay male couple work: The value of individual and group therapy. In J. V. Jordan, & J. Carlson (Eds.), *Creating connection: A relational-cultural approach with couples* (pp. 91-113). New York: Rutledge.

Shrewsbury, K. M. (2015). "Just like everyone else": Lesbians performing heteronormativity to create connection (Order No. 3718563) Available from ProQuest Dissertations & Theses Global. 1-242. San Francisco, CA: ProQuest Dissertations Publishing.

Solomon, M. (2014). *Winning marriage: The inside story of how same-sex couples took on the politicians and pundits--and won.* Lebanon, NH: University Press of New England.

Strah, D., & Margolis, S. (2004). *Gay dads.* New York, NY: Penguin.

Tasker, F. (2013). Lesbian and gay parenting post-heterosexual divorce and separation. In A. E. Goldberg, & K. R. Allen (Eds.), LGBT-parent families: Innovations in research and implications for practice. New York: Springer.

Tasker, F., & Patterson, C. J. (2007). Research on gay and lesbian parenting: Retrospect and prospect. *Journal of GLBT Family Studies,* 3(2-3), 9-34.

Tornello, S. L., & Patterson, C. J. (2012). Gay fathers in mixed orientation relationships: Experiences of those who stay in their marriages and of those who leave. *Journal of GLBT Family Studies,* 8(1), 85-98.

Tuazon-McCheyne, J. (2010). Two dads: Gay male parenting and its politicisation--A cooperative inquiry action research study. *Australia & New Zealand Journal of Family Therapy,* 31(4), 311-323.

Vittorio, G. (2005). Being like me: Self-other identity, mirror neurons and empathy. In S. Hurley, & N. Chater, *Perspectives on imitation: From neuroscience to social science* (Vol. 1, pp. 101-118). Cambridge, MA: MIT Press.

Walker, M. (1999). Race, self, and society: *Relational challenges in a culture of disconnection* (Vols. Work in Progress, No. 85). Wellesley, MA: Stone Center, Wellesley College.

Walker, M. (2005). Critical thinking: Challenging developmental myths, stigmas, and stereotypes. In D. L. Comstock (Ed.), *Diversity and development: Critical contexts that shape our lives and relationships* (pp. 47-66). Belmont, CA: Thomson, Brooks/Cole.

Walker, M., & Rosen, W. B. (2004). *How connections heal: Stories from relational-cultural therapy.* New York: Guilford.

Wells, G. (2011). Making room for daddies: Male couples creating families through adoption. *Journal of GLBT Family Studies,* 7(1/2), 155-181.

Dropping the Flag: Female Gang Members Deciding to Leave

··· ■ ■ ■ ···

LOUISA D. FOOTMAN, PhD, LCSW-C

Here I present the concluding chapter from my 2016 dissertation, "Dropping the flag: Female gang members deciding to leave." While thinking about this powerful topic, I instinctively knew the critical roles that relationships, positive and negative, would have on the brave choices of the women studied to change their lives. I also assumed (correctly) that relationships would have impacted the directions that their lives had taken, lives of violence, chaos, pain, losses, and grave consequence for self and others. The power of mutuality and connection was the guiding force for the women to change and grow, and those concepts are the heart of Relational-Cultural theory. They are also the heart of my life, my practice as a therapist and a social worker at The SEED School of Maryland, a public boarding school in Baltimore, MD. I am passionate about continuing the work of RCT, and about research related to women, forensics, and social justice matters. Always looking for connection. louisafootman@gmail.com.

Based on the concluding chapter of my 2016 dissertation, "Dropping the flag: Female gang members deciding to leave", this article addresses the important issue of gang violence from a relational-cultural lens, and summarizes how interviewing formerly gang-involved females and the ensuing data analysis answered the study's guiding question, What was your experience of leaving the gang? It incorporates the findings of the study with previous literature on the topic of female gang members and desistance, and highlights the implications of the study for the fields of counseling and human services. Throughout the chapter is discussion on how the research findings aligned with and differed from tenets of Relational-Cultural theory and the Age-Graded Theory of Social Control. Presentation of the study's limitations and implications for further areas of study conclude the chapter.

Summary of the Results

The Research Problem

Although violence is but one of many activities that gang members engage in, it is violence that generates the greatest public concern. It is agreed upon across the literature that "there is no better way to illustrate the distinctive characteristic of street gangs than to evaluate their disproportionate involvement in violence" (Decker et al., 2013, p. 390). Violence is the hallmark behavior that distinguishes gangs from other social groups. Gang activity is dangerous to all involved with gangs and all affected by gangs, on individual, community, and societal levels. Gang members are found responsible for crimes nearly 100 times more often than persons who are not gang involved (Sweeten et al., 2013). In the United States, the highest concentration of gangs remains in low-income neighborhoods of bigger U.S. cities but gang activity and gang influence have spread and continue to extend into suburban and rural areas. Gangs continue to grow their membership and gang membership continues to diversify its makeup (Miller, 2012).

Since early gang research, female members have been included in documentation of gang activity, but their involvement has been underreported. Gang research has focused on male gang members. To date, research including references to female members has minimized the level of their involvement, primarily studied female members in comparison to male members, and largely focused on reasons why female individuals join gangs. A more firm understanding of the prevalence of female gang members has risen over the past three decades, causing

114

a significant rise in stakeholders' attention to female gang participation. The current consensus is that female members represent close to one-third of all gang members, highlighting the ongoing need for diligence and dedication to the understanding of this population (Marsal, 2009; Maxson & Klein, 2006; Schram & Gaines, 2007; Wolf & Gutierrez, 2012).

Significance of the Study

It has been discussed at length that females join gangs following histories of sexual, physical, and/or emotional abuse, abandonment, neglect, familial discord, substance abuse, poverty, family gang history, and early sexual activity. What is not well understood is why female members decide to leave gangs and how they do so. This knowledge is crucial for the development of gender-specific prevention and intervention programming to assist gang-involved or gang-exposed females.

Substantial research on desistance from gangs, the process of making changes in one's lifestyle that lead to ceasing criminal activity, is lacking in general gang and criminology literature. This void is particularly seen in gender-specific studies, as most desistance research has focused on male gang members or does not distinguish gender as a factor. Some commonly cited reasons for male desistance from gangs are growing out of it, gaining employment, incarceration, marriage, and military service (Bovenkerk, 2011). Pregnancy and motherhood are the most commonly referenced reasons for female individuals to exit gang membership (Fleisher & Kreinert, 2004; Moloney et al., 2011). Spirituality, sobriety, and the desire to avoid future involvement with the justice system have also been found as determinants for desistance among criminally involved females (Michaelsen, 2011). This current study aimed to fill gaps in research by specifically focusing on the experience of female gang members who decided to stop being gang involved. It examined why they decided to leave gang activity, their processes of leaving, and how they accomplished not only leaving but also staying away from gang activity.

Literature Reviewed for the Study

Two theories were studied and utilized as frameworks for the study. Relational-Cultural theory, a theory focused on the significance of the impact of relationships on human development was used to examine the impact that relationships had on the participants, both during and after gang involvement (Miller, 1976). The Age-Graded Theory of Informal Social Control, a life-course theory often used to examine pathways out of criminal behavior, was used to compare, contrast, and explore the participants' process of moving away from gangs with predicted turning points typically found to lead people out of criminal lifestyles (Sampson & Laub, 1993).

The current study was conducted using Giorgi's (2009) descriptive phenomenology, a qualitative methodology that is well aligned with the discipline of counseling. As an interview-based method, phenomenology is suited for counseling research. In the counselor-client relationship, the practitioner carefully interprets the experiences of clients as told by clients; this is the foundation of the discipline of counseling, and this practice is also the basis of descriptive phenomenology, in which the interviewer seeks descriptions from participants from which they work to generate findings that are useful to gaining deeper understanding of the research problem (Hays & Wood, 2011).

Findings

For the formerly gang-involved female participants, the change process was typically a complicated process of changing and not a linear episode. As posited by Sampson and Laub (1993), accomplishments and events occurred across the trajectory of the participants' life courses, some of which were detrimental to participants and negatively impacted their lives, and some of which had significant meaning to them that allowed them to continuously refrain from criminal and gang activity. In life-course language, these events became transitions which led to increased or decreased gang activity (Sampson & Laub, 1993).

The participants often made multiple attempts to leave the gang before they found their individualized pathways to sustaining lasting changes that kept them away from gang activity permanently. Behaviorally, they had to learn how to refrain from criminality and violence as well as how to stop surrounding themselves with negative peer groups such as the gang—and in some cases, their families. Newly learned self-control required included resisting urges and temptations to commit crimes or acts of violence, to return to their old neighborhoods, to associate with gang-involved persons, or to engage in drug and alcohol use.

In the void of gang activity came productivity, the accomplishment of which was a slow and inconsistent process for the participants. Learning how to stop engaging in old, familiar behaviors went hand-in-hand with the addition of positive replacement behaviors. The participants' change processes were multifaceted and included working on themselves in the gang intervention program through self-help activities such as receiving psychotherapy, attending 12-step meetings or other need-specific groups, and working to gain deeper self-understanding. Another part of the change process was learning how to establish healthy interpersonal connections. Healthy relationships were developed with mentors, staff at the program, estranged family members, and their children and significant others. Growth occurred through developing relationships that fostered feelings of mutuality—one of the relational-cultural bases of healthy relationships which posits that relationships need to be mutually beneficial where caring and empathy are shared between both parties (Jordan, 1985).

Measurable accomplishments such as a legitimate income, high school or general equivalency diploma, driver's license, or positive terminations from probation were tangible benchmarks of the change process for the participants, or turning points in life-course framework. Turning points generated realizations of the value of possibility, while the accomplishments built momentum. Finally, incorporating the changes made within the program into their lives outside of the program was the pinnacle of the change process. Through it all, learning to be accountable and responsible for themselves was the outstanding gain of the change process for the participants.

Discussion of the Results

This study aimed to understand the processes leading up to the decision to leave a gang, the changes that each participant made in order to do so, what helped them with the decision, and how they facilitated leaving. The results of this study allowed for an understanding of why the participants first decided to leave gangs and how they then managed to do it. Previous efforts to leave the gang and stay away independently without outside help were not effective in the long run for the participants; frequent attempts at changing their lifestyles utilizing multiple supports from others were needed for achieving sustained success at desistance from gangs. Permanently staying away from the gang after leaving was far more challenging and complicated than the act of simply declaring oneself a non-gang member. Something different was needed to replace the significance of the gang in the participants' lives in order for them to remain continually abstain from gang activity, whether an accomplishment or a positive relationship.

Why Participants Left Gangs

Each of the participants experienced intensely difficult situations that were directly related to their gang involvement, sometimes many times over, before they felt sufficiently ready to attempt to leave. Painful consequences due to gang involvement were the main reasons for leaving the gang, which included experiencing and witnessing multiple traumas (often violent events), risking the loss or the actual loss of custody of their children, frequent encounters with law enforcement, and/or incarceration. It was during difficult times of pain and suffering that many of the women came to feel truly alone, and to realize that their gang-based relationships were far less supportive than they had previously believed. Relational cultural studies discuss the difficulty of experiencing the feeling of disconnection in relationships and the emotional damage that it causes. Disconnection is described by Jordan (2010) as occurring relationally "where mutual empathy and mutual empowerment do not occur; usually involves disappointment, a sense of being misunderstood, and sometimes a sense of danger, violation, and/ or impasse. Disconnections may be acute, chronic, or traumatic" (Glossary section, p. 2).

During times of crisis, feelings of disconnection to the gang heightened immensely. Incarceration was the experience most cited for this realization of experienced disconnection. For one participant, the experience of having both of her arms broken at once by rival gang members and being unable to take care of her physical needs showed her how truly isolated she was, as no one was there to care for her. The limited support that the participants reported receiving, if any, typically came from non-gang connections. Support often came from family members (even those family members who had been distant during the participants' gang involvement), or was found through programs. What was distinct was that there was typically no perceived support from fellow gang members.

Time in gangs and desistance.

Monti (1994) argued that the notion of gang youth "matur[ing] out" is antiquated—that it is so challenging for gang members to find successful pathways out of gang life that they now stay longer (p. 138). As previously stated, the average term for a gang member is thought to be two years or less; in this study, it was noted that the participants interviewed had stayed much longer than the two-year average in the literature. Gang research typically finds that young female individuals lose interest and drop out of gangs earlier than their male counterparts (Greene & Pranis, 2007; Maxson & Klein, 2006; Monti, 1994; Shelden et al., 2004). However, this concept of aging out of the gang was not something that occurred for any of the participants; each of them was of adult age when they decided to desist from gang activity. It appeared that their levels of

119

embeddedness and commitment to the gang did affect the amount of time that they stayed in their gangs. Devers (2011) correlated the length of time that one spends conducting violent activity with the perpetrator's willingness to commit violence; the more committed to the violence, the longer the person will stay criminally active, making it more difficult for them to disengage. The results of this study supported this theory: The cumulative time spent in gangs between the eight participants totaled 145 years of gang activity (7, 14, 15, 17, 18, 20, 22, and 32 years, respectively). With the minimum time spent by a participant being seven years, the time spent was far greater than the two-year average of female gang members. Each of the participants was deeply committed to gang activity.

In the sparse gang literature addressing the topic, the most frequently cited factors for female gang desistance were pregnancy and/or motherhood, spirituality, sobriety, and a desire to avoid future legal consequences (Fleisher & Kreinert, 2004; Michaelsen, 2011; Moloney et al., 2011). All of these factors were found to contribute to the decision to leave gangs for the participants interviewed, but it was a desire for opportunity and personal accomplishment that could come from moving on from gang involvement that was the uniting factor leading to change that was found in this study. Realizing that the negative direction that their lives were going in was not exclusively the fault of the participants themselves, but that this negativity was directly attributable to gang membership was a pivotal part of the change experience and prompted motivation to focus on regaining control of their lives as individuals. Encouragement came from healthy relationships and the feeling of kinship with the program community. After distancing themselves from gang involvement, they began gaining an awareness of the negative impact that gang activity had on their lives, including their own negative actions while gang involved. A powerful change agent for many of the participants was in their ability to learn how to separate or detach from being defined by their core identity as a gang member. They learned how to operate by making decisions in their own best interest by participating in growth fostering relationships. Through growth-fostering relationships, as emphasized in Relational-Cultural theory, they learned how to have better relationships with others as well as with themselves (Comstock, 2007). They also learned to change their approach to choosing daily activities and affiliations that were overall healthier for them.

What Helped Participants to Leave and/or Stay Away From Gangs

Although none of the participants came from the same gang, the themes that emerged from the data were the same—which speaks to the similarity of their experiences. The principal changes participants made to help them stay away from gang activity were:

* moving away from neighborhoods in which they had been active in gangs
* avoiding former gang associates
* establishing boundaries with relationships that they maintained with persons who had gang connections
* focusing on personal sobriety
* practicing self-reflection
* developing a desire for more or better opportunities
* fostering relationships based on compassion, respect, and mutuality

Understandably, relationships were often difficult for the participants to accept after years of conditioning themselves to be emotionally guarded and defensive, particularly with strangers or those in roles of authority. As Miller (1976) explained of RCT and the power of relationships that "The central point is that women's great desire for affiliation is both a fundamental strength, essential for social advance and at the same time the inevitable source of many of women's current problems" (p. 88).

The role of accumulating accomplishments and building off of the momentum from each positive step buoyed the women to continue progressing away from gang affiliation. Many of the

121

participants experienced intense periods of isolation that provided the time and space for reflection and some clarity. Later, through connection with others and the program, they began working to heal themselves. The program was a powerful tool for the women interviewed due to its focus on learning, responsibility, and accountability. As a part of the services received at the program, the participants were given the chance to reflect and were encouraged to make changes in their lives for the better. Transformation stories are shared in the facility's promotional literature, wherein the guiding framework highlights the concept of potentially transforming into one's "better self". While there were multiple expectations put upon them to remain successfully enrolled in the program, these expectations also came with accompanying support.

Studies of those who have desisted from gangs show them at higher risk for "violent victimization" since there can be violent consequences for leaving or trying to leave a gang (Decker et al., 2013, p. 382). Evidence shows that the more deeply embedded in gang activity the person, the more challenging it is to leave without consequence (Decker, Pyrooz, & Moule, 2014). For the women in the study, learning how to navigate the world without their gang identity or the sense of belonging that came from being in a gang required the participants to make new relationships and engage in different activities. None of the participants reported violent consequences for their decision to leave gangs. The guilt that they felt when they tried to set or keep boundaries with former gang associates was described for some as a highly challenging part of leaving gang affiliation. For this reason, creating their own boundaries and strengthening their non-gang voices by learning to say "no" to people who were historically unaccustomed to receiving this response from them became a powerful tool as they began the change process. This tool allowed them to create new relationships and grow away from toxic, gang-centered connections.

In terms of how they had come to seek services from the program, one surprising finding from the interviews was that several of the women interviewed were referred to the program by men in their lives—friends, relatives, or significant others. It was often men who had encouraged them to make the change and seek help with the change process, despite the initial presentation of admitted reluctance to change their lifestyle among many of the participants.

Discussion of the Findings

The study did not find a common strategy for change among participants. Repeat enrollments and episodic involvement with the program were common for many of the participants, as was repeat, episodic involvement with gangs and gang consequences. Participant 3 described the ease with which she returned to her gang after she was inactive for 10 years as, "You kind of jump in where you left off." Breakups, deaths, and the loss of custody of children frequently left them uncertain what to do and sent them back into dangerous lifestyles, often including the abuse of drugs and alcohol and participation in gang activity. These patterns are similar to those observed with relapses in drug or alcohol addiction, as the chronic resumption of dangerous, old behaviors were reported by many of the participants. This pattern was experienced many times over before they were prepared to apply the sustained effort needed to make a lasting change in their lifestyle.

The testimonies of the participants illustrated that there was a deep-rooted desire among them for connection to others and social attachment. It was also seen that commonly, this desire alone among the participants was not enough to make the sustained efforts to change on the first attempt. However, being given multiple chances raised the chances of success for those trying to change. The importance of attachment cannot be overstated in these findings. Hunt, Mackenzie, and Joe-Laidler (2000) found that "an overwhelming majority of gang members, when asked whether they would choose the gang over their family, chose the family" (p. 6). Repairs made with damaged familial relationships or new relationships that had familial qualities were among the accomplishments touted by participants that were helpful in their desistance process. As found by Benda

123

(2005), the significance of these bonds is not only fulfilling, but has an anti-criminogenic property; the "close bonds inspire a sense of responsibility toward loved ones and a hesitancy to act on impulses that could jeopardize relationships and familial security" (p. 338). A model of counseling based on incorporating core foundational relational cultural ideas including addressing issues of disconnection, real and perceived alienation from mainstream society, and the potential for growth through healthy relationships could benefit gang-involved women at all levels of gang embeddedness. Incorporating the use of mentors and peer-led guidance from predecessors who have successfully desisted has been recommended for this population to complement therapeutic services (Wolf & Gutierrez, 2012).

The cultivation of a sense of hope for the future was of utmost significance to the participants' successes and was often emphasized in literature about gang intervention strategies. Former gang member Victor Rios (now a professor at University of California), cited that during his difficult upbringing, "one adult was there for me" (a former teacher), and this had made the difference that mattered helping him to desist from gang membership (Fritz & Brown, 2012, m. 12). Monti (1994) observed, "Sometimes, however, even the toughest of gang members can be surprised by the rare flash of insight or sanity expressed by an adult" (p. 131). Father Gregory Boyle, founder of Homeboy Industries, a well-known gang intervention facility remarked that when working with former gang members, "you infuse kids with hope. Kids for whom hope is foreign" (Mock, 2012). Currie (2012) addressed the American Criminological Association with an emphatic message that "[h]ope is important because in its absence people can feel as if what they do or don't do doesn't matter, that consequences aren't very important" (p. 18).

In this study, the gang intervention program was a powerful tool for the women interviewed due to its focus on teaching them to accept responsibility and accountability. The program served as a replacement community, in which members were asked to show up just to better themselves. It wanted them to come simply because they desire to work on themselves; because they were broken and it sought to repair the broken elements and not capitalize on the damaged parts—which are the parts that often attract young people to join gangs. This program promotes peer support, assigns mentors, and fosters skills which are recommended for programs specific to gang-involved girls, but not included in many existing programs that are often "not designed with girls in mind" (Wolf & Gutierrez, 2012).

Relational-Cultural theory: Growth through relationship

In Relational-Cultural theory, the central idea is that particularly for women, there is an intrinsic need for positive relational connections with others, and this relational connection is what fosters a positive sense of self in women (Stiver, 1991). It proposes that it is within relationships that growth occurs, and particular significance is placed on relationships with attachment figures. Early histories of abandonment and/or unstable, inconsistent connections with caregivers were a shared experience for many of the participants. Strained, disconnected relationships with mothers was an experience found to be shared by several of the participants, and working to reconcile the emotional wounds felt by the absence of that relationship was discussed by several participants as part of their self-help process. Relationships were pivotal to the change processes undergone by the women.

At gang intervention program, the concept of kinship was frequently explained and a practice encouraged to persons enrolled. Kinship, the practice of feeling solidarity, compassion, caring for one another, and supporting each other's growth while making individual progress was the fabric of the program. In the spirit of Relational-Cultural theory, Walker (2002) quotes Miller as having "observed that growth requires engagement with difference and with people embodying that difference" (p. 3). Lasting changes are seen in program participants who are linked to others engaged in a similar change process while receiving support from the caring and compassionate staff.

125

Campana and Varese (2013) discussed how the creation of a feeling of kinship in organized criminal groups raises cooperation and loyalty among members by instilling in them a "future orientation that aligns their incentives with that of the organization" (p. 269). A notion that there is potential to grow with the organization can foster the creation of a community feeling, which contributes to loyalty of gang members. For some, it becomes a substitute family experience. During the course of attending the program, many of the participants spoke about their surprise at enjoying building positive relationships with other women, as trust-based friendships were not something that they had experienced previously. Hunt, McKenzie, and Joe-Laidler (2000) shared similar findings in their study of Latina gang-involved females, stating that during their gang-involved periods, "in the pursuit of respect, especially in their relationships with other homegirls, they were often disappointed in these relations" (p. 25).

In the ideal relational-cultural outcome, when authentic connections have been made, there are "The Five Good Things" (Miller, 1976) that emerge:

- an enhanced sense of zest for life
- feeling increasingly capable of taking action and then doing so
- a more advanced self-concept, improved feeling of worthiness
- deeper connection to others along with a desire for heightened connection. (p. 2)

Participants evidenced emerging awareness of these concepts in their post-gang lives which will hopefully continue as they move forward.

Age-Graded Theory of Social Control: Turning Points

As Sampson and Laub (1993) posited in their theory, the rewarding properties of building social capital were powerful motivators for the participants' continuing change processes. Regarding employment, one of the age-graded centrally mentioned turning points, feeling tied to their working relationship with the program was an effective agent in keeping the women away from gang activity. Securing employment had a positive impact economically and motivationally, and built the self-esteem of the participants. Stable work and attachment to a marital partner were the original predictors for desistance in the theory (Sampson & Laub, 1993). Participants gained social capital from relationships experienced at the program through connections made via the program (e.g., internships upon graduation, certificates, driver's licenses, scholarships), and through non-gang relationships in their lives outside of the program in which they were able to rebuild trust or establish healthier patterns of relations with new people. Sampson and Laub (1993) found that criminal behavior "declines monotonically with increasing levels of supervision and attachment" (p. 69). The connection the participants felt with staff and mentors at the program was tangible, and being held accountable by staff and mentors was important in strengthening their commitment to the program.

This study's participants experienced an opening of their minds to allow in new ways of thinking; being allowed to be vulnerable was a powerful, albeit frightening, experience that they learned through doing work on themselves in therapy, groups, and other components of the program. This vulnerability was not something they had experienced during gang involvement, and it created a pathway for emotional growth that led them to change their ways of thinking. Exposure to a new environment, either through moving or simply by daily attendance in the program, created the change. In the revised development of their theory, Sampson and Laub (1997) tout the importance of new environments on desistance, as well as the growth of human agency that follows accomplishment. Marriage (either legal marriage or long-term monogamous partnership) was cited by none of the participants as a reason for gang desistance, but improved supportive relationships were mentioned by all as motivators for continued desistance efforts.

Implications for Gang Intervention

From the literature and the varying gang statistics, it is evident that more frequent and efficient collaboration between multiple stakeholders and those working in gang intervention is critical. In the same sense that police departments and states and varying agencies and academics all have individualized ways of counting and defining gangs and gang members, different agencies each have their own ways to facilitate gang rehabilitation or intervention. All would benefit from collaboration and sharing of information (National Gang Center, n.d.).

In 2014, the Global Homeboy Network was founded, bringing together organizations across the world to discuss strategies being implemented in gang intervention, to brainstorm, and to transmit the idea of bringing skills training, therapeutic services, and a community element to international towns and cities (Homeboy Industries, n.d.). More programs following this logical model are needed, that all work to offer a combination of services in one space, minimizing barriers to services by making them more accessible physically. Fleisher and Kreinert (2004) discussed difficulties gang-involved female individuals often have with leaving their communities to receive services. The reduction in the amount of time and distance required to travel to different agencies for different services would mitigate this difficulty.

Leap (2012) wondered: "Why is it that no one who practices street intervention is discussing how to help people leave the gang?" (p. 144). A solid body of research on gang desistance has still not been compiled, although there is substantial evidence to support further research. The desistance process is highly individualized, and it takes time, dedication, patience, money, energy, and the provision of alternatives. Transparency and collaboration appear to work. Trust from gang members is notoriously difficult for outsiders to gain. If gang members are to be helped, they have to believe in those who are helping them. Community-based intervention programs such as CeaseFire in Chicago, Illinois, and Operation Safe Streets in Baltimore, Maryland, incorporate reformed gang members into street-based outreach to mediate conflicts and prevent violence. As noted by Leap (2012): "The experts are those people who have been or continue to be active gang members. Their voices are rarely heard" (p. 18). Creating a network of ex-gang members to support one another through the process of desistance will empower both the person leaving and the person who has already left successfully. A 12-step fellowship program called Criminals and Gang Members Anonymous has developed in prisons and gang-heavy areas. Modeled after the 12-step model of Alcoholics Anonymous, it works with the same principles: Fellowship, recovery, and gaining an understanding of what led to gang/criminal activity (Criminals & Gangmembers Anonymous, n.d.). Support and linkages to similar programs as supplements for those trying to desist are essential.

Debunking Myths About Female Members in Gangs

Although this study did not aim to define women's roles in gangs, one of the predetermined interview subquestions asked the participants to describe what it was like to be a female member in a gang. A brief discussion of the responses is relevant to the ongoing discussion about female gang membership. These responses provided insight into a major division among female gang members and gang affiliates, and was likely a contributing factor to the difficulty many of the participants acknowledged in getting along with other women. Many of the participants spoke about feeling a need to prove themselves because of being female, stating that they needed to act especially tough to earn respect from fellow gang members.

Participants described a division between gang-involved female individuals who were considered to be promiscuous and those who were not, and many of them spoke judgmentally about those considered to be promiscuous. Gang research that includes female members has often involved discussion of women's roles in the gangs, beginning with Thrasher (1927) suggesting that female

129

roles are divided into extreme categories of "tomboys" versus "sweethearts". This simplistic categorization/artificial spectrum harms the greater understanding of female presence in gangs. Participants pointed to a hierarchy among female individuals in the gang, shedding light on the differential status among them. It was stated that divisions exist between those female gang members who have male relatives who are also affiliated. Participants with male relatives spoke of receiving certain levels of protection that are not offered to non-related women and being granted respect that others who were not related to male gang members did not receive. Public assumptions about violent rituals celebrating entering and exiting the gang are overstated; the rumored ritual of "sexing-in", in which several male gang members are permitted to have sex with the girl or woman entering the gang, was denied by many participants. In the same way that it has also been found that many former gang members have quit gangs with very little consequence, the myth of sexual exploitation as an entrance or exit route into gang activity for women is exaggerated (Swift, 2011).

Recommendations for Future Research

Future research could study the depth of connections felt during gang desistance as women make their way into communities that they are also a part of (e.g., mother, recovering drug abuser, employee) without the gang identity, exploring how the relational tools gathered during their transformative experiences influence them in new roles and relationships. Conducting longitudinal studies of women with longer term separation from gang involvement to determine the long-term components of remaining inactive from gangs for five or more years would provide more understanding of successful desistance strategies. Another study could follow participants for years after their completion of the program, to determine what happens after the program successfully discharges the participants. Whether a person considers themselves active in a gang or not, gang history is not easily escapable—particularly for those who were deeply active with gang activity. There is still the pressure to continue living in the community, as relocating is difficult for many. Finding specific factors that allow a person to remain inactive without moving would be useful information for gang intervention. Lastly, a deeper qualitative study on the experiences of gang girls and their mothers, to gain further understanding of those relationships, is vital for their rehabilitation. Many of the participants spoke specifically to how painful this specific relationship had been over their life course. "Girls learn to grow in relationship through healthy interaction with their mothers and other significant people" (Surrey, as cited in Jordan, 1991). Being able to directly explore this experience is absolutely vital to gang research, particularly on females.

Conclusion

The study addresses the prevailing problem of female gang membership. The toll that gang membership and resulting consequences took on each individual who participated in the study was evident. Losses of relationships, of freedom, of opportunity, and of personal safety were experienced. To rebuild a foundation for positive growth in each of these areas was the journey that the participants took to reconstructing lives outside of gang membership. The participants' awareness of how harmful gang involvement had been to their lives allowed them to begin working on themselves as individuals. As explained by Currie (2012), "nurturing that ability to link their private angers and despairs with . . . exploitative institutions is absolutely central in helping people to move beyond their immediate problems and beyond individual solutions" (p. 17). Having dealt with significant losses, participants were able to express an awareness of the consequences of gang membership and express appreciation for their survival of gang activity. Just as gangs grow as "a natural resource for an undereducated and underemployed population who has been shut out from the labor market during the transition to adulthood" (Pyrooz, 2014, p. 352), providing supportive linkage to rehabilitative resources that led to the possibility of developing growth-fostering relationships with peers and professionals in a transformative community proved to be a strong alternative that allowed the women to become successfully independent. These newfound connections were shown to contribute to the decision to leave gangs for the participants interviewed, but it was a desire for opportunity and personal accomplishment that could come from moving on from gang involvement that was the uniting factor leading to the lifestyle change that was found in this study.

References

Benda, B. B. (2005). Gender differences in life-course theory of recidivism: A survival analysis. *International Journal of Offender Therapy and Comparative Criminology, 49*(3), 325–342. doi:10.1177/0306624X04271194

Bovenkerk, F. (2011). On leaving criminal organizations. *Crime, Law & Social Change, 55*(4), 261–276. doi:10.1007/s10611011-9281-x

Campana, P., & Varese, F. (2013). Cooperation in criminal organizations: Kinship and violence as credible commitments. *Rationality and Society, 25*(3), 263–289. doi:10.1177/1043463113481202

Comstock, D. (2007). Relational-Cultural theory. In B. Bank (Ed.), *Gender and education: An encyclopedia.* Retrieved from http:// search.credoreference.com/ content/entry/abcge/relational_cultural_theory/0

Criminals & Gang Members Anonymous (n.d.). *Introduction.* Retrieved from http://www.angelfire.com/id/CGAnonymous

Currie, E. (2012). Rethinking intervention: Consciousness, solidarity and hope as criminological principles. *Western Criminology Review,* 13(3), 15–20. Retrieved from http://www.westerncriminology.org/ documents/WCR/v13n3/v13n3.pdf

Decker, S.H., Melde, C., & Pyrooz, D.C. (2013). What do we know about gang members and where do we go from here? *Justice Quarterly, 30*(3), 369-402. doi: 10.1080/07418825.2012.732101

Decker, S. H., Pyrooz, D. C., & Moule, R. K. (2014). Disengagement from gangs as role transitions. *Journal of Research on Adolescence,* 24(2), 268–283. doi:10.1111/jora.12074

Devers, L. (2011). *Desistance and developmental life course theories: Research summary* (Contract No. GS-10F-0114L). Washington, D.C.: United States Department of Justice, Bureau of Justice Assistance.

Fleisher, M. S., & Krienert, J. L. (2004). Life-course events, social networks, and the emergence of violence among female gang members. *Journal Of Community Psychology, 32*(5), 607-622. doi:10.1002/jcop.20022

Fritz, M., & Brown, A. (Directors). (2012). One man's journey from gang member to academia [Television series episode]. In S. Just (Executive Producer), *PBS NewsHour*. Washington, DC: NewsHour.

Giorgi, A. (2009). *The descriptive phenomenological method in psychology: A modified Husserlian approach*. Pittsburgh: Duquesne University Press.

Greene, J., & Pranis, K. (2007). *Gang wars: The failure of enforcement tactics and the need for effective public safety strategies*. Retrieved from http://www.justicepolicy.org/images/upload/07-07_REP_GangWars_GC-PS-AC-JJ.pdf

Homeboy Industries. (n.d.). *What is the Global Homeboy Network?* Retrieved from http://www.homeboyindustries.org/ghn/

Hunt, G., Mackenzie, K., & Joe-Laidler, K. (2000). "I'm calling my mom": The meaning of family and kinship among homegirls. *Justice Quarterly* : JQ, 17(1), 1-31. Retrieved from http://search.proquest.com.library.capella.edu/docview/228160406?accountid=27965

Jordan, J. V. (1985). The meaning of mutuality. In J. V. Jordan, A. G. Kaplan, J. B. Miller, I. P. Stiver, & J. L. Surrey (Eds.), *Women's growth in connection: Writings from the Stone Center* (pp. 81–96). New York: The Guilford Press.

Jordan, J. (2010). *Relational-Cultural therapy*. Washington, D.C.: American Psychological Association.

Jordan, J.V., Kaplan, A.G., Miller, J.B., Stiver, I.P., & Surrey, J.L. (1991). *Women's growth in connection*. New York: The Guilford Press.

Leap, J. (2012). *Jumped in: What gangs taught me about violence, drugs, love, and redemption*. Boston, MA: Beacon Press.

Marsal, E. (2009). Spirituality as a protective factor against female gang membership. *Journal of Human Behavior in the Social Environment, 19*(3), 231–241. doi:10.1080/10911350802694584

Maxson, C., & Klein, M. (2006). *Street gang patterns and policies*. New York: Oxford University Press.

Michaelsen, V. (2011). Mothering as a life course transition: Do women go straight for their children? *Journal of Offender Rehabilitation, 50,* doi: 10.1080/10509674.2011.589887

Miller, J.B. (1976). *Toward a new psychology of women*. Boston: Beacon Press.

Miller, E. (2012). Gangs, contemporary. In W. Miller (Ed.), *The social history of crime and punishment in America: An encyclopedia* (pp. 668–672). doi:10.4135/9781452218427.n260

Mock, F. (Producer/Director). (2012). *G-Dog* [Motion picture]. United States: Chanlim Films.

Moloney, M., Hunt, G. P., Joe-Laidler, K., & MacKenzie, K. (2011). Young mother (in the) hood: Gang girls' negotiation of new identities. *Journal of Youth Studies,* 14(1), 1–19. doi:10.1080/13676261.2010.506531

Monti, D. J. (1994). *Wannabe: Gangs in suburbs and schools.* Cambridge, MA: Blackwell.

National Gang Center. (n.d.a). Frequently asked questions about gangs. Retrieved from http://www.nationalgangcenter.gov/About/FAQ#q1

Pyrooz, D. C. (2014). "From your first cigarette to your last dyin' day": The patterning of gang membership in the life-course. *Journal of Quantitative Criminology,* 30(2), 349–372. doi:10.1007/s10940-013-9206-1

Sampson, R. J., & Laub, J. H. (1993). *Crime in the making: Pathways and turning points through life.* Cambridge, MA: Harvard University Press.

Sampson, R. J., & Laub, J. H. (1997). A life-course theory of cumulative disadvantage and the stability of delinquency. In T. Thornberry (Ed.), *Developmental theories of crime and delinquency* (pp. 1–29). New Brunswick, NJ: Transaction.

Schram, P. J., & Gaines, L. K. (2007). Comparing the effects of treatment on female juvenile gang and non-gang members. *Women & Criminal Justice,* 18(4), 1–15. doi:10.1080/08974450802095937

Shelden, R. G., Tracy, S. K., & Brown, W. B. (2004). *Youth gangs in American society* (3rd ed.). Belmont, CA: Wadsworth/Thomson Learning.

Stiver, I. (1991). The meanings of "dependency" in female–male relationships. In J. V. Jordan, A G. Kaplan, J. Baker Miller, I. P. Stiver, & J. L. Surrey (Eds.), *Women's growth in connection: Writings from the Stone* Center (pp. 143–161). New York: The Guilford Press.

Sweeten, G., Pyrooz, D.C., & Piquero, A.R. (2013). Disengaging from gangs and desistance from crime. *Justice Quarterly,* 30I(3), 469-500. doi: 10.1080/07418825.2012.723033

Swift, R. (2011). *Gangs.* Berkeley, CA: Groundwood Books.

Thrasher, F. M. (1927). The gang: A study of 1,313 gangs in Chicago. IL: University of Chicago Press.

Walker, M. (2002). *How therapy helps when the culture hurts.* Unpublished manuscript, Jean Baker Miller Training Institute at the Wellesley Centers for Women, Wellesley College, Wellesley, Massachusetts.

Wolf, A. M., & Gutierrez, L. (2012). *It's about time: Prevention and intervention strategies for gang-affiliated girls.* Retrieved from http://www.nccdglobal.org/sites/default/files/publication_pdf/focus-its-about-time.pdf

Part II

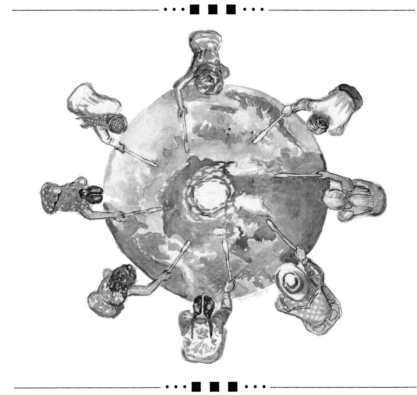

Transforming Community: Education

Dinner at Fitzwilly's: Intellectual Mattering in Developmental Relationships

—————————— ··· ■ ▧ ■ ··· ——————————

HARRIET L. SCHWARTZ, PhD

Original publication:

Schwartz, H.L. (2013). Dinner at Fitzwilly's: Intellectual mattering in developmental relationships. In Dominguez, N. & Gandert, Y. (Eds). Sixth Annual Mentoring Conference Proceedings: Impact and effectiveness of developmental relationship. Albuquerque, NM: University of New Mexico

Reprinted:

Schwartz, H.L. (2016). Dinner at Fitzwilly's: Intellectual mattering in developmental relationships. In Dominguez, N., Kailer, K., & Garcia, M. (Eds.). 6th annual mentoring conference proceedings (2nd ed.): Impact and effectiveness of developmental relationships [Special Issue 6]. The Chronicle of Mentoring and Coaching, 1(6). (Original work published by Dominguez, N. & Gandert, Y. (Eds.). 2013).

Reprinted here with permission.

Intellectual mattering, the experience that our thinking matters to another person, is an intention we can bring to our work with students and also an outcome of that work. The idea of intellectual mattering emerged from qualitative research on teaching and learning interactions and relationships and is further explicated by extant mattering literature and Relational-

Cultural theory as well as possible selves, authentic teaching, and interpersonal boundaries in teaching and learning constructs. I propose that experiences of intellectual mattering can increase student confidence and motivation and can also fuel the transition in which students move from seeing themselves as receivers of knowledge to seeing themselves as co-creators of knowledge. While based primarily on research in the higher education domain, intellectual mattering shows promise for application in youth and workplace mentoring contexts as well. Harriet L. Schwartz may be contacted at harrietschwartz14@gmail.com.

Students notice when we notice. This is to say that when we tell students that their thinking, ideas, and intellectual and academic work has impressed us, informed us, or inspired us, they notice and they may be influenced beyond simply feeling good that we have complimented their work. Intellectual mattering, the experience of knowing that one's ideas or work has touched or influenced another, can help to build the confidence of students who are struggling with memories of past failures or vague notions of imposter syndrome and can also help graduate students begin to see themselves as scholar-practitioners (Schwartz & Booth, 2013; Schwartz & Holloway, 2012, 2013).

The title of this paper "Dinner at Fitzwilly's" recalls what I now consider to be my first significant experience of intellectual mattering in the graduate context. While pursuing a master's degree at Springfield College, I approached Dr. Roberta (Heston) O'Connor who taught an elective course that was particularly engaging. I told her that I was considering an optional thesis and asked if she would be willing to discuss my ideas. She said yes and suggested that we meet to talk at Fitzwilly's, a restaurant in Northampton. We met regularly and each time, Roberta helped me expand and clarify my thinking and she almost always handed me a book to read before our next dinner as she introduced me to qualitative research.

At the time, I did not put language to the collaboration but I was clear that this was a different kind of relationship than I had experienced previously with faculty. This relationship was more collegial. My awareness of this and Roberta's interest in the content of my work began helping me to see myself as someone who could conduct research and contribute new knowledge. My master's research was not about faculty and student academic relationships. Recently, as I have developed the idea of intellectual mattering, I remember the quality of those meetings with Roberta.

Other examples of exchanges that convey intellectual mattering include a professor telling a student that her in-class presentation was particularly strong and asking if he may use her slides in future classes; and a student who upon meeting a professor's family at graduation realized that he had told them about her work (Schwartz & Holloway, 2013). In these exchanges, the student perceives not only that she or he did good work but also that the work touched or influenced the faculty member.

The concept of intellectual mattering emerges from research regarding teaching and learning as relational practice. As applied to education, relational practice is the process by which teaching and learning happen in relation, both in brief interactions and longer-term academic relationships. In this paper, I review mattering and other supporting literature and introduce the specific construct of intellectual mattering. I then address authenticity and interpersonal boundaries as related to intellectual mattering.

The scholarly path that led me to the concept of intellectual mattering is rooted in my ongoing inquiry of relational practice in graduate education. I began this work with a grounded theory study in which I interviewed matched pairs of master's alumni and faculty wherein both members of each pair agreed that they shared a meaningful academic relationship. Participants retrospectively described their relationships and particular interactions. Following this inquiry, I wanted to capture more immediate descriptions of meaningful exchanges between faculty and students. I wondered what kinds of exchanges students might identify as important in the midst of their academic work, exchanges that might not be memorable after graduation but that would seem important in a typical week of graduate study. To this end, I worked with a research partner and we conducted a critical incident technique (CIT) study with current master's students. In both of these studies, I noticed that not only did students describe incidents wherein professors complimented their work, but also incidents wherein they perceived that their ideas or work were important to the professor. These students cared not only that the professors thought positively of their work but also that their work held deeper importance for the professor. Wanting to identify this as a distinct phenomenon, I began to think of it as "intellectual mattering." I later discovered extant mattering literature which has deepened my understanding of this student experience. To provide context, I begin with background on relational practice.

Teaching and Learning as Relational Practice

Relational-Cultural theory (RCT) is the foundation for my work on teaching and learning as relational practice. Developed in the 1980s by Jean Baker Miller and her colleagues, Relational-Cultural theory countered the prevailing developmental theories that regarded autonomy and independence as the highest levels of human development. Instead, Relational-Cultural theory claims that people grow in relation to others and that the optimal state of human development is not to be fully independent but rather to be able to engage in healthy growth producing relationships (Jordan, 2010; Miller, 1986; Miller & Stiver, 1997). People involved in healthy growth-fostering relationships experience what Miller called The Five Good Things: increased energy, self-esteem, self-awareness, ability to take action, and a desire for additional connection (Jordan, 2010; Miller & Stiver, 1997). In addition, RCT reminds us to consider the cultural context that people bring to relationships and cultural dynamics that exist within relationships (Jordan, 2010; Walker, 2002). Finally, RCT also requires that we examine our assumptions about power in relationships and seek to develop a power-with rather than power-over approach (Jordan, 2010; Walker, 2002). Building on RCT, Fletcher (2001) used the language "relational practice" to study the workplace and found that work activities such as mutual empowering and team creating are not only treated as less important than other work in organizations but have "disappeared".

While RCT has been applied primarily in the therapeutic context, I saw it as relevant to teaching and learning as well and situated it as a sensitizing theory in my first study on relational practice in graduate education. Through that study and my subsequent empirical and theoretical work, I have come to see parallels between RCT and teaching and learning as relational practice. In healthy developmental teaching and learning relationships, educators and students experience something similar to The Five Good Things: energy, movement, intellectual mattering, increased understanding, and an appreciation for academic relationships. Teaching and learning as relational practice deepens engagement, facilitates challenge, and teaches transferable relational perspectives (helping students to rethink their assumptions about authority figures and also about the nature of faculty and student academic relationships) (Schwartz & Holloway, 2012, 2013). Educators engaged in relational practice seek to reduce but not eliminate hierarchy and express their authority as horizontal and not top-down; this calls for a nuanced understanding of interpersonal boundaries (Booth & Schwartz, 2012; Schwartz, 2011, 2012; Schwartz & Holloway, 2012, 2013). Through this ongoing inquiry, I seek to deepen my understanding of relational practice and find intentional approaches that we as educators can use to engage our students. I propose that authentic intellectual mattering is an intention we can bring to our work with students and also an outcome of that work.

Mattering: The Literature

Rosenberg and McCullough introduced the concept of mattering in a 1981 issue of *Research in Community and Mental*

Health with an article entitled "Mattering: Inferred significance and mental health among adolescents." Their theory was based on a theoretical replication study in which they explored relationships between adolescents and their parents, using data from four large-scale survey studies including participants from New York State, Baltimore, Chicago, and a nation-wide study (United States). In total, the combined studies included more than 6500 participants and data that was collected between 1960 and 1968.

Rosenberg and McCoullough (1981) determined that "the conviction that one matters to another person is linked to the feeling that: (a) one is an object of his attention; (b) that one is important to him; and (c) that he is dependent on us" (p. 163). *Attention* is the most basic form of mattering and its opposite, to go unnoticed, makes for a bleak human existence (Rosenberg & McCullough, 1981). Feeling *important* to another, that we are the object of another's concern is a stronger experience of mattering. When we believe that another cares about our thoughts, actions, goals, and fate, we experience mattering. Importance may also be experienced as ego-extension; the adolescent who senses that her or his successes or failures are felt by parents as their own, experiences being an ego-extension. Additionally, importance is conveyed by care and concern and may be expressed as approval or criticism; critical feedback does not communicate a lack of mattering but conversely shows that the parent cares about the adolescent's well-being or success (Rosenberg & McCullough, 1981). *Dependence* is the third form of mattering identified by Rosenberg and McCullough (1981). Perhaps unexpectedly, dependence as a form of mattering consists of knowing that others depend on us, not that we can depend on them; this particular experience of mattering, the idea that others depend on us, is a deep source of social integration and provides a bond to the larger society (Rosenberg & McCullough, 1981). In this initial theorizing, Rosenberg and McCullough (1981) clarify that we do not need to believe that another thinks well of us to feel that we matter, but rather we need to sense that we are the object of the other's attention and that we are important to that person. This distinction is particularly relevant to educators who may be charged with assessing student work and progress. In addition, Rosenberg and McCullough (1981) clarified that their study investigated adolescents' experience of mattering to their parents and thus their findings are not generalizable to students' relationships with siblings, teachers, or classmates. While their work is focused on adolescents and parents, it still remains the foundational study for all subsequent mattering research.

Following Rosenberg and McCullough's initial study, Schlossberg (1987, 1989) explored mattering in the lives of adult learners and college students. Schlossberg (1989) cited a study of adult learners by Schlossberg and Warren which found that mattering was meaningful to adult students who valued feeling important to an instructor, to their program, and to their institution. In later work, Schlossberg conducted a structured interview study with 24 participants (both men and women) ranging from age sixteen to eighty. Based on the findings, she added to Rosenberg and McCullough's (1981) original framework, contributing a fourth element of mattering, appreciation. Feeling that others appreciated their efforts was important to participants in the study. Schlossberg (1989) proposed that creating a mattering context for students will motivate them to engage, learn, and develop loyalty to the institution.

Several other scholars have studied mattering and undergraduates. Elliott, Kao, and Grant (2004) conducted a quantitative study with undergraduates and confirmed Rosenberg and McCullough's (1981) finding that mattering is "one of the primary motivators in the self-concept" (p. 353). Scholars have considered: Mattering over the course of undergraduate studies (Marshall, Liu, Wu, Berzonsky, & Adams, 2010); mattering and stress among undergraduates (Dixon Rayle & Chung, 2008; Gibson & Myers, 2006; Myers & Bechtel, 2004); and mattering among urban student populations (Tovar, Simon, & Lee, 2009).

Given that the current inquiry includes adult undergraduate and graduate students, two other studies are worth mention. In research with adults, mattering was shown to reduce risk for depression (Taylor & Turner, 2001) and to contribute to job satisfaction (Connolly & Myers, 2003).

Intellectual Mattering

After reviewing the mattering literature, I returned to the data from my two previous studies to see how I might more deeply understand the student comments that had originally moved me to identify intellectual mattering as important. After careful consideration of the data I determined that students described two distinct experiences of intellectual mattering, one that is content-oriented and a second that is process-oriented.

Students who described content-oriented experiences that reflect intellectual mattering recalled moments when professors responded to specific ideas or work; the student description is focused on the professor noticing the student's ideas or completed assignments. Examples include those cited earlier in this paper, a professor remarking that a student's presentation was exemplary and asking if he could use her slides and a student who realized that her professor had told his family about her work (Schwartz & Holloway, 2013). An additional student quote reflects this experience of intellectual mattering wherein the student notices early in her research process that the professor is engaged with her particular ideas:

> It also made me feel really good that she seemed very interested personally in the study from her own personal perspective; that she got excited about it and said, 'Wow, this is going to be great. We are going to get some really great information here, some new things'. So that made me feel good that she herself was excited about it more on a personal level than simply as my – my instructor. (Student 11)

148

Other students described experiences that reflect intellectual mattering, however the emphasis was on the process or the professor's approach rather than on the professor's response to their ideas. The distinction is subtle because all of these examples relate to students' experiences of interactions with faculty in the academic endeavor. In the first set of experiences, students seem struck primarily by their sense that the content has touched or resonated with the professor. Conversely, in the following examples, the students seem more moved by their experience of the professor's engagement with them in the process.

> But my experience was here's a person who's asking – who's asking a real effort of me. Here's a person who's asking me to really understand something and wrap my mind around it, and so like my – my – all of my urges for like I've got to deliver, like I – he's actually asking something of me, so I like want to pony up, and make it happen. (Student 7)

> He pushed me to the next level, you know? And so it was – that was a real turn in a lot of ways, and then I could ask more educated questions, you know, I could – I could – um, you know, instead of just going 'what is this theoretical model?' ... we can have a more intelligent conversations about the topic beyond – so, what is this thing? I: Yeah. You know, so it – it just – it was one of those real stepping off points for me. (Student 9)

Students described other faculty behaviors that reflect process-oriented intellectual mattering: spending additional one-on-one time with students to work on particular content or assignments; providing detailed feedback that is experienced by the student as specific to her or his work; suggesting additional readings, courses, research opportunities or doctoral study related to the student's interests; commenting on a student's sustained effort; and inviting student feedback about a course (Schwartz & Holloway, 2012, 2013).

All of these examples reflect attention and importance as identified by Rosenberg and McCullough (1981) as indicators of mattering and some also include appreciation as described by Schlossberg (1989). These examples also support earlier findings that mattering is a powerful motivator and influences self-image (Elliott, et al., 2004; Gibson & Myers, 2006; Rosenberg & McCullough, 1981; Schlossberg, 1987, 1989; Tovar et al., 2009). In addition, these examples parallel findings in Rossiter's (1999) phenomenological study of graduate students' experiences of caring. Elements of caring that graduate students experienced in relationship with faculty included: ...to be noticed... to be understood...to have one's concerns be a priority for another... to be shown one's best self" (Rossiter, 1999. pp. 209-210).

A student who experiences authentic intellectual mattering with a professor may not only receive a boost of energy and self-worth in that moment but may become more engaged in the larger learning journey (Schwartz & Holloway, 2012, 2013). Students reported that these moments increased their confidence, motivated them to want to produce higher quality work, and helped them see that they could engage in deep conversation with faculty and explore their ideas though original research (Schwartz & Holloway, 2012, 2013).

Intellectual mattering is also congruent with possible selves research. Possible selves are individuals' ideas of who they wish to become and who they fear becoming (Markus & Nurius, 1986) and "function as incentives for future behavior" (p. 955). I suggest that the possible selves construct offers one explanation of the motivational force of intellectual mattering; students who believe that they matter connect with their aspirational possible selves and are motivated to achieve. Educators can play a powerful role in the lives of students by helping students see new possibilities for themselves either through direct suggestion or through role modeling and other subtle expressions (Rossiter, 2007). I propose that when students experience intellectual mattering in the educational environment, their sense of self is enhanced particularly as it relates to their understanding of themselves as students and scholars. These moments have the potential to help students transition from seeing themselves as receivers of knowledge to seeing themselves as co-creators of knowledge.

Authenticity and Boundaries

Teaching with an intention to recognize and convey intellectual mattering calls on us to work from a place of authenticity and to recognize and navigate interpersonal boundaries with our students.

Authenticity

In a presentation to a class of undergraduates who were serving as mentors in the community, I was struck by the language that one of the students used in response to my description of my research. I paused for a minute and remarked that her language was particularly powerful and might help me think about my work in the future. Later in the session, one of the faculty members in the class commented that I walk my talk, in that I had "noticed" the student's use of powerful language. I had a similar experience in a session with faculty and staff when I acknowledged a faculty member's perceptive response. She smiled and pointed out that I was "noticing" her comment in a way that was consistent with my discussion of relational teaching and mattering. While it might seem positive that participants were sensing a consistency between what I was teaching and how I was facilitating the sessions, I had a lingering concern that because I had pointed to the importance of noticing and intellectual mattering, that the participants may have thought that my comments were strategic and not genuine.

These experiences remind me that authenticity is an important element of working intentionally in the area of intellectual mattering. "Authenticity is a multi-faceted concept that includes at least four parts: being genuine, showing consistency between values and actions, relating to others in such a way as to encourage their authenticity, and living a critical life" (Cranton

& Carusetta, 2004, p. 7). Whenever we comment that a student's ideas are powerful, we must mean it. The idea is not to look for opportunities to deliver compliments, but rather to recognize those moments when we are truly touched, informed, motivated, or inspired by a student's work and then to intentionally share our response with that student. Authentic teaching calls on us to be honest, trustworthy, and genuine in our interactions with students (Brookfield, 2006).

Interpersonal Boundaries

Telling a student that her thinking has been influential or that his presentation was inspiring reduces the hierarchy inherent in the teaching and learning relationship. Both RCT (Jordan, 2010; Walker, 2002) and relational practice approaches (Booth & Schwartz, 2012; Fletcher, 2004; Schwartz, 2012; Schwartz & Holloway, 2012, 2013) advocate reducing the power differential in helping and teaching relationships. These boundary dynamics are more subtle than many boundary questions such as those involving self-disclosure or availability. However, when we convey intellectual mattering we reduce the hierarchy and share the power in the relationship and thus our attention to boundaries is necessary.

To convey intellectual mattering to a student is to shift from what RCT calls a power-over stance to a power-with stance (Jordan, 2010; Walker, 2002). For some faculty this is a natural shift, particularly faculty who experience expertise as fluid (Fletcher, 2004). For example when I taught leadership and ethics to graduate nursing students, their in-the-field application of theory came from a base of medical knowledge that I simply did not have. I had to be comfortable with the ways in which their expertise joined with mine in the classroom.

I propose that faculty who are confident with an ebb and flow of expertise, experience their authority as horizontal, rather than top-down or vertical. Our authority is no longer based in being the keepers of the knowledge or seeing ourselves as intellectually superior to our students. Instead we activate our power horizontally as we seek to create safe, respectful, and energized learning spaces for students. While we work from a power-with stance, we also acknowledge that there is still an inherent power differential between teachers and students; we are comfortable with reducing the hierarchy, but we do not deny that a power differential remains.

Managing these subtle shifts in power and authority while also retaining the essence of our role as faculty is the boundary challenge inherent in working with intellectual mattering as a teaching intention. As long as we assess student work and have influence over students' academic and career progress, we hold power in the relationship. We are always and without exception teachers in the lives of students. Ultimately, we are more responsible than our students for the creation of the learning space and for the health and integrity of the educational relationship (Booth & Schwartz, 2012; Holloway & Alexandre, 2012; Schwartz, 2012; Tom, 1997).

Conclusion

The construct of intellectual mattering emerged from research on meaningful interactions and relationships between master's students and professors. I further developed this idea based on a review of extant mattering literature as well as Relational-Cultural theory, possible selves, authentic teaching, and interpersonal boundaries concepts. Through the early development of this construct, I suggest that students experience two forms of intellectual mattering: content-oriented and process-oriented. In addition, I propose that the experience of authentic intellectual mattering can give students increased energy, confidence, and motivation and can promote their transition from knowledge receivers to knowledge co-creators.

Fitzwilly's is a funky little restaurant located on Main Street in Northampton, Massachusetts. I remember meeting Roberta there for dinner, discussing ideas and books and possibilities. I remember the semi-dark pub lighting and I remember that those times felt important. I have come to understand our collaboration and connection in theoretical terms and yet I also recall those meetings on an emotional level. Roberta introduced me to qualitative research which was not yet taught in our program; I felt challenged. I left each meeting excited to read the next book or do the next piece of exploration; I felt energized. A professor was taking me seriously as a thinker; I felt important. My work mattered. My thinking mattered. I mattered.

The author wishes to thank Lisa Goldstein Graham, PhD, for her review of early drafts of this paper.

References

Booth, M., & Schwartz, H. L. (2012). We're all adults here: Clarifying and maintaining boundaries with adult learners. In H. L. Schwartz (Ed.), *New Directions for Teaching and Learning: Interpersonal Boundaries in Teaching and Learning* (pp. 43-55). San Francisco, CA: Jossey-Bass.

Brookfield, S.D. (2006). Authenticity and power. In P. Cranton (Ed.), *New directions for adult and continuing education: Authenticity in teaching* (pp. 5-16). San Francisco: Jossey-Bass.

Connolly, K. M., & Myers, J. E. (2003). Wellness and mattering: the role of holistic factors in job satisfaction. *Journal of Employment Counseling,* 40(4), 152–160.

Cranton, P., & Carusetta, E. (2004). Perspectives on authenticity in teaching. *Adult Education Quarterly,* 55(5), 5–22.

Dixon Rayle, A., & Chung, K. (2008). Revisiting first-year college students' mattering: Social support, academic stress, and the mattering experience. *Journal of College Student Retention: Research, Theory & Practice,* 9(1), 21–37.

Elliott, G. C., Kao, S., & Grant, A. (2004). Mattering: Empirical validation of a social-psychological concept. *Self and Identity,* 3(4), 339–354.

Fletcher, J. K. (2001). *Disappearing Acts: Gender, Power, and Relational Practice at Work.* Cambridge, MA: The MIT Press.

Fletcher, J. K. (2004). The paradox of postheroic leadership: An essay on gender, power, and transformational change. *The Leadership Quarterly,* 15, 647–661.

Gibson, D. M., & Myers, J. E. (2006). Perceived stress, wellness, and mattering: a profile of first-year citadel cadets. *Journal of College Student Development,* 47(6), 647.

Holloway, E. L., & Alexandre, L. (2012). Crossing boundaries in doctoral education: Relational learning, cohort communities, and dissertation committees. In H. L. Schwartz (Ed.), *Interpersonal Boundaries in Teaching and Learning New Directions for Teaching and Learning,* 2012(131), 85–97.

155

Jordan, J. V. (2010). *Relational-cultural therapy* (1st ed.). Washington, D.C.: American Psychological Association.

Markus, H., & Nurius, P. (1986). Possible selves. *American Psychologist, 41*(9), 954–969.

Marshall, S. K., Liu, Y., Wu, A., Berzonsky, M., & Adams, G. R. (2010). Perceived mattering to parents and friends for university students: A longitudinal study. *Journal of Adolescence, 33*(3), 367–375. doi:10.1016/j.adolescence.2009.09.003

Miller, J. B. (1986). *Toward a new psychology of women* (2nd ed.). Boston, MA.

Miller, J. B., & Stiver, I. P. (1997). *The healing connection: How women form relationships in therapy and in life.* Boston: Beacon Press.

Myers, J. E., & Bechtel, A. (2004). Stress, wellness, and mattering among cadets at West Point: Factors affecting a fit and healthy force. *Military medicine, 169*(6), 475–482.

Rosenberg, M., & McCullough, B. C. (1981). Mattering: Inferred significance and mental health among adolescents. *Community and Mental Health, 2,* 163–182.

Rossiter, M. (2007). Possible selves: An adult education perspective. *New Directions for Adult and Continuing Education,* 2007(114), 5–15.

Rossiter, M. (1999). Caring and the graduate student: A phenomenological study. *Journal of Adult Development, 6*(4), 205–216.

Schlossberg, N. K. (1987). Understanding and Reaching Adult Learners. McGill Journal of Education, 22(1), 9–18.

Schlossberg, N. K. (1989). Marginality and mattering: Key issues in building community. *New Directions for Student Services,* 1989(48), 5–15.

Schwartz, H. L. (2011). From the classroom to the coffee shop: Graduate students and professors effectively navigate interpersonal boundaries. *International Journal of Teaching and Learning in Higher Education, 23*(3), 363–372.

Schwartz, H. L. (2012). Reflection and Intention: Interpersonal Boundaries in Teaching and Learning. In H. L. Schwartz (Ed.), *New Directions for Teaching and learning: Interpersonal Boundaries in Teaching and Learning* (pp. 99 - 102). San Francisco, CA: Jossey-Bass Publishers.

Schwartz, H. L., & Booth, M. (2013). A relational approach to assessment. *Manuscript in preparation.*

Schwartz, H. L., & Holloway, E. L. (2012). Partners in learning: A grounded theory study of relational practice between master's students and professors. *Mentoring & Tutoring: Partnership in Learning,* 20(1), 115–133.

Schwartz, H. L., & Holloway, E. L. (2013). "I become part of the learning process": Mentoring episodes and individualized attention in graduate education. *Manuscript submitted for publication.*

Taylor, J., & Turner, R. J. (2001). A Longitudinal Study of the Role and Significance of Mattering to Others for Depressive Symptoms. *Journal of Health and Social Behavior,* 42(3), 310 – 325.

Tom, A. (1997). The deliberate relationship: A frame for talking about student-faculty relationships. *The Alberta Journal of Educational Research,* XLIII(1), 3–21.

Tovar, E., Simon, M. A., & Lee, H. B. (2009). Development and Validation of the College Mattering Inventory With Diverse Urban College Students. *Measurement and Evaluation in Counseling and Development,* 42(3), 154–178.

Walker, M. (2002). *Power and effectiveness: Envisioning an alternate paradigm.* Works in Progress (94). Wellesley, MA: Wellesley Centers for Women.

Cultivating Educator Hope to Support Development of Optimal Learning Communities

··· ■ ■ ■ ···

BETSY B. NORDELL

Cultivating the best possible environment for learning has been a focus of Betsy Nordell's work with educators and school communities since she joined Open Circle, a RCT action project at the Stone Center – Wellesley Centers for Women, in 1993. Central to that work is the foundational idea that teaching and learning occur within a rich relational cultural context. Betsy most recently has been exploring how the nature and quality of the relational cultural web influences what happens in schools and, in particular, how hope serves to enhance the lives of individuals and the functioning of groups. Betsy Nordell may be contacted at bnordell@wellesley.edu.

Teachers' Influence on Educational Outcomes

Research repeatedly shows that teacher quality is the preeminent schooling factor affecting student achievement (Goldhaber & Hannaway, 2009; Schmoker, 2011). According to Palmer (2007), teachers teach who they are. Nieto (2003) agrees and asserts,

> ...teachers bring their entire autobiographies with them: their experiences, identities, values, beliefs, attitudes,

159

hang-ups, biases, wishes, dreams, and hopes. It is useless for them to deny this; the most they can do is acknowledge how these may either get in the way of, or enhance, their work with students. (p. 24)

Relational Images and Controlling Images

According to Miller and Stiver (1997), Miller (2008), and Surrey and Kramer (2013) each person's relational images or individualized beliefs about relationships, forged from life experience, inform the logic of personal decision-making. Relational images "...define what we believe will happen to us. Not only do they portray what we expect will happen in relationships, they determine the meanings of this experience for our total conception of ourselves" (Miller, 2008, p. 110). These powerful inner constructions are modified throughout the life span (Miller, 2008). While relational images are individualized and live in the mind of each person, they are influenced by dominant cultural messages that help create and inform relational structures fostering stratification (Miller, 2008; Walker, 2008).

Collins (2000) references cultural messages when articulating her notion of controlling images. These images, created in diverse settings by the dominant cultural group, are intentional categories designed to identify, exclude, and marginalize people viewed as members of the nondominant group (Collins, 2000). Systems of oppression can cultivate a person's foundational belief that she/he lacks ability (Barr & Gibson, 2013). Within schools, both controlling images and relational images affect each person's sense of self, belonging, and connection that, in turn, influences individual performance, motivation, development, overall relational interest, engagement, and hope (Collins, 2000; Comstock et al., 2008; Miller, 2008).

Relational Cultural Interpersonal Moments

Each person's brain has powerful neural networks created over time that foster what each individual anticipates, predicts, expects, and assesses moment-by-moment (Olson, 2014). These habitual processes affect what each person notices and what she/he misses (Olson, 2014). They also influence the actions of all involved in a given co-created relational cultural moment (Chen & Bargh, 1997; Eagleman, 2015; Surrey & Kramer, 2013).

In a social context, behavioral expectancies guide perception priorities and inform the anticipated actions of other people, thereby enabling a person's appropriate reciprocal action (Chen & Bargh, 1997). A person's chosen action, deemed situationally appropriate in anticipation of another person's actions, plays a role affecting the other person's actions as well, because while people see, they also act (Chen & Bargh, 1997; Eagleman, 2015).

During each relational cultural moment, each person's perceptions have a powerful role to play in what aspects of self and other becomes amplified. Humans "… are interactive and interreactive creatures; conditioned reactivity in one triggers the patterns of reactivity in the other, impacting and influencing each other in an ongoing dance of interreactivity" (Surrey & Kramer, 2013, p. 106).

This interpersonal process is an in-the-moment, perception-action-reaction, co-created experience occurring between people (Eagleman, 2015). Therefore, Chen and Bargh (1997) assert that this anticipatory expectancy serves a causal function. It potentially creates a behavioral confirmation or self-fulfilling prophecy that would not have otherwise occurred (Chen & Bargh, 1997). Similarly, Jordan, Kaplan, Miller, Stiver, and Surrey (1991) refer to this mutual influence as bidirectional exchange; Bandura (1986) identifies it with the term reciprocal causality (Surrey & Kramer, 2013).

In addition, Miller and Stiver (1997) state "just as we can get a sense of how another person feels and thinks, so others can get a sense of how we feel and think" (p. 43). With this mutual empathy, there is a "…joining together in a shared experience that builds something new for both (or all) of the people involved" (Miller & Stiver, 1997, p. 43).

The relational cultural milieu of different groups, situations, places, and individuals amplify different facets of each person. Educators' expectations and perceptions profoundly affect each educator's ability to identify and nurture the best that students and other members of the school community have to offer (Chen & Bargh, 1997; Goleman, 2013; Little, 2014; Yamashita & Schwartz, 2012). Teachers' expectancies and perceptions also influence their access to what they see in themselves as well (Fredrickson, 2003; Larrivee, 2012).

Culture and Human Multiplicity

Culture permeates every setting (Hollins, 2008; Nieto, 2010a; Nieto, 2010b; Walker, 2008). Created, supported, and sustained by community members, this often unarticulated, but powerful variable affects all aspects of every human interaction (Gaitan, 2006; Hollins, 2008; Nieto, 2010a; Nieto, 2010b). It determines social acceptance and shunning, behavioral approval and reprimand, a sense of comfort and threat.

Culture animates all schools and every classroom (Gay, 2010; Hollins, 2008; Nieto, 2010a; Nieto, 2010b). Teachers, along with all other adults in the school community, have the unique opportunity to support student development by intentionally creating an inclusive and supportive educational context by identifying shared cultural priorities that they can strive to purposely transmit (Barr & Gibson, 2013; Carter, 2010; Fisher et al, 2012; Guthrie & Schuermann, 2010; Hollins, 2008; Martin, 2011). The school's culture is a powerful pervasive force that provides educator focus, informs motivation and commitment, and influences teacher productivity and effectiveness (Peterson & Deal, 2010; Saleh & Khine, 2014). When educators and students are part of such an intentional school community, they can become elevated and achieve their full potential (Carter, 2010; Fisher et al, 2012; Guthrie & Schuermann, 2010; Hollins, 2008; Martin, 2011). During their research in high-poverty, high-performance schools, Barr and Gibson (2013) identified hope as a central influence determining school success. Nolan and Stitzlein (2011) agree and argue that the pragmatic cultivation of hope and hopefulness via the application of imagination, gratitude, and intelligence provides a means to better confront the complex challenges facing education today.

A student's culture influences what, why, and how she/he learns. The teacher's personal culture also has a critical role in the educational context. It influences all aspects of the learning experience the teacher provides to her/his students (Gaitan, 2006; Hollins, 2008; Strouse, 2001). Tisdell (2003) asserts the educator's use of teaching practices that explicitly acknowledge and thoughtfully utilize student cultures, provides the teacher with a more complex foundation upon which to base her/his determinations of what each student needs, affecting interventions, educational methods, and the overall learning environment created, positively influencing educational outcomes. This inclusion of the familiar from the students' culture makes for a more positive school culture by lessening the disconnection, alienation, and/or invisibility that some students feel when their personal culture differs from the school culture (Gaitan, 2006; Strouse, 2001; Tisdell, 2003).

Barr and Gibson (2013) assert this student sense of invisibility is caused, in part, by an educational context devoid of belonging and meaning. This type of school environment facilitates student disengagement. Teacher appreciation of and inquiry into the alignment of the dominant classroom and school culture and its intersectionality with each student's personal culture, as well as the interpersonal dynamic of the classroom community (student-student, teacher-student, adult-adult), and the ways each affects student behavior and learning potentially leads to enhanced teacher determinations of what is occurring and why (Gaitan, 2006; Rothestein-Fisch & Trumbull, 2008). Nieto (2010a) and Hollins (2008) add that culture is not fixed or solid, it is in a state of flux. In every interaction, the cultural backgrounds of all are at play.

According to Pope, Reynolds, and Mueller (2014), every person is multidimensional and experiences the world, other

163

people, and the self in "...complex and dynamic ways. Part of [each person's] reality is influenced by...daily experiences with privilege, power, and prejudice" (p. xv). When a person experiences microaggressions or faces implicit and/or explicit bias, it diminishes self-image and blocks relational opportunities (Pope et al., 2014). In addition, intentional or unintentional unexamined privilege coupled with over-simplified notions of power dynamics serves to perpetuate existing inequities and inhibits empathic understanding of the lived experience of others currently marginalized within the status quo (Comstock et al., 2008; Pope et al., 2014). People create and utilize individualized strategies of relational disconnection and connection in order to negotiate uncertain relational cultural terrain (Jordan, Walker, & Hartling, 2004; Miller & Stiver, 1997). People have many different aspects of who they are; the environmental context, who they are with, and their treatment by other people profoundly influences what facet emerges and whether hope arises or is squelched (Eagleman, 2015; Little, 2014; Lopez, 2013; Walker, 2002).

What is Hope?

Hope has many definitions. *I hope today is sunny,* is a common, simple type of wish. To Scioli and Biller (2009), hope is highly complex. Their work with hope involves human biological needs, psychological traits, social aspects, and spiritual dimensions (Scioli & Biller, 2009). Snyder's (2002) cognitively based conception of hope emerged from qualitatively based research that, in part, asked participants to talk about their day. Snyder (2002) repeatedly heard general descriptions of what the participants needed to achieve or explicit goal statements. The research subjects were naturally consistently thinking about different routes or pathways to reach their goals for the day. In addition, the participants highlighted their motivation to take those particular routes or use those specific pathways (Snyder, 2002). Recent neuroscientific research has confirmed the naturally occurring future-oriented thinking structures and processes that feature so prominently in Snyder's (2002) hope work (McGonigal, 2012).

These natural thinking processes are what underlie Snyder's (2002) hope theory. Superseding these specific goal thoughts, people had self-appraisal thoughts that were self-referential and enduring. These thoughts concerned their perception of their personal capacity to create pathways forward toward goals, along with their capacity to find the motivation to pursue identified goals (Snyder, 2002).

Lopez (2013), building on Snyder's (2002) work, defines hope in action as having three parts (meaningful goals, agency thoughts, and pathway thoughts) that synergistically work together and act as a powerful feedback loop for human behavior. Goals are outcomes grounded in a sense of a desired future self – "...who [I] want to be...where [I] want to go.... what [I] want to [do]" (Lopez, 2013, p. 24). Agency thinking involves, in part, an awareness of outside supports as well as an appreciation of one's strengths, attributes, and skills. Agency thinking is a type of cause-and-effect-based belief in a personal ability to shape one's own life, to motivate oneself, and to persist when pursuing long-term, personally meaningful goals. Pathway thinking refers to an awareness of the existence of multiple routes toward a desired outcome, the evaluation of options, the monitoring of progress, the expectation of possible hardship and challenge, along with an open and curious stance that enables the uncovering and consideration of additional options forward (Lopez, 2013; Lopez & Snyder, 2009; Snyder, 2002).

Relational-Cultural theory asserts, in part, that a person's experience of hope is inextricably linked to her/his sense of connection within the relational cultural world (Jordan, 2011; Miller, 2008; Walker, 2002). People make meaning in a relational context and are hardwired to grow through connection with others (Banks, 2015). Throughout life, people understand their worlds through their movement towards or away from connection (Jordan, 2011; Miller & Stiver, 1997; Surrey & Jordan, 2012). Recent brain research supports this notion of the power of the relational context to influence growth and affect optimal human development (Banks, 2015; Eagleman, 2015).

Teacher Hope and Dormant Intelligence

A teacher's level of hope affects her/his access to the best of what she/he has to offer (Lopez, 2013). According to Rego, the leading researcher on workplace levels of hope (as cited by Lopez, 2013), a person's intelligence and hope reinforce each other to positively influence creativity and productivity. Hope provides a motivational energy that allows for greater utilization of a person's cognitive abilities. In hope's absence, Rego posits, intelligence remains dormant, an under-utilized resource (Lopez, 2013). This has important educational implications for both teachers and students.

Emotional Contagion

Humans are a social species with brains wired to work best when in the presence of other humans and thrive within a positive relational context (Banks, 2015; Eagleman, 2015; Goleman, 2006; Singer & Bolz, 2014). Highly developed human emotional attunement capacities create an understanding and resonant experience of another's potential feelings by sight (Banks, 2015; Lopez, 2013). Emotions (positive and negative) act as a contagion and spread between people (Banks, 2015; Fredrickson, 2003, 2004; Kashdan & Biswas-Diener, 2014).

According to Becker et al. (2014), due to emotional contagion, the teacher's emotional state affects educational outcomes. It acts as a significant emotional force in the classroom. Emotional contagion is not always positive (Becker et al., 2014).

Emotions, Perception, and Thinking Processes

Emotional states influence human perception processes affecting the breadth of information culled and interpreted from a situation (Fredrickson, 2003, 2004; Kashdan & Biswas-Diener, 2014). When people are in an authentically positive emotional state, they literally see their world and process information differently than when they are feeling negative emotion. Negative emotion causes a more narrowed perceptual field and more focused brain functioning. Positive emotions such as joy, gratitude, serenity, interest, hope, pride, amusement, inspiration, awe, and/ or love cause human brain functioning that is broader, more complex, less stereotypical, more relational, and creative. With authentic positive emotions, perception widens and people have a greater thought-action repertoire. Connections between disparate ideas become clearer. Positive emotions act as a buffer and enhance resilience as well as lead to an upward spiral of positivity (Fredrickson, 2003, 2004; Kashdan & Biswas-Diener, 2014).

Both negative and positive emotional states are valuable, necessary, and helpful for making valid, comprehensive, and complete sense of the world (Fredrickson, 2003, 2004; Kashdan & Biswas-Diener, 2014). However, due to a naturally occurring and evolutionarily important human negativity bias, negative states and situations seem more relevant, are more attentionally compelling, and are remembered more comprehensively and easily than positive states and situations, influencing hope's cultivation (Baumeister, Bratslavsky, Finkenauer, & Vohs, 2001; Kashdan & Biswas-Diener, 2014; Rozin & Royzman, 2001). In school settings, a teacher's negativity and/or loss of hope can spread to others (students, colleagues, administrators, student caregivers), thereby affecting their levels of hope (Barsade, 2002; Hatfield et al., 1994; Lopez, 2013).

Being able to see both the good and bad within a given good or bad circumstance, along with feeling both the corresponding positive and negative emotions requires emotional agility, can expand situational understanding, increase well-being, and cultivate hope (Kashdan & Biswas-Diener, 2014; Lopez, 2013). That said, emotional agility sometimes is difficult to put into practice (Ben-Shahar, 2012; Matta, 2012).

167

Things are Not Only What They Seem

Miller and Stiver (1997) and Miller (2008) assert even when people are alone, they think, feel, and act within a framework formed by relational images, controlling images, and their corresponding individualized meanings. In a given moment, a person's relational images and controlling images inform what is perceived and how that information is interpreted (Miller, 2008).

According to Kabat-Zinn (2005), moment-by-moment, once a person's sight and hearing engage, humans tend to swiftly conceptualize by categorizing, labeling, valuing, judging, and developing stories for what is seen and heard. These evolving, individualized, powerful, automatic, habitual, sense-making patterns in the brain, formed by beliefs, affect thinking, feeling, and acting (McGonigal, 2015; Smalley & Winston, 2010). In short, reality is personal (Achor, 2013; Eagleman, 2015; McGonigal, 2015; Schmidt, 1986).

Zimmermann (1986) suggests, during every second, the human brain receives eleven million pieces of environmental information. Since the conscious brain is limited to effectively processing only about forty bits per second, the brain filters and actively chooses what tiny percentage of inputs to notice, pay attention to, and process (Achor, 2013; Schmidt, 1986). The unconscious brain handles, ignores, disregards, or dismisses the rest (Achor, 2013; Schmidt, 1986).

As a result, things are not only what they seem. Perception is a highly complicated, incomplete, and individualized process (Achor, 2013; Chabris & Simons, 2010; Eagleman, 2015; McGonigal, 2015). However, most humans tend to embrace the strong illusion that they have a complete experience of the visual world, erroneously believing they process all information in the environment (Chabris & Simons, 2010). Repeatedly, researchers find people tend to seek information that confirms existing beliefs

PART II • EDUCATION

while ignoring contradictory information (McNerney, 2011). If a person has a foundational belief that all has been seen and is known, there seems to be no compelling reason to look any further than one's individual perception. This has powerful implications for the cultivation of hope.

According to Chabris and Simons (2010), while some of the world is, indeed, vividly experienced, humans have no awareness of what is occurring outside of their narrow focus of attention. People also typically have an accompanying mistaken assumption that they will notice objects that are unusual or distinctive, but in fact, often these remain unnoticed (Chabris & Simons, 2010; Simons, 2000). In educational settings, a teacher's expectation of misbehavior can lead to the educator's missing or undervaluing positive behavior exhibited by students who have historically been troublesome (Split, Kooment, Helma & Thijs, 2011).

A person's lack of humility concerning perception completeness coupled with confidence in current knowledge level and personal assessment proficiency can create blindness to unexpected nuances and larger changes in key aspects within an environment (Chabris & Simons, 2010; Staats, 2015; Staats & Contractor, 2014). A more humble appreciation of the nature and limits of habitual human perception processes may be helpful to consider and tend to in an ongoing way and perhaps most especially when current circumstances seem bleak and hope is desirable yet seems out of reach.

Teacher Stress and Burnout

Teaching is a complex task laden with many competing priorities (Singer, 2010). Burnout and teacher turnover are common (Richardson et al., 2014). Richardson et al. (2014), assert the teaching profession in the United States lacks social status and features a relatively low pay scale. The job requires personal, emotional, and intellectual efforts. Schooling processes emphasize individual student development, often via large and small group teaching methods, within a larger culture of public evaluation, judgment, and criticism. Some school systems provide teachers with an abundance of curricular materials. The breadth of content goals and objectives often negatively affects educator efficacy when too much is expected within too short a time (Richardson et al., 2014).

According to Singer (2010), this is a recipe for stress and potentially burnout. In the first study of its kind, researchers measured student cortisol levels (stress hormones) and found they were higher in students "...if their teachers reported higher burnout levels" (Sifferlin, 2016, para. 3). In the study, the teachers' references to burnout involved a greater experience of stress, reduced effectiveness in class management and teaching, reduced work satisfaction, and less connection to students (Sifferlin, 2016).

The Power of Hope

Hope is a powerful life sustaining force (Lopez, 2013; Scioli & Biller, 2009; Snyder, 2002). It is a source of purpose-driven action (Lopez, 2013; Snyder, 2002). Consequently, a person's hope level shapes what life she/he lives. Hope is predicated upon a personally felt and known perception of reality (Lopez, 2013; Snyder, 2002). Since humans are a social species, this sense of reality arises from within a pervasive and powerful relational cultural world (Banks, 2015; Eagleman, 2015; Goleman, 2006). The practices that follow provide options for educators interested in cultivating hope in themselves and others.

Stories, Positive Relationships, and Hope

Stories can enhance a sense of connection between people (Smith, 2016). Research suggests the learning about the positive stories of others fosters hope (Lopez, 2013). When a person experiences (hears, sees, reads) another's compelling story, it alters neurochemical processes and can serve as a vehicle for shaping and influencing behavior (Smith, 2016). Other people's stories of hope can act as a contagion, inspiring change, persistence, and transformation (Lopez, 2013; Smith, 2016).

Within the context of positive growth-fostering relationships people know themselves in a qualitatively different way than if they only consider self-created storylines informed by relational images or information found in the dominant culture (controlling images) and/or negative relationships (Frey, 2013; Miller & Stiver, 1997; Walker, 2008). In positive growth-fostering relationships, each person's habitual thinking and perceiving along with her/his corresponding individualized storylines are accessible to some degree and can be challenged, broadened, and deepened as a result of mutual empathy, vulnerability, and openness (Jordan, 2013; Miller & Stiver, 1997). There is mutual accessibility and interest in each other's growth (Jordan, 2013). Each person matters to the other, each affects the other, producing "...change in one another and in the relationship" (Jordan, 2013, p. 79). These relationships provide a supportive context where a person can expand beyond a narrow story of perceived situational understanding that creates her/his individualized sense of the way things are and what is possible (Jordan, 2013; Miller & Stiver, 1997).

Bransford et al. (2000) emphasize the significant role relationships play in education. Bryk and Schneider (2003), Bransford et al. (2000), and Bryk, Bender Sebring, Allensworth, Luppescu, and Easton (2010) highlight the importance of a positive relational environment in the adult community for optimal educator performance and enhanced educational outcomes. The relationships educators have with their students are also pervasively influential (McGrath & Noble, 2010; Wang, Haertel, & Walberg, 1994). Teachers need to know their students' intellectual and cultural backgrounds in order to improve academic interventions, effectively develop student interest, deepen curiosity, and make more valid and reliable subjective determinations (Bransford et al., 2000; Engel, 2015; Gaitan, 2006).

Frymier and Houseer assert higher levels of student motivation and learning occur when the relationship between teacher and student is a positive one (as cited in Edwards, Edwards, Torrens & Beck, 2011). Positive teacher-student relationships act as a buffer for students and support the development of resilience during hardship (Wang et al., 1994). McGrath and Nobel (2010) agree and view the social milieu and teacher-student relationships as powerful variables in learning contexts. Students closely observe teacher-student interactions. Importantly, McGrath and Nobel (2010) assert that what students notice about the teacher-student relationships affects the classroom student-student relationships. Teachers and students are highly complex social beings; different groups, people, and situations bring out different aspects of who they are, ultimately affecting how they are perceived by others, how they perceive themselves, how they perceive others, and how they act (Chen & Bargh, 1997; Eagleman, 2015; Little, 2014).

Miller (1986) asserts positive growth-fostering relationships create five good things: 1. an increased sense of self, other, and the relationship, 2. increased zest, 3. an enhanced sense of worth, 4. greater productivity, 5. a desire for more relational connection. Rich positive relationships provide vital information that informs and enhances a personal sense of capacity, affecting performance, risk-taking, growth, and development (Banks, 2015; Comstock et al., 2008; Edwards et al., 2011), all key features of hope (Lopez, 2013; Scioli & Biller, 2009).

Seeking out and developing mutually positive growth-fostering relationships within diverse groups is one way to broaden culturally bound perspectives and storylines (Comstock et al., 2008; Jordan, 2002; Miller & Stiver, 1997; Pope et al., 2014). If the consideration of diverse points of view occurs within a relational context of mutual empathy and vulnerability, more dimensional understanding is possible (Jordan, 2001, 2011). Without diversity, more similar key situational variables tend to pop out as most relevant to similarly-minded people potentially leading to the deep consideration of what is familiar and a blindness to variables that can be larger in scope or not immediately self-serving. In positive relational cultural contexts rich with a diversity of stories told and heard, new vistas can emerge (Comstock et al., 2008; Jordan, 2002). Qualitatively different aspects of current circumstance can come into clearer view potentially leading to a more expansive perception of possibilities influencing the cultivation of hope (Senge, Scharmer, Jaworski, & Flowers, 2004; Thatchenkery & Metzker, 2006).

Mindfulness, Humility, and Hope

Kozak (2009) asserts, "how reality seems to look, how it sounds, and how it feels is all relative to the system that apprehends it" (p. 44). Enhanced mindful awareness increases the opportunity to notice the content and trajectory of perception and thinking patterns. Smalley and Winston (2010) assert mindful awareness acts to clean the lenses of our experience to better understand how personalized filters affect perception, appraisal, corresponding experience, and thought-action repertoire. This different perspective potentially supports insight into and a broader understanding of situational factors and past situationally based conclusions regarding available choices, instead of falling into habitual behavioral responses (Ben-Shahar, 2012; Kabat-Zinn, 2005; Smalley & Winston, 2010). The workings of relational images and controlling images can come more clearly into focus. Once brought into awareness, better known, and understood, greater choices emerge as to how to notice, continue, or cease habitual perception and meaning making (Ben-Shahar, 2012; Goleman, 2013; Smalley & Winston, 2010).

Smalley and Winston (2010) view "… mindfulness [as] a means of seeing the conceptual frameworks by which you live – how your thoughts shape your worldview" (p. 174). Applied with educators, this process can affect teacher motivation and learning. It will provide a potential avenue for greater appreciation of the nature, origins, and influence of implicit and explicit bias possibly leading to a more nuanced discernment of what is happening in the classroom and potential reasons why (Kytle, 2004; Langer, 2014; Mason, Gunersel, & Ney, 2014; Staats, 2015; Staats & Contractor, 2014).

Langer (2014) asserts over-learned skills and habitual ways of being create a sense of confidence that influences a person's attention, awareness, and focus. A tension can exist between being confident about moment-to-moment assessments of the relevant situational factors that are causing a particular outcome, while being mindfully aware that humans do not see all there is (Simons, 2000). The simultaneous holding of both competence and a more humble lack of knowing can be a complicated process (Brookfield, 2009). However, as Laing suggests, "the range of what we think and do is limited by what we fail to notice" (as cited in Kabat-Zinn, 2005, p. 19). Once embraced, humility concerning perception completeness can foster increased curiosity about what is unnoticed, providing a rationale for learning ways to expand perception to gain a more complete picture of reality (Achor, 2013; Tangney, 2000).

Cultivating Hope through Applied Compassion Practices

According to Keltner, Marsh, and Smith (2010), compassion is a relational construct because it involves the acknowledgment of a person's suffering and offers kindness in response. Compassion practices enhance awareness and recognition of the commonality of human suffering and increase appreciation and understanding of common human imperfection (self/others) (Gilbert, 2009; Neff, 2012; Salzberg, 2010; Singer & Bolz, 2014). These ideas are similar to those articulated in Surrey and Jordan's (2012) descriptions of the cultivation of relational mindfulness and relational wisdom within therapeutic settings.

Compassion practices are a vehicle for trying to organize emotions, thoughts, and motives into habitual brain patterns that better support well-being for the self and others (Gilbert, 2009). Over time, practices like Tonglen's Transforming Suffering (when the commonality of human suffering is the singular attentional focus) and Just Like Me (when foundational human similarities are intentionally brought into deep awareness) potentially help support authentic human connection and interpersonal understanding (Barbezat & Bush, 2014; Bush, 2015; Chodron, 2000).

174

When compassion practices focusing on the deep suffering of others along with the desire to extend a kindness to alleviate suffering were studied using real-time functional magnetic resonance imaging (fMRI), a distinctive neural signature relating to positive emotions, love, and affiliation appeared (Singer & Bolz, 2014). Notably, compassion practices engage positively energizing biological systems and neural networks (Singer & Bolz, 2014). Research using compassion practices in health care settings have found potential implications for addressing caregiver burnout (Seppala et al., 2014). These research findings have an important connection to education in the United States. As mentioned previously, teacher turnover resulting from negative stress experiences and burnout is common and significantly problematic (Richardson et al., 2014).

In addition, compassion practices support the cultivation of positive relationships. Compassion directed at others influences perception processes that potentially augment how people think and feel about specific people and/or groups (Fredrickson, 2013; Singer & Bolz, 2014). While directing compassion to people we naturally care for is relatively easy, authentic compassion becomes harder when considering people who have done harm and/or committed a wrong (Singer & Bolz, 2014). Siegel (2010) agrees and suggests when humans identify others as not us, a lack of resonance occurs and the brain circuitry that sees another human being as "…having an internal mental life" is not activated (p. 257). This may facilitate the human ability to transform other human beings into objects thereby reducing a felt sense of their humanity. This compassion inhibition may help explain the inhumane and violent aspects of the human species (Siegle, 2010). Hicks (2011) concurs. In her experience working in war-torn parts of the world, the acknowledgement of the inherent dignity and worth of human beings is the critical starting point to resolving conflict in a sustainable way. That common understanding fosters hopefulness concerning possible relational shifts (Hicks, 2011).

Cullen, a Stanford University Center for Compassion and Altruism Research and Education trainer, found educators gained valuable insight into their relationships with students through cultivating compassion practices (Singer & Bolz, 2014). Singer and Bolz (2014) reported that after training with Cullen, some educators dealing with particularly difficult students reported they no longer found they needed to seek evidence to prove how difficult the students were in order to solidify their cases against them. Over time, the teachers found themselves softening and becoming more relationally open and aware. Teachers reported that this helped to shift negative relationship patterns developed with difficult students. They were able to release their focusing on habitual seeking and finding evidence of negative behavior and instead saw evidence of the positive, as well. The teachers' compassion practices allowed different information about their students to emerge into view thereby affecting the content of their subjective assessments. Given the teacher-student relationship is co-created in each moment, the shift in the teacher's behavior to an augmented, more compassionate perception and outlook shifted the relational outcome over time.

According to Neff's (2011) research, self-compassion practice, or the inward direction of compassion, featuring the interaction and combining of mindful awareness, a deepened sense of common humanity, and kindness, fostered a more self-compassionate frame of mind. A person's frame of mind affects what she/he deems worth noticing in a given situation and her/his subjective assessment concerning what is possible and true, thereby potentially affecting hope levels (Achor, 2013; McGonigal, 2015). Applied self-compassion serves to augment initial understandings (McGonigal, 2012; Neff, 2011, 2012; Singer & Bolz, 2014; Zakrzewski, 2012). In addition, people who practice self-compassion are better able to hold an emotional balance when faced with difficult situations. This self-kindness application helps reduce burnout because self-compassion promotes calmness and clarity (McGonigal, 2012; Neff, 2011; Singer & Bolz, 2014; Zakrzewski, 2012). Relatedly, Miller and Stiver (1997) refer to similar notions as self-empathy asserting, "when people develop greater self-empathy, they usually have begun to change their relational images and their meanings" (p. 135).

Cultivating Hope through Gratitude Practices

Gratitude practices support the expansion of perception by, in part, intentionally bringing into awareness an authentic acknowledgment of what is working well coupled with processes of intentional appreciation and savoring (Bryant & Veroff, 2007; Hlava & Elfers, 2014; Howells, 2012; Jonas, 2012; Watkins, 2014). These processes tend to foster positive emotions that result in expanded thinking (Fredrickson, 2003; Howells, 2012). Tsang (2006) suggests gratitude practices positively influence individual causal attributions, as well as psychological and physical well-being. In addition, Algoe, Haidt, and Gable's (2008) research indicates that gratitude practices promote the formation and maintenance of positive relationships.

Gratitude practices also provide information to base decision-making upon that is qualitatively different than that culled from the situation using negatively based perceptual processes (Howells, 2012, 2015). This information can be particularly helpful since humans have a natural negativity bias (Hanson, 2013). Information concerning the true positive that exists may serve to bolster a grounded sense of hope (Lopez, 2013; Scioli & Biller, 2009; Snyder, 2002).

To Howells (2012), gratitude is, in part, an expression of thanks toward another person, embedded within the relational context. Therefore, Howells (2012) views gratitude as fundamental to education due to the inherent interpersonal relationship between teacher and student. Teaching is a relational process that creates an interpersonal context (Howells, 2012; Palmer, 2007).

Howells (2012) offers gratitude practice as a vehicle for growth through reflection and does not suggest gratitude as a means of fixing difficult problems. Howells' (2012, 2015) work with teacher gratitude was oriented toward a purposeful direction of attention and intention, in a reliable, regular, and habitual way, as a consistent educator practice. One aspect of Howells' (2012) educator gratitude work was attentional focus augmentation. The teachers moved from a narrow and deep consideration of what they were not getting from students to intentionally noticing and considering the positive that they were receiving from students (Howells, 2012).

Some educators successfully used gratitude practices to negotiate complicated and historically negative relationships with difficult parents by focusing on the positive they received from those parents and considering what they appreciated about those parents (Howells, 2012). In some extreme family circumstances, all the educators could muster was practicing appreciating the parent's humanity. Even then, teachers reported it made a difference in what they thought and felt about the parent (Howells, 2012). This gratitude practice process of noticing and connecting to common humanity and the inherent dignity therein is a feature of compassion work as well (Barbezat & Bush, 2014; Hicks, 2011; Singer & Bolz, 2014). Howells (2012) found gratitude cultivation methods positively affected teacher "… presence, efficacy, and resilience" (p. 4).

Teachers working with Howells (2012) found through regular, intentional employing of gratitude practices, their habitual perception shifted. They saw more student actions and characteristics that they could appreciate and give thanks for, that were previously imperceptible. The teachers reported that their gratitude acted as a block to the narrow habitual negative thoughts about the student (Howells, 2012), thereby influencing the teacher's development of hope (Lopez, 2013; Snyder, 2002). This outcome is congruent with Emmons' (2007) findings that with consistently practiced gratitude comes positive psychological, interpersonal, and physical benefits. Gratitude practices influence a person's ability to perceive what is working well, positively affects relationships and well-being, and fosters a more hopeful sense of reality (Howells, 2012, 2014).

Conclusion

Lopez (2013) asserts hopeful people have four foundational beliefs. They believe their future will be better than their present, they have power to influence their future, there are many possible pathways leading to desired outcomes, and all potential paths contain some obstacles (Lopez, 2013). Therefore, the cultivation of hope has an important role to play in teaching and learning environments.

Teaching is a complex profession. During difficult times, when hope seems out of reach, stories, positive relationships, applied humility, mindfulness, compassion, and gratitude offer possibilities for augmenting an individually felt and known sense of personal truth concerning what is possible. This expanded perception of reality provides an opening into new vistas and offers novel ways of seeing and experiencing the world.

Through naturally occurring human emotional contagion processes, authentically experienced hope has the power to spread between people. Educators who understand hope and methods for its cultivation will be better equipped to foster hope in themselves and others, thereby helping to create optimal, uplifting, and hopeful learning communities (Barr & Gibson, 2013; Lopez, 2013).

References

Achor, S. (2013). *Before happiness: The hidden keys to achievement.* New York: Random House.

Algoe, S., Haidt, J., & Gable, S. L. (2008). Beyond reciprocity: Gratitude and relationships in everyday life. *Emotion.* 8, 425-429.

Bandura, A. (1986). *Social foundations of thought and action: A social cognitive theory.* Englewood Cliffs, NJ: Prentice Hall.

Banks, A. (2015). *Four ways to click: Rewire your brain for stronger, more rewarding relationships.* New York: Penguin.

Barbezat, D. & Bush, M. (2014). *Contemplative practices in higher education.* San Francisco, CA: Wiley.

Barr, R.D. & Gibson, E.L. (2013). *Building a culture of hope: Enriching schools with optimism and opportunity.* Bloomington, IN: Solution Tree Press.

Barsade, S.G. (2002). The ripple effect: emotional contagion and its influence on group behavior. *Administrative Science Quarterly.* (12) vol. 47, no. 4, 644-675.

Baumeister, R.F., Bratslavsky, E. Finkenauer, C. & Vohs, K.D. (2001). Bad is stronger than good. *Review of general psychology.* Vol. 5. No. 4, 323-370.

Becker, E.S., Goetz, T., Morger, V. & Ranellucci, J. (2014). The importance of teachers' emotions and instructional behavior for their students' emotions - An experience sampling analysis. *Teaching and Teacher Education.* 43: 15-26.

Ben-Shahar, T. (2012). *Choose the life you want: The mindful way to happiness.* New York: Workman.

Bransford, J.D., Brown, A.L., & Cocking, R.R. (2000). *How people learn.* Washington, D.C.: National Academy Press.

Brookfield, S. D. (2009). *The skillful teacher: On technique, trust, and responsiveness in the classroom.* San Francisco, CA: Wiley.

Bryant, F. B. & Veroff, J. (2007). *Savoring: a new model of positive experience.* Mahwah, NJ: Lawrence Erlbaum Associates.

Bryk, A.S. & Schneider, B. (2003). Trust in schools: A core resource for school reform". *Educational Leadership.* 60(3): 40-45.

Bryk, A.S., Bender Sebring, P., Allensworth, E., Luppescu, S. & Easton, J.Q. (2010). *Organizing schools for improvement: Lessons from Chicago*. Chicago, IL: The University of Chicago Press.

Bush, M. (2015, August). *Contemplative practice: Just like me*. 11th Annual Summer Session on Contemplative Pedagogy, Smith College, Northampton, MA.

Carter, S. C. (2010). *On Purpose: How great school cultures form strong character*. Thousand Oaks, CA: SAGE.

Chabris, C. F. & Simons, D. J. (2010). *The invisible gorilla: and other ways our intuitions deceive us*. New York: Random House.

Chen, M. & Bargh, J.A. (1997). Nonconscious behavioral confirmation processes: The self-fulfilling consequences of automatic stereotype activation. *Journal of Experimental Social Psychology*. 33: 541-560.

Chodron, P. (2000). *When things fall apart: Heart advice for difficult times*. Boston, MA: Shambhala Publications.

Collins, P. H. (2000). *Black feminist thought: Knowledge, consciousness, and the politics of empowerment*. New York: Routledge.

Comstock, D. L., Hammer, T. R., Strentzsch, J., Cannon, K., Parsons, J., & Salazar II, G. (2008). Relational-Cultural theory: A framework for bridging relational, multicultural, and social justice competencies. *Journal of Counseling & Development*. (86): 279-287.

Eagleman, D. (2015). *The brain: The story of you*. New York: Penguin Random House.

Edwards, C., Edwards, A., Torrens, A., & Beck, A. (2011). Confirmation and community - the relationships between teacher confirmation, classroom community, student motivation, and learning. *Online Journal of Communication and Media Technologies*. 1(4): 17-43.

Emmons, R.A. (2007). *Thanks!: How the new science of gratitude can make you happier*. New York: Houghton Mifflin Company.

Engel, S. (2015). *The hungry mind: The origins of curiosity in childhood*. Cambridge, MA: Harvard University Press.

Fisher, D., Frey, N., & Pumpian, I. (2012). *How to create a culture of achievement in your school and classroom*. Alexandria, VA: ASCD.

Fredrickson, B. (2003). The value of positive emotions. *The American Scientist*, July-August 330-335.

Fredrickson, B. (2004). Gratitude, like other positive emotions, broadens and builds. In R. Emmons & M. McCullough (Eds.). *The Psychology of Gratitude* (pp. 125-166). Oxford: Oxford University Press.

Fredrickson, B. (2013). Love 2.0: *How our supreme emotion affects everything we think, do, feel, and become*. New York: Penguin.

Frey, L. L. (2013). Relational-cultural therapy: Theory, research, and application to counseling competencies. *Professional Psychology: Research and Practice, 44*(3), 177-185.

Gaitan, C. D. (2006). *Building culturally responsive classrooms*. Thousand Oaks, CA: Sage.

Gay, G. (2010). *Culturally responsive teaching*. New York: Teachers College.

Gilbert, P. (2009). *The compassionate mind: A new approach to life's challenges*. Oakland, CA: New Harbinger Publications.

Goldhaber, D. & Hannaway, J. (2009). *Creating a new teaching profession*. Washington, DC: The Urban Institute Press.

Goleman, D. (2006). *Social Intelligence: The new science of human relationships*. New York: Bantam Dell.

Goleman, D. (2013). Focus: *The hidden driver of excellence*. New York: HarperCollins.

Guthrie, J. W. & Schuermann, P.J. (2010). *Leading schools to success: Constructing and sustaining high-performing learning cultures*. Thousand Oaks, CA: SAGE.

Hanson, R. (2013). *Hardwiring happiness: The new brain science of contentment, calm, and confidence*. New York: Random House.

Hatfield, E., Cacioppo, J. T., & Rapson, R. L. (1994). *Emotional contagion*. New York: Cambridge University Press.

Hicks, D. (2011). Dignity: *The essential role it plays in resolving conflict*. New Haven, CT: Yale University Press.

Hlava, P. & Elfers, J. (2014). The lived experience of gratitude. *Journal of Humanistic Psychology*. Vol. 54(4) 434-455.

Hollins, E. R. (2008). *Culture in school learning: Revealing the deep meaning*. New York: Routledge.

Howells, K. (2012). *Gratitude in education: A radical view*. Boston: Sense Publishers.

Howells, K. (2014). An exploration of the role of gratitude in enhancing teacher-student relationships. *Teaching and Teacher Education*. 42: 58-67.

Howells, K. (2015). Researching the place of gratitude in the personal domain of the educator: Tales from the field. In K. Trimmer, A.L. Black, & S. Riddle (Eds.), *Mainstreams, margins, and the spaces in-between: New possibilities for education research*. (pp. 36-49). New York: Routledge.

Jonas, M.E. (2012). Gratitude, Ressentiment, and Citizenship Education. *Studies in Philosophy and Education,* Vol. 31, Issue 1, 29-46.

Jordan, J.V. (2001). A relational-cultural model: Healing through mutual empathy. *Bulletin of the Menninger Clinic*. 65(1): 92-103.

Jordan, J.V. (2002). *Learning at the margin: New models of strength* (work in Progress No. 98). Wellesley, MA : Stone Center Working Paper Series.

Jordan, J. V. (2011). The Stone Center and relational–cultural theory. In J. C. Norcross, G. R. VandenBos, & D. K. Freedheim (Eds.), *History of psychotherapy: Continuity and change* (2nd ed.) (pp. 357-362). Washington, DC, US: American Psychological Association.

Jordan, J.V. (2013) Relational Resilience in Girls. In S. Goldstein & R.B. Brooks, *Handbook of Resilience in Children* (pp. 79-90). New York: Springer.

Jordan, J.V., Kaplan, A.G., Miller, J.B., Stiver, I.P., & Surrey, J.L. (1991). *Women's growth in connection: Writings from the Stone Center*. New York: Guilford Press.

Jordan, J.V., Walker, M., & Hartling, M.L. (2004). *The complexity of connection: Writings from the Stone Center's Jean Baker Miller Training Institute*. New York: Guilford Press.

Kabat-Zinn, J. (2005). Coming to our senses: *Healing ourselves and the world through mindfulness*. New York: Hyperion.

Kashdan, T. & Biswas-Diener, R. (2014). *The upside of your dark side*. New York, NY: Penguin.

Keltner, D. (2009). *Born to be good: The science of a meaningful life*. New York W.W. Norton.

Keltner, D., Marsh, J., & Smith, J. A. (2010). *The compassionate instinct: The science of human goodness*. New York: W.W. Norton & Company.

Kozak, A. (2009) *Wild chickens and petty tyrants: 108 metaphors for mindfulness*. Somerville, MA: Wisdom.

Kytle, J. (2004). *To want to learn*. New York: Palgrave Macmillan.

Langer, E. J. (2014). *Mindfulness*. Boston: Da Capo Press/Perseus Books.

Larrivee, B. (2012). *Cultivating teacher renewal*. Plymouth, UK: Rowman & Littlefield.

Little, B.R. (2014). *Me, myself, and us: The science of personality and the art of well-being*. Philadelphia, PA: Perseus.

Lopez, S. J. (2013). *Making hope happen*. New York: Simon & Shuster.

Lopez, S. J. & Snyder, C. R. (2009). *The Oxford handbook of positive psychology*. New York: Oxford University Press.

Martin, J. R. (2011) *Education reconfigured: Culture, encounter, and change*. New York: Routledge.

Mason, B. A., Gunersel, A. B., & Ney, E. A. (2014). Cultural and Ethnic Bias in Teacher Ratings of Behavior: A Criterion-Focused Review. *Psychology In The Schools*, 51(10), 1017-1030.

Matta, C. (2012). *The stress response*. Oakland, CA: New Harbinger.

McGonigal, K. (2012). *The neuroscience of change*. Boulder, CO: Sounds True.

McGonigal, K. (2015). *The upside of stress*. New York: Penguin.

McGrath, H. & Noble, T. (2010). Supporting positive pupil relationships: Research to practice. *Education & Child Psychology*. 27 (1): 79-90.

McNerney, S. (2011). Confirmation bias and art. *Scientific American*. Retrieved from http://blogs.scientificamerican.com/guest-blog/confirmation-bias-and-art/

Miller, J.B. (1986). *What do we mean by relationships?* (Work in Progress No.22). Wellesley, MA: Stone Center Working Paper Series.

Miller, J.B. (2008). How change happens: Controlling images, mutuality, and power. *Women & Therapy*. 31(2-4): 109-127.

Miller, J. B. & Stiver, I. P. (1997). *The healing connection: How women form relationships in therapy and in life*. Boston: Beacon Press.

Neff, K. (2011). *Self-Compassion*. New York: HarperCollins.

Neff, K. (2012). The science of self-compassion. In C.K. Germer, R.D. Siegel, & The Dalai Lama (Eds.). *Wisdom and Compassion in Psychotherapy*. (pp. 79-92). New York: Guilford.

Nieto, S. (2003). *What keeps teachers going?* New York: Teachers College Press.

Nieto, S. (2010a). *Language, culture, and teaching: Critical perspectives*. New York: Taylor and Francis.

Nieto, S. (2010b). *The light in their eyes: 10th anniversary edition*. New York: Teachers College Press.

Nolan, C., & Stitzlein, S. M. (2011). Meaningful Hope for Teachers in Times of High Anxiety and Low Morale. *Democracy & Education,* 19 (1): 1-10.

Olson, K. (2014). *The invisible classroom: Relationships, Neuroscience, and mindfulness in school*. New York: W. W. Norton.

Palmer, P. (2007). *Courage to teach*. San Francisco, CA: Jossey-Bass.

Peterson, K.D. & Deal, T.E. (2010). *The shaping school culture fieldbook*. New York: Wiley.

Pope, R.L., Reynolds, A. L., & Mueller, J. A. (2014). *Creating multicultural change on campus*. San Francisco, CA: Jossey-Bass.

Richardson, P. W., Karabenick, S. A., & Watt, H. M. G. (2014). *Teacher motivation: Theory and practice*. Hoboken, NJ Taylor and Francis.

Rothestein-Fisch, C & Trumbull, E. (2008). *Managing diverse classrooms: How to build on students' cultural strength*. Alexandria, VA: ASCD.

Rozin, P. & Royzman, E.B. (2001). Negativity bias, negativity dominance, and contagion. *Personality and social psychology review*. Vol. 5, No. 4, 296-320.

Saleh, I.M. & Khine, M.S. (2014). *Reframing transformational leadership: New school culture and effectiveness*. Rotterdam, Netherlands: Sense Publishers.

Salzberg, S. (2010). *The force of kindness: Change your life with love and compassion*. Louisville, CO: Sounds True.

Schmidt, R.F. (1986). *Fundamentals of Sensory Physiology*. New York: Springer.

Schmoker, M. (2011). *Focus: Elevating the essentials to radically improve student learning*. Alexandria, VA: ASCD.

Scioli, A. & Biller, H. B. (2009). *Hope in the age of anxiety*. New York: Oxford University Press.

Senge, P., Scharmer, C.O., Jaworski, J., & Flowers, B.S. (2004). *Presence: An exploration of profound change in people, organizations, and society.* New York: Random House.

Seppala, E.M., Hutcherson, C.A., Nguyen, D. T.H., Doty, J.R., & Gross, J.J. (2014). Loving-kindness meditation: A tool to improve healthcare provider compassion, resilience, and patient care. *Journal of Compassionate Health Care.* 1(5): 2-9.

Siegel, D. J. (2010). *Mindsight: The new science of personal transformation.* New York: Random House.

Sifferlin, A. (2016, June). Stress is contagious in the classroom. Time. Retrieved from http://time.com/4384135/stress-burnout-teachers/

Simons, D. J. (2000). Attentional capture and inattentional blindness. *Trends in cognitive Sciences.* Vol. 4 (4): 147-155.

Singer, J. (2010). *The teacher's ultimate stress mastery guide.* New York: Corwin.

Singer, T. & Bolz, M. (Eds). (2014) *Compassion. Bridging practice and science.* Munich, Germany: Max Planck Society.

Smalley, S. L. & Winston, D. (2010). *Fully present: The science, art, and practice of mindfulness.* Phil., PA: Perseus.

Smith, J.A. (2016, June). The science of the story. *Greater Good.* Retrieved from http://greatergood.berkeley.edu/article/item/science_of_the_story

Snyder, C. R. (2002). Hope theory: Rainbows in the mind. *Psychological Inquiry,* Vol. 13, No. 4, 249-275.

Spilt, J. L., Koomen, H. M. Y., & Thijs, J.T. (2011). Teacher well-being: The importance of teacher-student relationships. *Educational Psychology Review,* 23(4): 457-477.

Staats, C. (2015) Understanding implicit bias: What educators should know. *American Educator.* American Federation of Teachers, AFL-CIO. Retrieved from http://www.aft.org/ae/winter2015-2016/staats

Staats, C. & Contractor, D. (2014). *Race and discipline in Ohio schools: What the data say.* Columbus, Ohio: Kirwan Institute for the Study of Race and Ethnicity at Ohio State University.

Strouse, J.H. (2001). *Exploring socio-cultural themes in education.* Columbus, OH: Prentice-Hall.

Surrey, J. & Jordan, J. (2012). The wisdom of connection. In C.K. Germer, R.D. Siegel, & The Dalai Lama (Eds). *Wisdom and Compassion in Psychotherapy.* (pp. 163-175). New York: Guilford.

Surrey, J. & Kramer, G. (2013). Relational Mindfulness. In C.K. Germer, R.D. Siegel, & P.R. Fulton (Eds). *Mindfulness and Psychotherapy.* (pp. 94-111). New York: Guilford.

Tangney J.P. (2000). Humility: Theoretical perspectives, empirical findings and directions for future research. *Journal of Social and Clinical Psychology.* Vol. 19, pp.70-82.

Thatchenkery, T. & Metzker, C. (2006). *Appreciative intelligence.* San Francisco, CA: Berrett-Koehler.

Tisdell, E.J. (2003). *Exploring spirituality and culture in adult and higher education.* San Francisco, CA: Jossey-Bass.

Tsang, J. (2006). Gratitude and prosocial behavior: An experimental test of gratitude. *Cognition and Emotion.* 20(1), 138-148.

Walker, M. (2002). *How therapy helps when the culture hurts* (Work in Progress No. 95). Wellesley, MA: Stone Center Colloquium Series.

Walker, M. (2008). Power and effectiveness: Envisioning an alternate paradigm. *Women & Therapy.* 31(2-4): 129-144.

Wang, M.C., Haertel, G.D., & Walberg, H.J. (1994). Educational resilience in inner cities. In M.C.Wang & E. Gordon (Eds). *Educational resilience in inner-city America: Challenges and prospects.* (pp. 45-72) Hillsdale, NJ: Erlbaum.

Watkins P. C. (2014). *Gratitude and the good life: Toward a psychology of appreciation.* New York: Springer.

Yamashita, M. & Schwartz, H.L. (2012). The coconut and the peach: Understanding, establishing, and maintaining interpersonal boundaries with international students. In H. Schwartz (Ed). *New Directions for Teaching and Learning.* Vol. 2012, Issue 131, p. 57-69.

Zakrewski, V. (2012). How self-compassion can help prevent teacher burnout. *Greater Good The Science of a Meaningful Life.* Retrieved from http://greatergood.berkeley.edu/article/item/self_compassion_for_teachers

Zimmerman, M. (1986). Neurophysiology of sensory systems. In R. F. Schmidt (Ed). *Fundamentals of Sensory Physiology.* (pp. 68-116). New York: Springer.

Relational-Cultural Theory in Practice: The Power of Connection Through Student and Professional Mentorship

———— ···■■■··· ————

CONNIE GUNDERSON, PhD, JANE LARSON, MSW,
CORRIE EHRBRIGHT, MSW, VANESSA THOENNES, MSW,
AMY ANDERLY-DOTSON, MSW, ANTHONY KLAR, MSW,
ASHLEY TUVE, MSW, WILL WALES, MSW

Relational-Cultural theory (RCT) recognizes the primacy of relationship, and emphasizes the intrinsic human desire for connection through mutual empathy, radical respect, community and social justice. The purpose of this paper is to share the voices and experiences of MSW students who completed an advanced practice course in Relational-Cultural theory at The College of St. Scholastica in Duluth, Minnesota with the instruction of Dr. Connie Gunderson. Core aspects of learning included the opportunity for students to collaborate with faculty at the Jean Baker Miller Training Institute at Wellesley College in Boston, Massachusetts and participate in a mentorship program with RCT practitioners throughout the USA and Canada. Their experiences demonstrate that with the power of connection and the value of intrinsic inter-relationship mutual learning, growth and change are possible as students integrate Relational-Cultural theory into field placements and other professional settings. Connie Gunderson, PhD, LISW may be contacted at cgunderson@css.edu.

Informed by Benedictine heritage and its dedication to hospitality, respect, stewardship, community, and the love of learning, The College of St. Scholastica (CSS) is committed to fostering a learning environment that contributes to the well-being of persons and the planet. Students recognize that these values are based on the centrality of relationship. They guide theoretical and practical approaches to address the needs of persons and the environments in which they live.

At CSS, the Master of Social Work (MSW) program introduces students to diverse theoretical and clinical approaches to address the needs of persons, families, and communities. One approach that exemplifies the Benedictine values is called Relational-Cultural theory (RCT). RCT recognizes the primacy of *relationship,* and emphasizes the intrinsic human desire for connection through mutual empathy, radical respect, community and social justice.

The purpose of this paper is to share the voices of MSW students who completed a course in Relational-Cultural theory at The College of St. Scholastica. This paper will briefly describe the course curriculum. The paper will focus on students' learning and reflections of their professional growth during the course, and the implications of applying RCT in clinical social work practice. It will also describe how the CSS MSW program continues to integrate RCT into its academic setting.

Brief Introduction to Relational-Cultural Theory

Relational-Cultural theory evolved as a developmental and psychological model in the 1970s through the collaboration of four women psychologists, Jean Baker Miller, Irene Stiver, Judith Jordan, and Jan Surrey, in Boston, MA. These women, along with other scholars and practitioners, began to challenge mainstream, traditional psychologies of human development that were grounded in a belief of the *separate-self.* From their perspectives, psychological theories that valued and fostered a *separate-self* worldview, based on individualism and autonomy, promoted a culture that was fundamentally antithetical to the health and well-being of persons and communities. In refute, the women posited that health, well-being, and growth are based on the primacy and centrality of *relationship* and *relational movement* rather than the focus of *acting in one's sole interests* (Miller, 1976). This paradigm shift in thought and action has affected how counseling, therapy, organizational development, and policy changes are understood and practiced. In 2012, an editor at the American Psychological Association recognized Relational-Cultural theory as one of the top ten psychological theories of our time (Carlson, 2012). This is a tribute to the scholarship of the women who dared to challenge the status quo in the field of psychology.

Relational-Cultural Theory: An MSW Course Curriculum

In the fall of 2014, MSW students at the College of St. Scholastica had the opportunity to study Relational-Cultural theory and its approach to human development, clinical practice, and social justice.

The course curriculum included an in-depth exploration of RCT theory, collaborative mentorship with RCT clinical practitioners, an introductory training experience at the Jean Baker Miller Training Institute at Wellesley College in Boston, MA, and two community based educational events, hosted by the College of St. Scholastica and the Duluth community, featuring Dr. Judith Jordan and Dr. Connie Gunderson. The course was designed to engage students to learn about growth fostering relationships with each other, RCT mentors, and RCT scholars. The students were encouraged to reflect and practice the tenets of RCT in all aspects of the course. To assist in this process, students worked in small groups with RCT mentors to examine RCT through comprehensive literature reviews and collaborative discussions. Each small group critically reflected on how the theory and tenets applied to clinical social work practice.

191

A student reflected that RCT mentorship was a unique way to build relationships and foster learning:

> I feel very fortunate to have had the opportunity to work with our mentors. They brought a wealth of experience, wisdom, knowledge, and fun to the table. They were willing to answer questions, share resources, and offer guidance. Most importantly, they brought themselves to the relationship and, I believe, we did as well. In true RCT fashion, our mentoring relationship was one of a reciprocal nature with all of us engaged in mutual learning.

This next section includes brief summaries of the students' learning and reflections of some of the primary RCT tenets.

Basic Tenets of Relational-Cultural Theory

Mutual Empathy

Mutual empathy is one of the essential factors necessary for growth in relationships (Jordan, 1986). According to Hartling and Miller (2004), mutual empathy is not a static one-way process, nor is it a relational courtesy, but rather a complex skill that helps us "know" another person's experience. To be empathic requires vulnerability. Jordan (1992) likens mutual empathy to a "life-giving empathic bridge" where people with different views and perspectives can come together and engage in dialogue that creates change (p. 2).

The practice of mutual empathy in therapy encompasses not only empathizing with clients' experiences but also with their strategies of disconnection (Miller & Stiver, 1994). It is also a corrective experience allowing clients to build positive relational images and know they can have an impact on the world and the people in their lives which, in turn, contributes to a sense of empowerment (Walker, 2004). As clinicians, being mutually empathic also means identifying and empathizing with our own experiences and strategies of disconnection which can interfere with the ability to be fully present and engaged with our clients (Jordan, Walker, & Hartling, 2004).

Walker (2004) notes that all people deserve to be treated with dignity. Radical respect is a key aspect of mutual empathy. Without radical respect it is unlikely that clients would allow themselves to be vulnerable enough to authentically engage in a relationship. The practice of mutual empathy is paramount – without it, healing cannot take place. A student allowed herself to experience mutual empathy as she wrote:

> Boston was an opportunity for me to join and experience the special bond the class already seemed to have. I wasn't sure what to expect. When I walked into the airport the morning we were flying out, ready to cry over the fact I had to leave my babies, two of my classmates greeted me immediately with smiles, hugs, and words of reassurance. It was in that moment that I knew I was going to part of something special. Special seems like an understatement here. The bond we all created in Boston was nothing short of extraordinary, and that bond continues to grow.

Authenticity

Authenticity is being able to fully represent oneself honestly in relationships (Jordan, 2004). When we are able to be authentic we are able to better know, understand, and discuss our thoughts and feelings with others (Miller & Stiver, 1997). The benefits of authenticity have been stressed in many fields including psychology, sociology, philosophy, and spiritual traditions (Chen, 2004). For example, a recent study on authenticity, life satisfaction, and distress indicated that the ability to be authentic in relationships was connected to an increased feeling of life satisfaction and decreased levels of distress (Boyraz, Waits, & Felix, 2014). As an example of this, a student wrote:

193

Authentic interpersonal relationships are critical to
client health. Yet so many clients come to therapy in a
state of profound isolation. RCT is refreshing because
the focus is on healthy and authentic relationships,
rather than on symptoms of mental illness.

Another student reflected:

The RCT class was like nothing I expected. The class
was small and intimate. We got to know each other's
quirks and personalities on a deeper level. This was
something new for me, since I was used to blending in,
and being unnoticed. In the RCT class I was visible.
When I spoke, people heard me, and that was something
I had never experienced before. In this environment
I learned my voice was accepted. For the first time,
I realized I could make a difference outside of the
classroom, and connect with others on a deeper level.

These results support the importance of helping clients share
their personal stories, explore thoughts and feelings, be true to
themselves, and feel free to engage in meaningful ways with
others.

Social Justice

As clinicians it is important to understand that chronic
exposure to social disparities, such as race, gender, and class
based stereotypes, are painful and foster self-doubt and feelings
of unworthiness (Comstock et al., 2008). RCT invites clinicians
to think beyond symptom reduction and remedial helping
interventions (Comstock et al., 2008). Clinicians are encouraged
to explore the social challenges and barriers clients may deal with
on a daily basis. For example, Birrell and Freyd (2006) describe
in their article, *Ethics and Power,* how cultural oppression, social
exclusion, and other forms of social injustices underlie the pain
that individuals in marginalized and devalued groups routinely

experience in their lives. During the training in Boston, Dr. Maureen Walker explained that although oppression is often institutionalized at societal levels, it is necessarily enacted in the context of interpersonal relationships, therefore the fragmentation caused by the violation of human bonds can only be healed by new and healing human bonds (Walker, 2014). While at the training in Boston, a student became more aware of an important social justice issue while attending a lecture by author, Allan G. Johnson, who wrote *The Gender Knot*. The student noticed:

> During the training, I was introduced to new perspectives about gender and privilege in our culture. I began to understand how white males have a status of unearned privileged in our society. As a white male with this unearned privilege, I became increasingly aware of how I may be perceived by others based on this unearned privilege alone. For example, I recognized how women are often discounted in our culture by being referred to as "guys." This demonstrated how "male dominant" our society is.

As a clinical social worker, it is critical to be cognizant of the deep-rooted issues of power and privilege and to be able to address clients' experiences with their environments and systemic assumptions and practices from a relational human rights perspective.

Boundaries

Many traditional therapeutic models view boundaries as a rigid line of separation. Clients may be subject to what the therapist determines as rules or boundaries. This perspective often carries connotations of control and separateness. From an RCT perspective, boundaries are viewed as an opportunity for connection and a place of meeting and exchange (Walker & Rosen, 2004). One method that fosters a *power-with* relationship is a conversation initiated by the therapist with a client at the beginning of the relationship. To create an environment that is mutually respectful and safe, therapists and clients need to discuss and clarify the purpose and focus of their therapeutic relationship. Here, boundaries are discussed and mutual agreements are developed to establish a constructive therapeutic relationship. For example, therapists respect clients by focusing on the clients' needs during the therapy hour, and only use a "judicious use of self" when offering feedback and responses. Clients respect therapists by honoring the therapists' need for personal privacy inside and outside of the office. This is critical in establishing a positive relational connection (Walker & Rosen, 2004). During the semester, there were discussions about the need for healthy professional boundaries. A student reflected:

> I have struggled with the some of the traditional models of mental health treatment. For example, a therapist who is intentionally aloof and objective (if that is even possible) exudes judgment and superiority. Sadly, I have witnessed clinicians who repeatedly tell clients what is wrong with them, interpret clients as manipulative and treatment resistant, and unilaterally design treatment plans that clients must follow or face significant consequences. This does not model a growth fostering relationship, or offer a client a safe place to be vulnerable. An RCT clinician tries to relate with a client in a professional manner with mutual empathy, fluid expertise, a judicious use of self, clear boundaries and clarity of purpose.

Power

RCT focuses on safe and healthy therapeutic relationships. So the concept of power is central to RCT. Power is present in every relationship. How power is perceived and manifested is critical. RCT suggests that power is defined as the ability to facilitate change (Jordan, 2010). For example, relationships that strive to acknowledge and respect each person's ability to contribute, while recognizing the different roles and needs each person may have creates an environment that supports empowerment, connection, and growth (Miller & Stiver, 1997).

The students explored how they experience power in their work with clients and in their organizations. Recognizing how people use power to interact in relationship has been insightful. One student wrote:

> The privilege of going to Boston to learn from the founding scholars of RCT was life changing for me. It's not every day that someone, like myself, has the opportunity to meet people like Dr. Jordan, Dr. Banks, and Dr. Walker. They generously supported our efforts, and they invited us into mutually responsive relationships. How amazing to be invited to call or e-mail them with a question, or a thought, and get a response! How amazing to be asked to share our personal experiences, so they could learn from us.

Constructive Conflict

Relationships are not static. They are quite dynamic. In therapy, clients and therapists naturally move along a continuum between connection and disconnection (Comstock et al., 2008). Disconnections and resulting conflicts may cause fear. Conflicts in therapy can be seen as pathways for transforming misunderstandings to empathy, and for building bridges between one another through collective relational struggle (Comstock et al., 2008). RCT suggests that with increased mindfulness and a willingness to address inevitable conflicts that occur in therapy in a constructive "win-win" manner, clients can feel safe, become more attentive and responsive to relational movement, and gain confidence in their ability to grow in relationship. A student reflected on her insights about the importance of providing a safe climate for conflict and struggles to occur:

I have learned so much about the value of relationships and the importance of building them with clients. Many clients have experienced loss and trauma and are searching for safety, so it is important to be able to provide that for them.

RCT has changed my interactions with others – I find myself listening more and asking more questions rather than offering solutions right away, which has always been my instinct. I have learned how to create a space that is open and safe. Through this course I have found my voice and been able to share what I have learned about RCT outside of the classroom.

RCT has also taught me the importance of fostering and maintaining relationships that have already been established, to know when disconnections occur, and how to work through them in respectful ways.

Connection and Disconnection

Therapists will likely work with clients who have been referred by social services, the courts, and other programs. Clients may wish for connection with a therapist and hope that the therapist will care enough to listen and understand their story, and, at the same time, clients may feel ambivalent and guarded about treatment. The desire for connection and authentic engagement may be overshadowed by protective strategies to stay out of relationship and to feel safe – to be relationally disconnected (Jordan, 2005).

A disconnection is defined as a psychological rupture that occurs when a child or adult is prevented from participating in a mutually empathetic and mutually empowering interaction (Miller & Stiver, 1997). According to Miller and Stiver (1997), two key features are necessary to bring about re-connection. A person must be able to take some constructive action within the relationship to make one's experience known. And the other person in the relationship must be willing and able to empathically respond in a way that supports a new and better connection.

Clients' disconnections are not the only ones that need to be respectfully responded to. Therapists bring their own strategies of disconnection to a therapeutic relationship. The need for connection, based on mutual empathy, with other professionals is recommended for all who are working in clinical practice. Thus, it is important for therapists to participate in professional supervision to support their own personal and professional growth. One of the fundamental beliefs in RCT is that one never needs to be isolated because of the power of connection. A student wrote about her struggles with connection:

> I had a profound life changing experience when I went to the Jean Baker Miller Training Institute. Before leaving for the trip to Boston, my hope tank was on empty. I had been compassionately working for a rural agency. I was devastated when the agency suddenly eliminated my position. When I left for Boston with my cohort, I wanted to isolate. It was what I knew. However, while in Boston, I rediscovered who I was as an individual, a spouse, a mother, and as a social work professional. I realized I had been lost for over two and a half years. My life had been weighed down with shame and guilt. The environment I had been working in created these lonely and negative feelings. I noticed that the most fearful and difficult part of my journey in Graduate School has been exploring who I am and who I am becoming. I have had to force myself to look at the positive attributes, skills, and passions that are inside of me.

The Five Good Things

A culture that fosters growth and is grounded in radical respect, hospitality, and community offers an environment that provides us with The Five Good Things: a sense of zest, clarity about ourselves and our relationships, a sense of worth, an enhanced capacity to participate in our world, and a desire for more connection (Jordan, 2010). From this perspective, life's journey is inherently relational. For example, we grow through and towards relationships during our lifetime, rather than towards separateness and independence (Jordan, 2010). One student expressed her ideas: "We wish to feel safe and to offer safety to others. We wish to give and receive love and kindness. We strive to increase our capacity for relational growth by developing mutual empathy, mutual empowerment, and resilience." Another student wrote about her experience with The Five Good Things:

> Because of this course, I have zest in the face of the most trying time of my life. I have the most clarity about myself, others, and my relationships than ever before. I have a sense of worth and an enhanced capacity to be productive. Most of all, for the first time in my life, I have the desire for more connection, and for that I am grateful.

Another student added how RCT concepts are intertwined:

> Last year, at the beginning of my RCT journey, Dr. Gunderson spoke about The Five Good Things, growth fostering relationships, mutual empathy, and authenticity. Until then, I had never heard how these concepts could be linked together. I knew instantly, I found a "theoretical home". Everything, from that point on, has been moving me towards learning how to live and practice RCT in my personal and professional life.

The course taught students to apply theory to real life situations. Students were able to engage with peers, mentors, clinicians, educators, and scholars. They created a safe place to explore, struggle, and support each other to develop personal and professional skills critical for comprehensive clinical practice.

Future Collaborations

The College of St. Scholastica has integrated RCT into the Masters of Social Work curriculum. There are plans to offer RCT as an undergraduate course to first year students to assist them as they adjust to college life. It is clear, scientific studies are continuing to emerge with data that supports RCT and demonstrates that humans are neurologically wired for connection (Banks & Hirschman, 2014). To assist in providing ongoing evidence in this field of study, Graff, Gunderson, and Larson completed and are in the process of publishing a study on the C.A.R.E. program with MSW students (Graff, Gunderson, & Larson, 2017). This is in the process of being published. This study focused on the relevancy of the C.A.R.E. assessment tool and specific C.A.R.E activities for the relational health of students.

In addition, in collaboration with the Jean Baker Miller Training Institute and Wellesley Centers for Women, engaged CSS faculty and staff, current students and alumni, along with other professionals organized the Transforming Community: The Radical Reality of Relationship Conference in June, 2016. We are currently establishing the cornerstone at the college and with our community to offer ongoing training in Relational-Cultural theory/therapy in Duluth, MN.

Clearly, the "relational movement" is alive and well on this northern Minnesota campus and in our local community as CSS faculty and students introduce RCT in field placements, professional settings, and with clientele. Collaboration between the College of St. Scholastica and the RCT scholars and practitioners from Boston and elsewhere in the USA and Canada demonstrate that change is possible as we work collaboratively to foster healthier relationships for students, clients, and professionals.

Conclusion

Professional social work education integrates theory and practice and teaches students to engage, assess, and intervene with clients in a wide range of settings. RCT suggests working from a paradigm that places the focus of clinical assessment and intervention on relational development and interaction. From a relational perspective, we approach persons and their environments with a belief in intrinsic inter-relationship. We see the challenges for human rights through a relational lens. We incorporate a relational perspective into how we make policy decisions. For some, this is a significant shift in thought and action.

As the St. Scholastica MSW students graduate and move into the clinical world, integrating the tenets of RCT into their work may not always be easy. A student noted that she has much to learn as she embraces a relational paradigm in her personal and professional life.

> I still feel like an infant or a toddler with RCT. I am still in wonder of everything. I am learning and exploring. I realize that RCT is not based on a set of facts to memorize, or quick steps to follow. It is a way of living and being with everyone and everything around me. This theory takes time to develop and understand.

Yet, as more practitioners and organizations truly recognize the centrality of relational interdependency, and as research continues to confirm that we, as humans, are literally hardwired to connect, and as persons consistently challenge power-over systems that intentionally isolate and marginalize "others", a relational movement, that is already underway, will be ever-present to foster well-being for all persons and for the planet in which we live.

Acknowledgements

The students of the advanced course in Relational-Cultural theory would like to thank those who offered their assistance while writing this publication. We thank Dr. Gunderson for her endless support throughout the course. Her guidance challenged each of us to explore new ways to connect and relate with others.

We thank our mentors. We are grateful for their willingness to stand with us as we explored the tenets of Relational-Cultural theory. Their experience and insight enhanced our learning and broadened our perspective of social work.

Finally, we thank Dr. Amy Banks, Dr. Judith Jordan, and Dr. Maureen Walker. The training experience was life changing for us. We are moved by your passion for intrinsic human connection and your willingness to support each of us as people and professionals.

●

References

Banks, A., & Hirschman, L. A. (2015). *Four ways to click: Rewire your brain for stronger, more rewarding relationships.* New York: Penguin.

Birrell, P.,. & Freyd, J. (2006). Betrayal and trauma: Relational models of harm and healing. *Journal of Trauma Practice, 5*(1). doi: 10.1300/J189v05n01_04

Boyraz, G., Waits, J.B., & Felix, V.A. (2014). Authenticity, life satisfaction, and distress: A longitudinal analysis. *Journal of Counseling Psychology, 61*(3), 498-505. doi: 10.1037/cou0000031

Carlson, J. (2012). In e-Connections Newsletter. Spring, 2012. Wellesley, MA: Jean Baker Miller Training Institute, Wellesley Centers for Women

Chen, X. (2004). *Being and authenticity.* New York: Rodopi.

Comstock, D., Hammer, J., Strentzsch, J., Cannon, K., Parsons, J., & Salazar, G. (2008). RCT: A framework for bridging relational, multicultural and social justice competencies. *Journal of Counseling and Development. 86,* 279-287.

Graff, D., Gunderson, C., Larson, J. (2017). [Assessing MSW student's health and wellness with the C.A.R:E. program]. Unpublished raw data.

Hartling, L. M., & Miller, J. B. (2004). Moving beyond humiliation: A relational reconceptualization of human rights. Excerpts from a paper presented at the Summer Advanced Training Institute: Encouraging an Era of Connection, Wellesley College, Wellesley, MA.

Jordan, J. V. (1986). The meaning of mutuality. *Work in Progress, No.23.* Wellesley, MA: Stone Center Working Paper Series.

Jordan, J. V. (1992). Relational resilience. *Work in Progress, No. 57.* Wellesley, MA: Stone Center Working Paper Series.

Jordan, J. V. (2004). Relational resilience. In J. V. Jordan, M. Walker, & L. M. Hartling (Eds.). *The complexity of connection: Writings from the Stone Center's Jean Baker Miller Training Institute.* New York: Guilford Press.

Jordan, J. V. (2005). Commitment to connection in a culture of fear. *Work in Progress No. 104*. Wellesley, MA: Stone Center Publications. doi: 10.1080/02703140802146423

Jordan, J. V. (2010). *Relational-Cultural therapy*. Washington D.C.: American Psychological Association.

Jordan, J.V., Walker, M., & Hartling, L. M. (Eds.). (2004). *The complexity of connection*. New York: Guilford Press.

Miller, J.B. (1976). *Towards a new psychology of women*. Boston: Beacon Press.

Miller, J.B., & Stiver, I.P. (1994). Movement in therapy: Honoring the "strategies of disconnection. *Work in Progress, No. 65*. Wellesley, MA: Stone Center Working Paper Series.

Miller, J. B., & Stiver, I. P. (1997). *The healing connection: How women form relationships in therapy and in life*. Boston: Beacon Press Books.

Walker, M., & Rosen, W. B. (2004). *How connections heal: Stories from Relational-Cultural therapy*. New York: The Guilford Press.

Walker, M. (2004). How relationships heal. In M. Walker & W. Rosen (Eds.). *How Connections Heal: Stories from relational-cultural therapy*. New York: Guilford Press.

Walker, M. (2014). The Power of Connection. Jean Baker Miller Training Institute Lecture. 24. - 26. October 2014. Wellesley, MA: Wellesely College.

205

Caretaking the Radical Reality of Relationships: A Relational-Cultural Framework for White Faculty Mentoring Minority Students at Predominantly White Institutions

— · · · ■ ■ ■ · · · —

KRISTEN SHREWSBURY, PhD

"Caretaking the Radical Reality of Relationships: A Relational-Cultural Framework for White Faculty Mentoring Minority Students" is a reflection on applications of Relational-Cultural theory in my life and work. I have found RCT to provide a rich framework for anti-racism and social justice efforts. The RCT community is of equal importance to my ability to stay in connection while working in a non-relational cultural context. Kristen Shrewsbury, PhD may be contacted at shrewskm@gmail.com.

Working at a predominantly white institution (PWI) of higher education inherently affords many privileges to me, a white faculty member. I know how to interact with administrators because the unwritten cultural protocols align with those I learned in my K-12 and higher education experiences. Additionally, I was a majority-status undergraduate at the institution where I now find employment. The (easily observable) perks of my whiteness include sharing a race with almost all the senior administrators and the majority of fellow faculty, staff, and students, having aligned culturally-informed notions of interaction expectations, and hearing my English dialect used daily and in all formal and most informal exchanges.

While I claim membership in non-privileged identity groups as a queer woman, my marginalized identities are impacted by my whiteness and cannot be considered without acknowledging I am of the majority-status race and hold a position of power as a professional with a terminal degree. I have brought this self-awareness in varying degrees to my role as a faculty supervisor and mentor to students working in an English-language tutoring center that I coordinate. In my nine years, one third of these student tutors were from non-dominant racial identity groups and held international visas to attend higher education in the United States. I have struggled with and grown in providing culturally competent and responsive cross-cultural mentorship, where I, as a white American faculty member, serve as mentor to marginalized students (Merriweather & Morgan, 2013). I offer this article as a reflective guide for my future mentoring relationships, a mile marker in my journey, and an invitation to other white faculty to the critical conversation of how to develop cross-cultural consciousness so that we might better serve our minority-status students and colleagues.

In the past 30 years, United States higher education institutions have shown increases in racially and ethnically diverse faculty and students, though at a slower rate than the increase in numbers of white students (Aud, Fox, & KewalRamani, 2010; Student Exchange Visitor Program, 2004; 2016). Increasingly diverse campus populations along with administrative initiatives in response to legislative directives have called for the examination of the conventionally white, Anglo-Saxon, protestant traditions that maintain intellectual stratifications and reserve education for a privileged class. More recently, visa-holding international students enrolled in U.S. higher education have increased exponentially, more than tripling between 2004 and 2016 to approximately 1.18 million students in the United States in March 2016 (Student Exchange Visitor Program [SEVP], 2004; 2016). Marginalized students at predominantly white institutions are tasked by virtue of their minority status to negotiate majority-status values and expectations for access to the majority-status normed educational practices. Visa-holding international students enrolled in higher education face a unique and at times additional level of cultural navigation during their academic tenure in the U.S.

Culturally responsive interventions at predominantly white institutions are slow and incremental, relying on the work of generations who have engaged the rigid hierarchies that maintain majority-status norms. Affirmative action legislation and practices have created pathways of access for marginalized students who otherwise do not have historically direct pathways into higher education. Accessibility, however, has not meant inclusion. Beyond gaining admittance, retention practices for minority students endeavor to address the systemic and social inequalities that contribute to marginalized student attrition. Transforming university communities from assimilationist ivory towers to dynamic sites of acculturation and learning that value diversity requires interventions that uproot marginalization and exclusion, which are often put forth as social norms and intellectual stratifications.

Cross-Cultural Mentorship

Popular at four-year institutions and widely practiced in both student affairs and academic units, Millennial retention and engagement practices hinge on relationships (Espinoza, 2012). In both student-faculty relationships and student worker-faculty supervisor relationships, mentorship serves as a meaningful avenue to provide insider connections and framing of the institutional culture while encouraging personal relationships (Handelsman, 2005) and intellectual mattering, the notion that one's thinking matters to another person (Schwartz, 2013). Defining an effective stance toward retaining and engaging Millennials includes viewing teaching as a personal growth opportunity in which faculty learn *with* their students (Espinoza, 2012). Especially in predominantly white institutions, marginalized students benefit from mentorship in reframing negative institutional messages about race and gender (Hinton, Grim, & Howard-Hamilton, 2009). Both race and gender influence the mentorship relationship (Griffin & Reddick, 2011), and thus cross-cultural mentorship must acknowledge them through continuous and honest dialogue, which requires mutual trust and empathy (Johnson-Bailey & Cervero, 2004).

A challenge to the critical work of mentorship is the reality that minority students often significantly outnumber minority faculty. These faculty are often asked to serve or informally end up serving as the mentors, advisors, supporters, and primary contact for marginalized students, a demand that serves as a cultural taxation with real and tangible implications such as impeded career progress and diminished job satisfaction (Joseph & Hirschfeld, 2011). Existing departments can have a socially just response to this cultural taxation by requiring majority-status faculty to personally and professionally develop cultural competencies that serve the broader student body.

However, developing the cultural competence of majority-status faculty requires deep personal conviction, high tolerance for ambiguity, capacity for vulnerability, humility, and commitment to the work, of which Bonilla-Silva (2015) point out that most white faculty are unable to do effectively. McCoy, Winkle-Wagner, and Luedke (2015) researched white faculty beliefs and attitudes toward marginalized students whom they mentor and identified a consistent gap between the espoused beliefs of white faculty that they are advocates for students of marginalized and a pervasive colorblind racism: the belief that race should not and does not matter (Worthington, Navarro, Loewy, & Hart, 2008). Race-neutral, colorblind language serves to reinforce racial biases (Bonilla-Silva, 2010) because it renders structural racism invisible from the more powerful position in the relationship and unburdens white faculty from examining their own privilege (McCoy et al, 2015). Colorblind racism perpetuates templates for interaction derived from "socially inscribed histories" that disallow the authentic connection and vulnerability required for a mutually empathic mentoring exchange (Merriweather & Morgan, 2013, p. 3). Over time, chronic disconnection can occur when the faculty mentor repeatedly dismisses a student mentee's racialized or gendered experience causing isolation, hopelessness, and disconnection in the relationship (Walker, 2008), a clear mentoring failure.

More research is needed on cross-cultural mentorship of minority students, with comparisons between white faculty and minority faculty mentoring practices (McCoy et al, 2015). In the meantime as minority faculty numbers grow with diversity efforts, a temporary option for a more socially just campus climate and to address the cultural taxation on these faculty is for white faculty to actively work on their cross-cultural competencies and responsiveness. Minority students deserve excellent mentorship and minority faculty deserve to be tasked fairly. For majority-status faculty to expand their consciousness and humility in meeting the challenges marginalized students face, self-work around power and privilege is required. The development of this racial consciousness supports a human desire for healthy connection (Banks, 2011), and thus promises deep rewards for both the white faculty and the communities in which they take part.

Seeing Whiteness And Taking (Faltering) Action

Early in my career, I recognized that my position providing academic support to English language learners on a predominantly white campus meant more than delivering sound instruction using pedagogically appropriate methods. I was developing relationships with these learners and in earning their trust, began to hear story after story of marginalizing experiences. In the privacy of my office, my students processed the burdens and pain of acts of racism, linguicism, microaggressions, and overt xenophobia through their writing both for formal class essays and as a means to develop as writers in English. While monolithic thinking about people of color and assumed exposures, values and belief systems reinforces the assumption of differing values and expectations about higher education among students of color and those of majority status faculty at PWI's, the experiences non-native English speaking students consistently share with me is evidence that many white faculty embedded in the cultures of power at our PWI are at best tone deaf to the diversity of thought available in a cross-cultural classroom, and at worst disappointed to have to expand their teaching to provide accessibility beyond the dominant cultural norms.

I tried to help in our sessions, like most well intended white people tend to do. I faltered often; the students may have remained hurt and were possibly further marginalized by my mistaken words or assumptions. I was frustrated. I regularly took action outside of our private conversations, doing what white people do when they spy injustice – I reported it to the proper authority with every conviction that the system would respond wholeheartedly to correct these transgressions. I was confronted with inaction, placation, and a strong reminder to follow the script – the unwritten, liberal colorblind, "look how far we've come" script. These responses opened my eyes to the regular responses these students received, and gave me insight into the institutional way of handling reports of marginalization. I saw that I had to go outside the institution to learn what I could do to support the students, work to effect systemic changes, and manage my expectations and disappointments without burdening the students with my emotional needs. I was accepted to participate in a five-day race immersion experience for higher education employees designed to bring equal numbers of people of color and white people together to process race.

The experience was excruciating and changed my life. I wrestled with white fragility for the first half of the experience, using defensive moves to avoid talking about or acknowledging race (DiAngelo, 2011). When I could no longer rest in the quiet collusion of ignorance my world paradigm shifted for good to knowing at a soul level that I perpetrate racist attitudes and beliefs. I can't un-know that I will most likely always be a perpetrator of racism. I learned what I can do is commit to the slow, incremental, humbling, at times infuriating exercise of listening, sitting with discomfort, guilt and pain, and staying in awareness to change my core beliefs and actions, when I would love to take a break and just fall back into the comfort of my privilege. There I don't have to think about "this stuff" anymore.

I don't always succeed. Sometimes I do take a break. This is hard to admit, but the truth. When I do come back to actively resisting collusion, I must remember that I can stay open and it will not kill me; I know what the defensive moves of white fragility look and feel like, and I can name them when I succumb to them, using the tools I have to move through them. I can read books and attend community meetings. I can use my energy to influence local policies and practices to build a more socially just system. I can act in my power to provide connection in places of disconnection. I can stop acting and talking and taking up space to allow others who have been silenced a chance to be heard. I can walk away with integrity when I am not invited to the table of activists and friends marginalized in the dominant system. I can respect people with whom I disagree or don't like. I can focus my scholarship on social justice and talking to other white people about our role. It's a lifetime of choosing to stay in the struggle and I own it because I benefit from the construct of whiteness. The self-work is my responsibility and I make mistakes all the time. I am vulnerable and sometimes quick to anger because this is hard work, but I owe it to myself to stay the course. I am right to be angry that the entire community suffers because of the collusion of well-intended and not-so-well-intended white people. Self-compassion has become a critical aspect of my self-work because I misstep despite my best efforts.

Coming back to campus, I acknowledged my spheres of influence and began to examine my hiring practices by seeking the support of our Office of Equal Opportunity to write job descriptions that reduced my white tone deafness and blind spots in recruiting a diverse workforce. I found a Social Justice and Diversity Plan from another predominantly white institution and invited visa-holding international and racial minority students to shape it with me so that I might carry out a strategic plan in our tutoring center to better serve the English language learners on campus – a virtually invisible group at only about two percent of the overall population. I began to hire marginalized students who were invested in the services for English language learners and whose identities and experiences could inform their work in culturally appropriate ways. My employees had tremendous autonomy in providing services, and we explicitly addressed power dynamics to create together hierarchies constructed to support their actualization rather than subordination.

Here is where my well-intended efforts became trickier. I take the supervision of all my employees very seriously. I attempt to match their daily work and professional development to their long-term career goals and to support their job-search efforts after graduation. I get to know them and take real interest in their ideas, their families, and their plans for their lives. This engagement came very easily for the white, female students who were so similar to me and aligned with the culture of the predominantly white institution. For a visa-holding Chinese student employee, only here for four years to get her undergraduate degree before returning home, I had a much harder time. I was only beginning to see how much I did not know. The grammar of Chinese culture was foreign to me just as my workplace practices were steeped in an unfamiliar structure to my employee and were firmly situated within a grammar of whiteness that she had to decode (Bonilla-Silva, 2012). How could I mentor her well and provide the structure to invite the mutually beneficial outcomes of mentorship when I was unable to appreciate and negotiate our differences? I reverted to color blindness. I fell back on the privileged notion of equality – treat all students the same.

I cognitively knew the difference between equity, or providing access necessary to meet the individual's circumstances, and equality, or providing one form of access intended to fit all cases, but the dissonance between my goals and how to get there was too great. This visa-holding Chinese student only worked with me for one semester and then quietly went her separate way. I knew I had failed her and had failed myself in the process. I was deeply ashamed that after "coming so far" I had not been able to apply what I had learned in time to offer mentorship. I applied for and was accepted to a research trip to China the next summer. I worked hard to learn more about the culture with lower stakes than in-the-moment mentorship. I also took the time to examine my colorblind racism. I sought allies in my quest to be better than yesterday, to keep working for anti-racist outcomes even as I uncovered and began uprooting my own racist attitudes and beliefs. The experiences that continue to lead me to further self-work around racism are grounded in empathic failures but are also examples of resilience and the humbling experience of pressing on. In my social justice research, Relational-Cultural theory is a psychological framework I have come to rely upon to cultivate my resilience and guide my interactions to promote healthy connection and heal transgressions across difference (Jordan, Kaplan, Miller, Stiver, & Surrey, 1991).

Relational-Cultural Theory

Relational-Cultural theory (RCT) posits that people grow through and toward relationships throughout the lifespan, and that culture powerfully impacts relationships (Jordan et al, 1991; Jordan, 2010). RCT takes into account the cultural context that guides interactions toward or away from connection within a given power structure and offers an alternative theory of human development (Collins, 1990; Miller, 2008, Walker, 2008a). Rather than the traditional view that differentiation, autonomy, and independence are goals for maturation, RCT posits that human development is through and toward healthy, mutual relationship (Jordan, 2010). Neuroscience is providing exciting evidence that

215

humans are in fact hardwired for connection and that the pain of social exclusion, isolation and disconnection is processed in the same area of the brain that physical pain is processed (Banks, 2011; Eisenberger & Lieberman, 2005). With healthy relationships as the goal, a metric for authentic connection is the production of what Jean Baker Miller (1986) defined as The Five Good Things: zest, a sense of worth, clarity, productivity, and a desire for more connection. Authentic connection promotes the notion of strength in vulnerability, or the openness to being moved through the relationship (Jordan, 1992; 2002).

Cultural context powerfully and profoundly shapes the social structure that fosters connections and disconnections across human and social difference (Jordan, 2010). Majority-status groups construct and operationalize controlling images, dominant representations that distort the non-dominant cultural group being depicted with the intent of disempowering them and perpetuating the majority-status fear of losing rank in any number of ways including economically, socially, and politically (Collins, 1990; Miller, 2008). Modern examples of controlling images include constructs such as Black criminals, white saviors, smart Asians, welfare queens, rapist immigrants, and Latina maids. These images are not only false, but also insidious and become subconscious templates for oppressive attitudes and beliefs (Collins, 1990; Miller, 2008a). Controlling images impact how to act and how to construct relationships, offering a powerfully binding set of criteria for interactions (Miller, 2008). Colorblind racism as an ideology defends these controlling images as reality and further disempowers dissenting (often minority) voices that attest to the contrary (Bonilla-Silva, 2010). The integration of RCT with cross-cultural mentorship practices provides a framework to explore the caretaking, and the intentional actions of checking the health and mutual beneficence of the radical relationship between white faculty and minority students that ultimately creates in the relationship a sense of belonging and The Five Good Things: zest, a sense of worth, clarity, productivity, and a desire for more connection (Miller, 1986).

An Integrated Framework for Feminist Cross-Cultural Mentorship

Applying RCT to mentorship goals provides meaningful guidance for faculty mentors, and is particularly effective in addressing the isolation experienced by students with minority identity memberships (i.e., first generation college students), marginalized racial and ethnic identities, and emergent bilingual or non-native English speakers (Cokley, McClain, Enciso, & Martinez, 2012). When students enter an institution, the systemic biases are often revealed in how culturally aligned the student's home experience is with that of the institute. Students hailing from the dominant group of the institution often find little disruption to their adjustments, even rallying around the similarities as evidence of "fit." For minority students, the observation period is longer, the stakes higher to find the perceived "fit," and the threat of invisibility greater. "In a culture that stratifies human difference, that systematically rank orders human beings according to their racial group membership, it is inevitable that anxiety about racial difference would be the source of much human suffering" (Walker, 2008b, p.72). The feminist tenet that the personal is political applies to the cross-cultural mentoring relationship in that healthy processing of racial anxiety between mutually empathic, racially different people and across power positions is radical and can be healing to the individuals within a community.

A university setting can be paradoxical in promoting a strong sense of in-group belonging categorized by school spirit while also encouraging the development of individuated young adults who think critically. The network of formal and social relationships a student creates bridges assimilationist school spirit and critical thinking, allowing influential relationships to guide the student's development. Faculty mentors provide social support that is a strong predictor of academic persistence (Gloria, Castellanos, Lopez, & Rosales, 2005). The caretaking of the healthy cross-cultural mentoring relationship requires attention to the context of the predominantly white institution as evidenced through

217

controlling images and power stratifications, both observable and subtle (McCoy et al, 2015). Chronic disconnection happens when the student mentee is repeatedly and systematically prevented from representing his/her hurt or disconnection to the faculty mentor. The repeated disconnection teaches the students that it is unsafe to bring authentic aspects of self or experience into the relationship, and the mentoring relationship further marginalizes the student.

In student employment situations, explicitly offering mentorship and quality professional experiences for racial, social, and linguistically diverse students begins to address the empirical evidence that non-white students have fewer opportunities to engage with faculty at predominantly white institutions (McCoy et al, 2015). In mentoring and professional experiences, a closer relationship between student and faculty can create consistent experiences of intellectual mattering (Schwartz, 2013). An effective mentoring relationship is characterized by mutual trust, understanding, and empathy, and is a personal as well as a professional relationship (Handelsman, 2005). Assessing the success of the cross-cultural mentorship experience over time includes accounting for the mentee's socialization into the discipline or work culture, along with Jean Baker Miller's (1986) five good things: zest, a sense of worth, clarity, productivity, and a desire for more connection. Critical mentorship as a practice calls for the mentor "to continually examine areas of personal strength and growth, alongside hidden biases and privilege that can influence perspective and actions across many layered contexts" (K. Craddock, personal communication, March 23, 2017). Pervasive colorblind racism among white faculty ideologically can shield the faculty member from attending to the racial realities of cross-cultural mentorship.

Mutuality in mentorship is the ability for the relationship to move both parties and is contingent on mutual empathy and supported vulnerability (Miller, 2008). Mutuality is not the false notion that the faculty member and student mentee are equally powerful. The faculty mentor holds a position of greater power than the student mentee. Naming the power differential and agreeing to ways that the power differential will be acknowledged and negotiated provides a template for discussing positionality and its impact on experience. As with all privileged positions, faculty trying to bring self-consciousness to their mentoring practice must be vigilant in reflecting on ways in which "verbal, nonverbal, obvious, and subtle power is reinforced" (Miller, 2008, p. 3). Failure to recognize their own power is one way faculty mentors may act in marginalizing ways without realizing it creating barriers to authentic connection (Miller, 2008). Assuming notions of power based only in the white faculty's majority-status position can also lead to distorted views of power (Walker, 2008a). Listening and hearing a mentee's experience of power in the relationship creates a more comprehensive assessment of power (Brock, 1993; Walker, 2008a). Further, the recognition of power dynamics within the mentoring relationship must attempt to support the mentor and mentee to challenge and change power imbalances in the greater workplace and world (Alvarez & Lazzari, 2016). Modeling empowerment as a means to operate within a biased system while trying to change that system is an artistic subversion that requires further inquiry.

Expect to make mistakes. Founding RCT scholar Jean Baker Miller (2008) addressed the human fallibility involved in taking risks to be vulnerable in professional practices so that growth could occur. RCT emphasizes the cultivation of resilience required to move back into connection when disconnection happens; *because it will happen.* As careful and considerate as one can attempt to be, as much self-work as a white faculty mentor pursues, as mindful of the situation, context, and health of the relationship as is possible, practitioners "do not have to know and do everything right. Instead, the main thing is to stay in the immediacy of the moment-to-moment movement of the relationship" (Miller, 2008, p. 117). Being committed to handling the next steps after the transgression with humility and vulnerability takes practice and maybe even a break to regroup, but must be addressed in a timely and conscientious manner in order to preserve the functionality of the mentoring relationship. Following up with a supportive colleague or friend within a trusted network to process the mistake and take action to grow from it is essential. Strength in vulnerability, or supported vulnerability is paramount to authentic connection and a core concept in the caretaking of the radical reality of these cross-cultural relationships (Jordan, 1992; 2002).

The Threat of Cross-Cultural Mentorship

White people in North America are insulated from racial stress and unfamiliar with the taxation associated with racial stamina experienced by marginalized people who regularly contend with racially-based transgressions (DiAngelo, 2011). White fragility aims to disempower the acknowledgement of racism as a power structure operating in cultural norms, institutional systems, and relationships (DiAngelo, 2011). Every aspect of white privilege is called into question when racism is known to exist; therefore a protective strategy often used is to deftly or even bluntly move to a defensive stance at the mention of racism or even race. From a place of defense, vulnerability is by definition out of the question. For healthy connection to occur, one must be in a place of mutual empathy, of which the very foundation is vulnerability. A white person deciding to acknowledge racism is dangerous and may be perceived as treasonous to an entrenched racial order required for the white supremacist status quo to perpetuate. Bringing racial consciousness to mentoring relationships fosters resistance that comes from "transforming disconnection into stronger connection" and lays the foundation for building communities of resistance (Jordan, 2002, p. 3).

As a white faculty member committed to self-work around my white racial identity and collusion in white supremacist systems, I have engendered anger, professional subversion, and questions of my worth and value to the institution by talking about my worldview, my advocacy, and my scholarship. I know white educators who have lost their jobs, been demoted or undesirably reassigned as punitive measures for taking action to promote racial and social justice. An RCT approach challenges established psychological aims of independence and can be threatening when applied in a non-relational work setting (Hartling, 2008). Doing cross-cultural mentorship within a rigid, individualistic system also comes at a cost. In my experience, friends in the work are invaluable. The connections to other people who are committed to pursuing racial justice help to build funds of knowledge and strength from shared strategies, successes, failures, and professional networks that may be called on in times of need. I am driven by a profound desire to grow and an abiding belief that minority students deserve excellence in their educational and work experiences. In the same way, minority faculty deserve to excel in their own right, providing unique and meaningful contributions to their fields and our communities without the burden of excessive assignments in mentoring.

Transforming Community through the Radical Realities of Mentorship

Relational-Cultural theory offers a way to heal relationships situated in damaging cultural contexts. Relationships network into communities that span the globe in their reach. Social justice aims to transform communities to serve all members, not just the privileged few who maintain social dominance. As relationships provide space for connection and healing to occur, so do communities begin to heal and transform into more socially, just environments as resilience across divisions becomes more possible. As predominantly white institutions become more socially inclusive to marginalized students, healthy mentorship relationships are key instruments to reframing institutional bias and marginalization. Minority faculty must be supported fairly to achieve career milestones and advancement. White faculty who choose a journey of self-work toward greater racial consciousness must contend with white fragility, marginalization because of their threat to the status quo, and inevitable missteps along the way. The radical reality of a cross-cultural mentoring relationship involves consistently interrogating privilege, power, racism, and sexism in an effort to maintain a connection across difference to engage in a mutual connection that serves to elevate relational consciousness.

References

Alvarez, A. R., & Lazzari, M. M. (2016). Feminist mentoring and Relational-Cultural theory: A case example and implications. *Affilia: Journal Of Women & Social Work,* 31(1), 4154. doi:10.1177/0886109915612512

Aud, S., Fox, M, & KewalRamani, A. (2010). *Status and trends in the education of racial and ethnic groups.* United States Department of Education, National Center for Education Statistics.

Banks, A. (2011). The mythic reality of the autonomous individual: Developing the capacity to connect. *Zygon Journal* 46(1), 168–182.

Bonilla-Silva, E. (2010). *Racism without racists: Colorblind racism & racial inequality in contemporary America* (3rd ed.). Lanham, MD: Rowman & Littlefield.

Bonilla-Silva, E. (2012). The invisible weight of whiteness: The racial grammar of everyday life in contemporary America. *Ethnic & Racial Studies,* 35(2), 173-194.

Bonilla-Silva, E. (2015, Dec 4). The racial taxation of workers of color. I am tired of ALL the work I'm expected to do on the "diversity front." I'm asked to be on all sort of diversity-related Committees, help recruit Black and Latino undergrad students, assist with the recruitment of faculty of color in other units, and much, much more. [FaceBook status update]. Retrieved from https://www.facebook.com/eduardo.bonillasilva.7/posts/10153847446904668

Brock, R. N. (1993). *Journeys by heart: A christology of erotic power.* New York: Crossroads Press.

Cokley, K., McClain, S., Enciso, A., & Martinez, M. (2013). An examination of the impact of minority status stress and impostor feelings on the mental health of diverse ethnic minority college students. *Journal Of Multicultural Counseling And Development,* 41(2), 82-95

Collins, P. H. (1990). *Black feminist thought.* New York: Routledge.

DiAngelo, R. (2011). White fragility. *The International Journal of Critical Pedagogy* 3(3), 54-70.

Eisenberger, N. I., & Leiberman, M. D. (2005). Why it hurts to be left out: The neurocognitive overlap between physical and social pain." In K. D. Williams, J. P. Forgas, & W. von Hippel (Eds.) *The Social Outcast: Ostracism, Social Exclusion, Rejection, and Bullying,* 109–27. New York: Cambridge Univ. Press.

Espinoza, C. (2012). Millennial values and boundaries in the classroom. *New Directions For Teaching & Learning,* 2 012(131), 2941.

Gloria, A. M., Castellanos, J., Lopez, A. G., & Rosales, R. (2005). An examination of academic nonpersistence decisions of Latino undergraduates. *Hispanic Journal of Behavioral Science,* 27(2), 202-223.

Griffin, K. A., Reddick, R. J. (2011). Surveillance and sacrifice: Gender differences in the mentoring patterns of Black professors at predominantly white research universities. *American Educational Research Journal,* 48, 1032-1057.

Handelsman, J. (2005). *Entering mentoring: A seminar to train a new generation of scientists.* The Wisconsin Program for Scientific Teaching.

Hartling. L. M. (2008). Strengthening Resilience in a Risky World: It's All About Relationships, *Women & Therapy,* 31(2-4), 51-70.

Hinton, K.G., Grim, V. & Howard-Hamilton, M.F. (2009). Our stories of mentoring and guidance in a higher education and student affairs program. In M.F. Howard-Hamilton, C. Morelon-Quainoo, R. Winkle-Wagner, S.D. Johnson & L. Santiague (Eds.), *Standing on the outside looking in: Underrepresented students' experiences in advanced degree programs* (pp. 184-202). Sterling, VA: Stylus Publishing.

Johnson-Bailey, J. & Cervero, R. M. (2004). Mentoring in Black and white: The intricacies of cross-cultural mentoring. *Mentoring & Tutoring: Partnership in Learning,* 12, 7-21.

Jordan, J. V. (1992). Relational resilience. *Working Paper No. 57.* Wellesley, MA: Stone Center Working Paper Series.

Jordan, J. V. (2002) Learning at the margin: New models of strength. *Working Paper No. 98.* Wellesley, MA: Stone Center Working Paper Series.

Jordan, J. V. (2010). *Relational-cultural therapy* (1st ed.). Washington, D.C.: American Psychological Association.

Jordan, J. V., Kaplan, A. G., Miller, J. B., Stiver, I., and Surrey, J. (1991). *Women's growth in connection: Writings from the Stone Center*. New York: The Guildford Press.

Joseph, T. D., & Hirshfield, L. E. (2011). Why don't you get somebody new to do it? Race and cultural taxation in the academy. *Ethnic & Racial Studies, 34*(1), 121-141. doi:10.1080/01419870.2010.496489

June, A. (2015 Nov 8). The invisible labor of minority professors. *The Chronicle of Higher Education*.

McCoy, D., Winkle-Wagner, R, & Luedke, C. (2015). Colorblind mentorship? Exploring white faculty mentoring students of color. *Journal of Diversity in Higher Education, 8, 4*, 225-242.

Merriweather, L. R. & Morgan, A. J. (2013). Two cultures collide: Bridging the generation gap in non-traditional mentorship. *Qualitative Report, 18*, 1-16.

Miller, J. B. (1986). *What do we mean by relationships?* (Work in Progress No. 22). Wellesley, MA: Stone Center Working Paper Series.

Miller, J. B. (2008). How change happens: Controlling images, mutuality, and power. *Women & Therapy, 31*(2-4), 129-137.

Miller, J. B. (2008a). Telling the truth about power. *Women & Therapy, 31*(2-4), 145-161.

Padilla, A. (1994). Ethnic minority scholars, research, and mentoring: Current and future issues. *Educational Researcher, 23*(4), 24-27.

Schwartz, H.L. (2013). Dinner at Fitzwilly's: Intellectual mattering in developmental relationships. In Dominguez, N. & Gandert, Y. (Eds). *Sixth Annual Mentoring Conference Proceedings: Impact and Effectiveness of Developmental Relationship*. Albuquerque, NM: University of New Mexico.

Student and Exchange Visitor Program (SEVP). (2004, September 30). *SEVIS by the Numbers*. Washington, DC: SEVIS.

Student and Exchange Visitor Program (SEVP). (2016, March). *Student and Exchange Visitor Information System: General Summary Quarterly Review*. Washington, DC: SEVIS.

Walker, M. (2008). How therapy helps when the culture hurts. *Women & Therapy, 31* (2-4), 87-105.

Walker, M. (2008a). Power and effectiveness: Envisioning an alternate paradigm. *Women & Therapy, 31*(2–4), 129–144.

Walker, M. (2008b). When Racism Gets Personal: Toward Relational Healing, *Women & Therapy,* 31(2-4), 71-85.

Walker, M., & Miller, J. B. (2000). Racial images and relational possibilities. *Talking paper 2.* Wellesley, MA: Stone Center Working Paper Series.

Worthington, R. L., Navarro, R. L., Loewy, M., & Hart, J. (2008). Color-blind racial attitudes, social dominance orientation, racial-ethnic group membership and college students' perceptions of campus climate. *Journal of Diversity in Higher Education,* 1, 8-19.

Part III

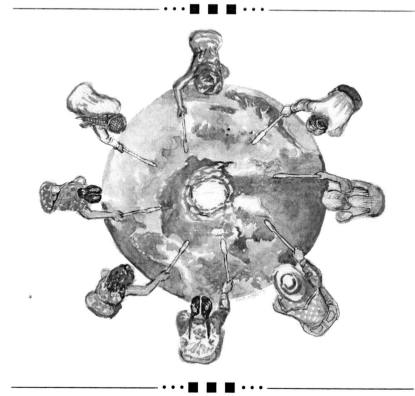

Transforming Community:
Social Justice

Weaving a Fabric for Transformative Social Justice Learning: Integrating Critical Race and Relational-Cultural Theories

—————————— ··· ■ ■ ■ ··· ——————————

CYNTHIA RENEE DONNER, MSW, LGSW

Prior to teaching in the Undergraduate Social Work Program at The College of St. Scholastica and being Coordinator of that program delivered at Fond du Lac Tribal Community College, Cynthia Donner worked for over two decades with non-profits in the Duluth area. In merging a life-long passion for social justice with the role of educator, she strives to create spaces and opportunities for people to discover the transformative potential of connecting with and contributing to shared stories. Cynthia Renee Donner may be contacted at Cdonner@css.edu.

The Transforming Community conference held June 2016 in Duluth, Minnesota, engaged people representing different realms of social justice work including young and life-long activists, therapists, educators, environmentalists, and managers. Instead of the focusing on analysis of facts and concepts presented and debated across single interest fronts, a practice typical in most social justice conferences, participants were invited to engage in empathic dialogue around intersecting ideas, experiences, and stories. The discourse shifted away from what stifles most cross-cultural organizing; namely, the inability to move beyond intrapersonal isolation that permeates the dominant discourse

229

and keeps people separated. The participants in this conference moved toward authentic dialogue, establishing insights that were validating and at the same time moved them to new levels of understanding.

What was it about this conference that made it possible for people to engage in connecting with each other in compassionate and meaningful ways? Reflecting on answers to this question might offer ways to enhance transformative social justice learning circles in academe and the community.

Freire views transformative social justice as a process that involves people in a cyclical collective process of self-reflection, critical analysis, and action he called *concientization* (Torres, 2007). In summarizing Freire's concept, Torres (2007) describes concientization as:

> A process of social transformation…an invitation to self-learning and transformation in its most spiritual and psychological meaning. A process in which our past may not wholly condition our present. A dynamic process that assumes that by rethinking our past we can fundamentally gain an understanding of the formation of our own self, the roots of our present condition, and the limits as well as the possibilities of being a self-in-the world. (p. 3)

The June conference offered a different yet seemingly familiar way for people to come together, where individual stories were both heard and felt, and new understandings emerged from a foundation of human connection and solidarity. People reflected on the presentations to glean meaning for their lived and shared experiences in facilitated dialogue sessions. They practiced empathic compassion and listened for the heartbeat of humanness. Vulnerability met trust and carried the process of connecting through valleys of uncertainty as strangers found solidarity. Participants felt safe enough to risk opening themselves up to reverently witnessing others pour out their stories. Understandings were deepened as these stories were shared and both the tellers and the insights exposed were honored. Participants committed to quiet their minds so their hearts could hear, and a new fabric of collective consciousness seemed to form from individual strands of understanding that was both felt and known. As the hours passed, the sharp edge of tension typically associated with expertise and defense in formal learning environments diminished to compassionate acceptance and reverence for self and others. Aha moments of self-validation and critical shifts in consciousness were reported by many participants, along with a growing sense of solidarity between and among people in attendance.

What made this conference different from most was not a new framework for analyzing oppression, but rather a relational context was established for guiding participants through a committed process of attending to and learning from each other. Relational-Cultural theory was the foundational pattern on which new connections and consciousness were woven together interpersonally and collectively. Concepts, ideas, and experiences were introduced and critically reflected on through empathic listening and authentic dialogue. People reached deeper levels of connections with each other in subsequent dialogue sessions, and in the process, they discovered new insights and deeper levels of shared experience.

Critical Race Theory and Relational-Cultural Theory

Critical Race Theory (CRT) emerged in the 1970s in response to changing forms of racial oppression, drawing from earlier movements and philosophers in critical legal studies and radical feminism (Delgado & Stefancic, 2012). Delgado and Stefancic (2012) define CRT as a movement "of activists and scholars interested in studying and transforming the relationship among race, racism, and power" (p. 3). They also state that most social activists agree racism is a common experience, yet difficult to address because of color-blind perceptions of equality that advance white privilege in perceived and real experiences. A prominent base which CRT evolved out of is the "social construction thesis" that "holds that race and races are products of social thought and relations" (Delgado & Stefancic, 2012, p. 8).

Relational-Cultural theory (RCT) is a modern psychological theory developed by Jean Baker Miller, and an initial group of scholars—including Judith Jordan, Alexandra Kaplan, Janet Surry, and Irene Stiver through the Stone Center at Wellesley College in Boston (M. Walker, personal communication, March 6, 2017). RCT posits growth-fostering relationships are central to human development (Jordan, 2010). Social justice activists have joined psychotherapists and educators in applying this theory in conjunction with other critical post-modern theories and advances in neuroscience to strategies that promote justice and healing. In particular, RCT examines the oppressive forces and related trauma and social isolation (Jordan, 2010).

CRT is concerned with disparities resulting from forces of structural oppression and was influenced by feminist views on the relationship between power and the social construction of roles and privileges that support patriarchy and domination (Delgado & Stefancic, 2012). These concerns with disparities are also reflected in what Jordan, Frey, Schwartz, and Walker presented on RCT in the June conference. CRT examines oppressive social stratification; "it seeks to uncover the mechanism and structures that actually disadvantage people, even those ostensibly designed by institutions to serve the needy" (Ortiz & Jani, 2010, p. 183). Carillo, Hernandez and Fitch propose that the lived experiences—and understandings of those experiences—leave diverse teachers/learners in a place of "ideological dislocation, in which their interests and passions are neither consistent with Eurocentrically-based curricula nor fit well as acceptable research questions" (Ortiz & Jani, 2010, p. 181). According to Ortiz and Jani (2010), this ideological dislocation is manifest in higher education in in three ways: there is lack of curriculum content that speaks directly to the experiences of students and faculty of color; students frequently lack mentors who can assist them in successfully navigating the learning environment; and having few faculty of color likely affects the overall research agendas of universities. They write: "Racial assumptions become a part of the development of the psyche for members of all groups through internalization, the phase of social construction by which 'facts' become a part of the conscious and unconscious" (p. 181).

Jordan (2010) writes that RCT examines the trauma, isolation, and social shame resulting from human disconnection that accompanies forces of oppression. She further poses the basic premise of RCT that justice is served when interpersonal relationships and institutional alignments are grounded in empathy, respect, and mutuality. Both RCT (Walker, 2008) and CRT (Delgado & Stefancic, 2012) consider the role of stories and empathy as significant features of their philosophical dimensions and related practice approaches.

Transforming Community:
The Radical Reality of Relationship

The June 2016 conference sparked a unique synergy. People from diverse communities representing many histories of oppression and privilege convened with Jordan and other current leaders in RCT over the three days to listen, share and reflect. There were heartfelt stories of struggle and transformation, and many individuals reported a renewed strength or clearer vision resulting from the connections made with new people and testimonies during conference sessions and dialogues. It was evident that several presenters and attendees were well steeped in theoretical and/or experiential understanding of oppression and related traumas and disparities from their respective fields of psychotherapy, education, health care, and social activism. But the focus on and practice of RCT over the three days seemed to launch both RCT followers and newcomers into previously uncharted territory rich in meaningful connections that generated substantive qualities of relief, validation, and hope for many in attendance.

Because these kinds of outcomes are not common among professional conferences or circles of learning and action, they merit particular consideration if the desire is to move communities beyond critical analysis to transformative change through shifts in individual and collective consciousness. Through dialogue that adhered to principles of RCT, conference participants demonstrated how the practical application of this theory facilitates growth-fostering relationships among diverse people and deepen engagement among those pursuing transformative change. This has been a significant missing piece in the curriculum and analytical approaches to social justice organizing in the past.

Implications for Social Justice Education

CRT is important to social work education. Like other critical perspectives, it promotes an understanding of racial segregation and the functions of postmodernism that is described by Ortiz and Jani (2010) as a "refusal of positivism, recognition of intersectionality, deconstruction of social constructions, understanding of categorization, and rejection of totalizing categories" (p. 177). In their argument for CRT as a transformational model for teaching diversity, they point out that because race-based ideology is woven into the fabric of the dominant culture, "research methods, theories, and practice techniques taught in social work education rest on the assumptions and values of dominant culture, which, unless subjected to critique, will have questionable applicability to non-Euro-American populations" (p. 182). In a discussion of explicit and implicit curriculum requirements associated with CRT, they further argue that in addition to teaching students about culture they also need to be taught how to "analyze the institutional arrangements of society, assess how they are shaped by dominant cultural assumptions, and recognize how they may disadvantage members of nondominant cultural groups" (p. 189). They conclude by declaring that CRT is a paradigm that calls forth action across all spectrums of social work curriculum with its use of socially conscious indicators, the nature of questions it poses, and the patterns of interaction it promotes can be conceptualized as social work competencies and be concretized into practice behaviors—with some creativity particularly on the part of social work educators.

RCT offers a framework for transformative learning that can be applied across social work curricula (as demonstrated in the June 2016 conference dialogue sessions) to facilitate understanding of CRT in engagement, assessment, planning and evaluation in a context of growth-fostering relationships. As Ortiz and Jani (2010) assert, "teaching diversity is more complex than trying to attend to the various differences among people in society and the resulting 'isms'" (p. 190). They further cite the need for students to be prepared to move outside of their prescribed roles and/or comfort zones, and be ready to engage in dialogues that lead to transformative evaluation and outcomes on micro/mezzo/macro levels. RCT's foundational principles for cultivating growth-fostering relationships can facilitate integration of CRT learning and development in cognitive, affective, value, and skill dimensions. These principles are grounded in what Jean Baker Miller proposed as Five Good Things which have been described as "Attributes of a growth-fostering relationship: zest, sense of worth, clarity, productivity, and a desire for more connection" (JBTMI, 2017, para. 15). The leading scholars of RCT have contributed research and curriculum in the fields of neuroscience, psychology, social work, education, social and environmental justice with practice methods that can be integrated into curricular approaches with CRT and other post-modern theories to prepare teachers/learners for the challenges of today's fragmented world.

At the June conference, Jordan suggested the "social prescription of self-interest" (how we have been socially conditioned to identify with a separate individual self) is a major consideration in examining the isolation that is prevalent among people and in accounting for the increasing disparities along lines of race and class. The separate self that we are conditioned to identify with is constructed along lines of race, class, and gender which creates an isolating fabric of internalized notions of privilege and oppression around our psyche that prevents us

235

from engaging in growth-fostering relationships. Internalizing that isolated separate self is restricting on both cognitive and emotional levels. It requires intentional reflective work to be aware of how these restrictions impact our worldview and relationships. Conscious effort is required to be fully open, empathically present, and responsive with others who are different.

Learning how to connect with others in growth-fostering relationships may be the glue to hold movements together that are focused on transformative justice. People who benefit from or succumb to the dominant individual-centered mindset are not typically invested in transformative social change; and yet they regularly challenge our classroom, professional, and community learning circles. Individuals who expect to be taught what will be on the test, so that they can pass it and receive the degree that will land the desired job are conditioned to do so. The "what's in it for me" worldview competes with critical thinking to the degree that people adhering to this mindset are not easily motivated beyond personal self-interest to examine the role of structural power and privilege affecting social conditions across micro-mezzo-macro practice fields. The separate individual self-interest orientation combined with privilege that comes with perceived or real socioeconomic status inhibits some people from stepping outside of the comfort zone of conformity and, in the June conference, what Walker called the field of anxiety between right and wrong. CRT suggests this results from internalized social construction of race and the real socioeconomic benefits afforded people who fit the categorical expectations of white—including behaviors as well as skin colors. Walker further discussed how people are often willing to learn how to talk in politically correct "pseudo-empathy" terms (i.e., Minnesota Nice), but not necessarily willing to walk in the field which demands critical curiosity void of judgment and the courage to be vulnerable.

For some the shame of identifying with a privileged group's discriminatory beliefs or the inability to overcome one or more experiences with oppression is an additional layer of socially prescribed separateness that perpetuates isolation and suppression of voice. As Schwartz and Frey asserted in their presentation at the June conference: "shame is a social emotion," and too often shaming is a public experience for people in classroom and professional/field encounters. They proposed that learners benefit from a context of authentic and caring relationships, with clearly defined boundaries of dependence and mutuality (especially within the dynamics of power in the learning process), and appreciation that their thinking and efforts matter.

The experiences of trauma and shame associated with structural forces of oppression permeate lived experiences of both teachers and learners in a way that influences cognitive understandings of those lived experiences. The socially conditioned orientation toward a separate-self places the challenge of transcending these experiences and related beliefs deep in our individual and collective psyches. Schwartz and Frey went on to state at the conference that we all have "possible selves"— images of who we want/don't want to be. They suggest that "feedback loops" are a powerful way to learn from and deal with our possible selves and the disconnection in emotional reactions to others' thoughts and actions—providing the teacher/mentor is grounded in genuine openness to learning and utilizes reflection and support from colleagues.

Jordan cited the importance of relationship in her discussion of relational resilience. She wrote that it is "Movement to a mutually empowering, growth-fostering connection in the face of adverse conditions, traumatic experiences, and alienating sociocultural pressures; the ability to connect, reconnect, and/or resist disconnection. Movement toward empathic mutuality is at the core of relational resilience" (JBTMI, 2017, para. 39).

Implications for Marginalization

Jordan suggested at the June conference that "closed hearts are taught" through socialization of the separate self in a society where "unacknowledged privilege is embedded in every social structure and system of the U.S. culture". She further stated that capitalism has woven the fabric of U.S. history since early colonization, and stories of injustice continue as the interconnected threads of oppression have tightened under extreme corporate-capitalist control of global economies and political systems. Banks and Craddock pointed out in their presentation at the conference that "social exclusion and perceived social exclusion can be deadly". They proposed that the psychological resistance to marginalization and other forms of social pain (e.g. overt and covert microaggressions, stereotype threats, exclusionary policies) is a part of the lived experience of people who occupy our classrooms, community, and professional circles. Pain can be enhanced by the combination of ideological dislocation and human disconnection that compels silence while inducing fear and isolation.

How might more inclusive policies and practices transform organizational and institutional systems if they ensured people coming together were grounded in analytical dimensions of RCT and relational dimensions of CRT? Social work values and guiding principles demand that implicit and explicit curriculum ensures inclusion of experiences and perspectives. As teachers, we have more to learn and can be transformed by students. As teacher-learners we must recognize as Frey stated at the conference that "expertise is fluid" and therefore must "be aware of our own disconnection to emotional reactions" to students and others with different in views or experiences.

Walker suggested in her keynote presentation at the June conference that our "embodied difference—or racialized bias/ narrative" is part of the human experience and yet we seldom acknowledge this in ourselves, much less make it part of our classroom discussions, nor hold each other accountable through institutional or community dialogues. Empathic dialogue is increasingly rare in our sociopolitical realms today, with rancorous debate dominating in public discourse and social media. It seems challenging for most people to actively listen to a speaker or connect interpersonally for any length of time, evidenced by the constant need to ask people to turn their communication devices off during class or professional meetings. Dialogue enables us to make meaning of our stories and experiences. Mutual compassion and genuine empathic listening, unconditional positive regard and courageous curiosity are important elements of dialogue that can take us to deeper levels of understanding. The conference dialogue sessions incorporated these elements, and demonstrated the cognitive and emotional levels of understanding that can be reached toward individual and collective transformation.

Ortiz and Jani (2010) emphasize CRT principles of asking the right questions, focusing on structural transformation, honoring contextual competence, refusing assumptions. Walker in her conference address identified five practical steps for respectful and courageous engagement with each other: Embrace the whole brain, all voices; pause, breathe; question normalcy; learn about people who've resisted racialized power systems; and develop a community of allies. Perhaps more focused and deliberate integration of both these approaches in classroom and community learning circles can foster transformative justice. Given the social and interpersonal isolation in current times, a firm base of knowledge and skills for growth-fostering relationships with diverse people is central to social work education. We are social beings, wired for connection; but unfortunately we are dealing with social systems that challenge this core aspect of humanity. Combined, both theoretical paradigms could help us through the struggles of transformative change—CRT for analysis to help us deconstruct oppressive forces and understand the complexity of intersecting systems, and RCT for building growth-fostering relationships into new and better ways of understanding and being with each other and the world.

References

Delgado, R. and Stefancic, J. (2012). *Critical race theory*. New York: New York University.

Ortiz, L. and Jani, J. (2010). Critical race theory: A transformational model for teaching diversity. *Journal of Social Work Education,* 46 (2). Council on Social Work Education.

Jean Baker Miller Training Institute (2017). Glossary of key terms. Retrieved from: https://www.jbmti.org/Our-Work/glossary-relational-cultural-therapy

Jordan, J. (2010). *Relational-Cultural Therapy*. Washington, DC: American Psychological Association.

Torres, C. A. (2007). Paulo Freire, education and transformative social justice learning. Retrieved from http://www.ipfp.pt/cdrom/Pain%E9is%20Dial%F3gicos/Painel%20A%20-%20Sociedade%20Multicultural/carlosalbertotorres.pdf

Reflections on the Time In-Between

···■ ■ ■···

MARY URSULA VICARIO

In 1979, my senior year of high school, my father's response to finding out that I was dating the prom queen was a disconnection we were not able to heal before he passed weeks later. The shame with that unrepaired disconnection drove me back into the closet where I stayed for 15 years. After coming out a second time and being out just shy of 15 years, the final piece of context that I needed to understand, heal, and grow from that ruptured relationship had finally arrived. When the last day of the Transforming Community conference in 2016 was also the morning after the shooting at the Pulse nightclub in Orlando, I knew then that I needed to share the healing I had received through the gift of viewing the disconnection with my father through the lens of his relationships and culture. Mary Ursula Vicario may be contacted at findinghopeconsulting@gmail.com.

**I had so much fun coming out when
I was in high school in the late 1970s
that I went back into the closet and did it again 15 years later.
This is a reflection on moving through the time in-between.**

I don't remember when I first heard the word lesbian, but I know I heard it often as a child for whenever my mother was driving and her focus snapped from the road to a woman in a short skirt (there were quite a few of those in the 1960s), my father would bellow, "Keep your eyes on the road, you stupid (expletive) lesbian!" I never really knew what a lesbian was, but I knew it made you a really bad driver.

My father arrived in this country in 1914 an Italian immigrant "without papers," which made him a true WOP. As such, he experienced life as a fight for survival and often prefaced things he wanted me to learn with "To survive in this country...." One of his favorite phrases was, "To survive in this country you must never let your gender precede your person." And to that end Daddy and I were glued to the TV while Billy Jean King played Bobby Riggs in the tennis battle of the sexes. We both rooted for Billy Jean. I only found out later that my father had bet on Bobby Riggs because "You never put your money where your heart is." When Billy Jean won, my 5'2", 220-pound father jumped out of his easy chair, pumped his fist in the air and shouted, "Big Dyke!" I remember thinking, "I don't know what that is, but I am gonna be one when I grow up!"

In junior high school, I started slipping off the playground into the woods with Lynnie, to hold hands, exchange secrets, and sneak kisses. It's funny, I don't remember the date I was married, June 23 or 24, 1983 or 1984, but I do remember the day Kim fell into my arms crying over some girls making fun of her. It was July 5, 1976, the summer of my freshman year in high school, and the minute I held her I knew I was going to be a "lousy driver" just like my mother.

When I was a senior in high school, Kim was the prom queen; and somehow my father found out about us dating. It was amazing, this man who knew all too well what it was like to be marginalized, who had watched his mother die of strep throat in 1932 because no doctors would come to the Italian ghetto, who called me into the room to watch the civil rights protestors on the news explaining to my mother, "I want her to see what her country is doing to its own people," turned on me in a manner I never expected or understood. The Reverend Sharon Dittmar's Rainbow

242

Sunday sermon about the Italian mobsters who owned the bar
that the Stonewall riot was named for helped me understand my
father's reaction for the first time. She described the early morning
hours of June 28, 1969 when a particularly oppressed group of
minority and Hispanic transgender men and women, and gays and
lesbians fought the unloving and unrighteous system (in this case
represented by the police) and won. They fought with rocks and
purses and high heels, and they still won. She described how many
of these bars were run by the Mafia who detested their clientele
so much that they did not even wash the dishes they served their
substandard and over-priced food and drink on. Bars were raided
by the police on a monthly basis. The police arrested and roughed
up anyone without identification, people dressed in clothes of the
opposite gender, and the employees.

My father, and best friend up until that time, died that year a
few days after my prom and a few weeks before my high school
graduation. He had a dying wish that I did not know about until
I went to visit his brother in Boston that Christmas. My uncle
kept fixing me up with pretty blond Irish boys from Southie, an
unpleasant combination for an Italian girl who had a mind of her
own. I finally told my uncle, "The next time you fix me up with
someone make sure she has long brown hair, high cheek bones and
green eyes." "No," he said, "because your father's dying wish was
that you'd marry a man."

With that knowledge came a sense of failure I had never
experienced in connection with my father. So later that year when
I met a 6'2" 170 pound man who said to a family member that
was bothering me, "If you do that again, I'll break your (expletive)
arm." I thought, hmmm… a bodyguard and a way to grant my
father's dying wish all in one. With my gender not preceding my
person, I asked him out. Three years later after negotiating a deal
that included me keeping my name, wedding and engagement rings
that were really cocktail and dinner rings (so no one would mistake
them for what they really were) and an agreement not to have kids
(he didn't want them and I didn't want mine to see me living a lie),

we decided to marry. Kim, my prom queen and real love, was to be my maid of honor. She called a few days before the wedding to say she just couldn't do it. I was as relieved as I was disappointed. I remember trying to lighten the moment with, "It's probably a good thing or else I would say my vows to the wrong person."

My husband was protective, even kind and funny for a while; and I teased that he made a lovely ornament on my arm. He bought me fabulous clothes while I mused, "If I have to act like a straight girl, I should at least have the costumes for it." He conveniently worked out of town five days a week and we traveled extensively to places like Bermuda, Europe, and Australia. We even got season tickets to Kim's theatre in Chicago, so I could at least see her several times a year. Yet no matter what the concession, the contract, the adventure, or even the fun, there was this emptiness and anger in me that always bled through everything—my friendships, my marriage, my work, my dreams.

Then came Issue Three, the proposed amendment to change Cincinnati's charter and make it illegal to pass any laws that would protect the rights of gays and lesbians—actually codifying our second-class citizenship. I told my husband: "This law applies to me." I joined the campaign against Issue Three, and in the process I discovered Crazy Ladies Bookstore (whose motto was, "If a woman questions too many of society's values, she is often deemed crazy") along with a whole community I did not know existed 15 years earlier when I was struggling to come out and stay out. I started coming to life during that campaign. I joined groups and even hung out at a church that would accept "us." While my husband knew all along I was a lesbian and was even used to me being alive whenever I was with Kim, he wasn't ready to see me fit into my skin every day. Ironically, I still had no plans to leave for I am a woman of my word; but when his feeling threatened translated into him threatening me, I began to make a plan to go. He slowed my process somewhat by threatening to expose me to my family; but in the end, his rage at me and my rage at myself propelled me forward—July 13,1995 became my

Independence Day. He kept his promise, outed me to my family, and mailed excerpts from my journals to illustrate his point. My mother disowned me and kept him as her son. My friends were torn. Some stayed, some went, and some risked getting to know the real me which has brought us closer than we ever were.

Kim is still in my life—although she is a straight girl now. I like to joke that I turned her straight. She likes to say, "When I think of Kinsey's six point scale (with one being completely heterosexual and six being completely homosexual) in high school you were a four and I was a three and for one brief, shining moment there was Camelot. Now you're a five and I'm a two and we will be friends forever."

Bill, the head of the Italian family, on my mother's side (I am the head of the Italian family on my father's side; my "gender could not precede my person"), called and told my mother:

> Aunt Joann, you are going to call your daughter and tell her that you love her even if she is a lesbian. Then you are going to bring her, not her ex-husband, to the next family function, which is my birthday. Be there Saturday at 2:00. I'll be calling you back in 10 minutes, to make sure it's finished.

She called and quoted him verbatim. I lovingly call that, "the one time the patriarchy worked in my favor." When I asked Bill, "Where the hell were you 15 years ago when I was trying to come out?" He said: "To survive in this country a woman needs a man's income. And since you have had one for 15 years, own property, and are self-sufficient, you can date whoever you want now." He clearly was unaware of one of my father's other strictures: "To keep her freedom, a woman must never earn less than her husband," something I followed the whole 15 years of my marriage.

Over time, my mother noticed the change in me and that my partner was far kinder to her than my husband ever was. She even commented that I was like a new person—like someone she never knew before. She said, "It was like you used to be playing dress up and under your mask was an anger I never understood." I told her "Now I fit into my skin, and it feels so good. Like coming home, nothing feels better!" Shortly before she died, she said to me, "I wonder what my life would have been like, if I had had the courage to fit into my skin?"

It's All About the Relationship

··· ■ ■ ■ ···

JULIE KIM, MSW, LICSW

As a student counselor with Health Services at the University of Minnesota, Duluth, my submission is a personal story about insights and experiences about surviving systems of oppression to living. Learning about Relationship-Cultural theory (RCT) clarifies the impacts of racism and oppression and helps people of color move from survival and isolation to building a foundation to live a meaningful life. RCT reflects my values, validates my personal experiences, and has taught me about the power of connection and healing. Julie Kim may be contacted at juliek@d. umn.edu.

"It's all about the relationship" is a phrase Connie Gunderson says quite often. It couldn't be more true, as I reflect on my life journey so far. Relational-Cultural theory (RCT), developed by the work of Jean Baker Miller, identifies the concept of *chronic disconnection,* a disconnection which promotes *condemned isolation* to such a degree that relationships are feared and persons have a sense they do not deserve loving relationships filled with understanding.

As a Korean girl, adopted at a young age into a white family, and growing up in a predominantly white community, I began my journey into *condemned isolation*. Being told daily that I didn't belong, I wasn't wanted, and I needed to go back to my country was reinforced through people's attitudes and by systems I was involved in every day. Always feeling a sense of being left out,

247

of being different, I was a label of ridicule, especially because of my appearance. Hearing comments such as: "Chink, you would be cute if your eyes were bigger. Can you see out of your eyes?" was a normal occurrence. I experienced an additional sense of condemned isolation because, since I was not fully Korean, I didn't fit into the American culture and I did not belong in my home country. "Where do I belong?" and "Where do I fit in?" were common questions that continued until I reached my early 30s.

Learning about racism and beginning to understand the personal consequences of racism turned my world into wonder, curiosity, and the unknown. "What am I supposed to do with this information?", and "Will it change my life?" At the time I remember thinking: "It was never my fault." This was a defining message that promoted internal change. I began to seek people who would support me for the way I looked; who understood my life experience; and who accepted my authentic self; an authentic self no longer ruled by fear, people's glares, or by people asking me personal questions about whether or not I was a "foreigner", or why I was in the United States.

Living authentically didn't come easy at first. I constantly questioned myself about whether or not my perceptions and ideas were valid. However, as I moved into deeper questions and reflections, my relationships became deeper and more intentional. Feeling accepted and understood was so profound and life changing and I started to believe "I do matter" because my relationships reinforced this every day.

My journey continues and I am constantly reminded of my story as I listen to college students of color share their experiences which are very familiar to my own. My goal is to help them recognize that they are enough, their multiple identities matter, and to teach them to live authentically. I say this because I know that no one can do this work alone or in isolation. For example, I was provided the opportunity to teach an all student of color course and in doing so, we created an environment that was not influenced by institutionalized systems already in place. In looking back, the students and I created an environment from the basic tenets of Relational-Cultural theory that modeled interdependence, empathy, mutuality, and connection. SunNy Vang, a class participant, summed up the learning experience for all by stating:

> My experiences with relationship building in our class began from a place of vulnerability. As a person of color, I struggle tremendously with a sense of belonging. Knowing that I do not "fit" nicely with what is considered normal or customary, I learned to appreciate it and to acknowledge that I have more to contribute to my community. These awarenesses did not happen overnight. We had discussions every day that reflected our reactions, thinking processes, and how we felt about a number of awesome and sad things. We all came from different places and our stories were welcomed. We connected on a far deeper level compared to other classes.

The students and I focused on building empathic relationships, and it truly fostered a responsive and relevant teaching and learning environment in ways that included much more than racial, social, and ethnic demographics. We supported each other by validating and embracing each other's knowledge, values, experiences, and differences. We all became more mutually responsive persons. I'm truly grateful for the students, as their insights and experiences have helped me to grow and continue to heal. Connie Gunderson was right, "It's all about the relationship".

Relational-Cultural Social Justice Advocacy: A Personal Journey

··· ■ ■ ■ ···

AMY C. MAKICE, MSW, LCSW

Amy Makice began her career in 1992, providing social work for late stage AIDS patients before AZT. Amy's commitment to social justice has deepened over the course of her career, and expands beyond her profession to the community in which she is a member. Ever since participating in a field practicum in graduate school based on the Relational-Cultural theory Works in Progress, Amy has held Relational-Cultural theory as her guiding philosophy of mental health work, advocacy, parenting, and life. She currently employs and teaches Relational-Cultural theory in her practice with women and families, in social justice advocacy, and through her Unitarian Universalist congregation to create community connections across differences that empower LGBTQA+ individuals in her home state of Indiana. You may contact her at amy@bloomington.cc.

In traditional power-over systems, a lot of social justice advocacy would end with forced vulnerability that is described by Jordan (2008) as a form of humiliation, with the victor convincing the other of the inherent wrongness of their position. She further writes that Relational-Cultural theory (RCT) shifts the focus to one of mutual vulnerability, in which both parties are open to being moved by the other's experience. Because social justice work is fraught with passionate disagreement, RCT's emphasis on

251

relational repair after empathic disconnection increases resilience and possibility (Hartling, 2009; Jordan, Hartling & Walker, 2004;).

When seeking connection through social justice work, several core components of RCT are evident, including power over/power under, authenticity, reconnection, relational neuroscience, and leveraging Jean Baker Miller's Five Good Things (Miller, 1986). The Jean Baker Miller Training Institute (JBMTI, 2016) proposes that authenticity includes the ability to say the One True Thing, the truth in the moment that allows for movement in the relationship while honoring the speaker's experience. Relational neuroscience reminds us that the work of being human does not happen in isolation; that relationships are vital to our well-being and meaning-making (Cozolino, 2006). The Five Good Things—the hallmarks of growth fostering relationships—are zest, a sense of worth, clarity, productivity, and a desire for more connection (Miller, 1986). These core components of RCT work together to strengthen connections both between advocates and across differences.

RCT and Personal Advocacy Work

LGBTQA+ work has long been important to me; my career started working with late stage AIDS patients before AZT. My work changed the first time I saw tears in my son's eyes because of who he loved. The afternoon he told me he couldn't participate in track because the gym class boys who threw around the words fag and homo were also walking in the locker room for practice, and he couldn't bring himself to deliberately put himself in proximity to them. My social justice work shifted then from a passion, to personal. I am as deeply connected to LGBTQA+ advocacy as I am to my son.

The summer between middle and high school, my son came out as gay, both to me and his community. His seventh and eighth grade years had been at a small progressive school, celebrating and affirming all gender identities and sexual orientations. Students were permitted to miss school to visit the statehouse to protest the anti-gay marriage amendment. His high school was a large institution, serving both the progressive university community and conservative rural southern Indiana. As a parent, I balanced between wanting my son to feel free to discover and express his true self, and wanting him to be safe.

His transition to high school was mostly smooth; partly due to upper class alumni of his middle school going out of their way to welcome him and pull him into their protective social groups. There were moments that scared me more than they did him: the kids taunting his best friend in the stairwell, asking if he was a homosexual, drawing out the word and leering at his ironed pink shirt. Carter stepped forward and said, "No, but I am," and the kids dispersed.

Most of the troubling events happened in gym class. Repeatedly, I offered to accompany him to the school to talk to the administration, help him write an email to the gym teacher, or otherwise advocate for himself; but he turned me down, wanting to handle it himself. After his third pair of gym shoes disappeared, he agreed I could request a meeting with his vice principal, marking the beginning of my formally trying to bring RCT and local advocacy together.

Saying One True Thing

I sat in the vice principal's office, bolstered with research about LGBTQA+ youth, bullying and education. My son, Carter, selected this administrator as the most likely to be helpful to us. "He wants to help, he just needs the information," Carter assured me. "He's the first step. Once he understands, he'll be a huge ally."

I described Carter's experience in gym class: constant name-calling and harassment, being blocked out of the attendance line resulting in tardiness, three pairs of gym shoes "missing," and being cornered on the National Day of Silence while a fellow student aimed body spray at him, demanding he break his silence in order to not be sprayed.

The vice-principal responded by asking for names, asserting it was one bad kid—an anomaly. Swift consequences would fix it. RCT doesn't sidestep consequences for actions, but it does call us to reach for a higher goal. My goal was not to add more rules to the student handbook, or to shame wrongdoers, but to honor every student's dignity and humanity. I replied by talking about the system; the atmosphere that made calling someone a *pussy* or a *fag* an acceptable part of the social norm. Our back and forth continued, getting nowhere.

"You're basing your entire opinion of this school on one kid's whining," he complained. "I can't do my job if you don't give me names."

"My son isn't interested in getting individuals in trouble. We're interested in changing the environment." I reached for my notebook. "You know, there's some research." His eyes rolled. I derailed. "Did you just roll your eyes because I said the word research?"

"Yes."

"Why?"

"Because we live in the real world here. We have real problems to solve."

I took a deep breath. I reminded myself that my goal was to build a relationship, and through that relationship, create a more supportive world for my child—for all the kids in my community. I remembered Carter's optimism and conviction that this administrator just needed a better understanding of LGBTQA+ students' experience to be an effective ally.

"Listen," he leaned forward, "it's a high school. There are more horses' asses here than there are horses. Just give me the names and I'll fix it."

"Again, my son isn't interested in tattling. We're interested in a school that models and teaches cultural competence to faculty and students. A school that welcomes and celebrates diversity."

He pushed back, repeating the horse's ass comment, getting Carter's name wrong. I could feel heat rising. How could I connect with someone who couldn't even hear me? How could I build a bridge with someone who had no interest in systematic change and approached me as though I were a trouble-maker?

As I had prepared for this meeting, I leaned on my training in RCT. I imagined a mutual conversation, each of us hearing the other. I imagined taking risks, being authentic. There are relational rewards to risking honesty; but I struggled in this moment to know how to be authentic and stay grounded in my love for my son, how to honor my convictions and connect with someone who couldn't hear them.

Irene Stiver, one of the founding scholars of RCT, emphasized the importance of sharing One True Thing (Walker, 2008). The JBMTI (2016) defines One True Thing as reaching beyond reactive authenticity and offering truth while inviting connection—something authentic and mutual. An emotional reaction would have been easy. Verbal smack downs, intellectual triumphs backed by research and progressive opinion, were also readily available. I had colleagues doing exactly that—trying to shame the administration into behaving better, but RCT demands something different than shaming those with whom we disagree. Shame pulls us out of connection plus impedes mutual empowerment and relational well-being (Walker, 2002). What was it that was true for me (authentic) and could create space for movement in this relationship (mutual)?

In her call for disruptive empathy during her keynote speech at the Transforming Community conference, Walker emphasized that connection does not require us to say one perfect thing, but to exercise the power to say One True Thing. Change, particularly institutional change, can be slow. Finding One True Thing to say in the face of disempowering comments may help move us toward greater authenticity (Hartling & Sparks, 2010).

"Wow. This meeting is not going how I'd hoped, and I'm not sure what to say. I'm not communicating at all what I intended when I scheduled this meeting." Picking up my notebook, I concluded, "I'm going to leave now, and maybe we can reschedule when it can be productive. I appreciate your time, and I wish this had gone better."

Back in my car, I wept. Fifteen minutes later, a text from Carter indicated the vice principal called him into his office immediately after I left and asked him to identify the troublemakers—using the same horse's ass analogy and calling him the same wrong name.

Reconnecting

A key piece of RCT is reconnecting after empathic failure (Jordan, Hartling & Walker, 2004). In social justice work, it is not always possible to reconnect with the same individual, but it is essential to regain a willingness to return to the work, to reconnect with possibility, as well as to continue listening and working on relationship. Resilience emerges in a relational context. As Hartling (2009) writes, "Taking an RCT perspective might ultimately lead to defining resilience as the ability to connect, reconnect, and resist disconnection in response to hardships, adversities, trauma and alienating social-cultural practices" (p. 63).

In the weeks that followed, I reached out to community and received support. Through connecting with trusted allies, I was able to recoup relational energy. Growth-fostering relationships offered me strength and fostered resilience—providing clarity and productivity that helped me return to social justice advocacy.

I met one-on-one with stakeholders—including teachers, counselors, parents and youth. We focused on learning and connecting. I asked questions, and I listened. When flummoxed,

I strived to return to the One True Thing of that moment. I was willing to stay in the MUD, a concept Jordan used in the Transforming Community conference to describe the mystery, uncertainty and doubt that is required in order to empathize across difference. With each new connection, we were closer to creating a school I wanted my kids to attend.

None of RCT's practices—connecting, building bridges, and emphasizing relational resilience—involve being bullied or allowing yourself to be beat up. Miller (1986) wrote "Authenticity and subordination are totally incompatible" (p 98). Being in an authentic relationship demands integrity and courage. Nice, polite behavior is a common strategy of disconnection; having the courage to enter conflict can signal a commitment to the relationship (Walker, 2002). As Walker (1999) described, The One True Thing I said in many meetings did not constitute an agreement or acceptance of a culture of disconnection.

Courage and Vulnerability

Jordan (2013) proposed a new definition of courage: "the capacity to act meaningfully and with integrity in the face of acknowledged vulnerability" (p. 207). She later defined vulnerability as "an experience in which we are open to others at the same time that we are open to our need for others" (p. 206). Jordan (2009) also described vulnerability as a means to growth-fostering connection that requires courage. The experience of daily life in an environment of name-calling and harassment while being assured that the high school is welcoming requires LGBTQA+ youth to either call on their own internal opposition—the ability to hold firm to their own moral truth in the face of a different reality—or to internalize the hostility (Ward, 2000). LGBTQA+ youth gain resilience from supportive relationships and through this resilience, courage emerges (Sadowski, Chow & Scanlon, 2009).

As a result of these meetings, our community of allies formulated a plan: Carter, along with peers from a local

LGBTQA+ teen group, myself, and another adult would surprise our school board meeting during the public comment portion. This was the same time Indiana was immersed in turmoil over the Religious Freedom Restoration Act (RFRA), which offered legal protections to businesses choosing to deny services based on religious objections to sexual orientation or perceived gender identity. This was also the summer the United States Supreme Court ruled in favor of marriage equality across the nation. Our community had made national headlines for a high school "Straight Pride Club" that failed to launch (Keck, 2015). LGBTQA+ rights were hot topics in public discourse.

During our planning of school board advocacy before attending that meeting, several teachers and public school administrators suggested to me that Carter would be happier at a high school across town with a reputation for being more inclusive. An adult participating in the discussion warned him that speaking in a publicly archived meeting would result in damage to his reputation—a permanent record that would follow him into adulthood. It would have been easy to disconnect from the struggle, to lose courage. The school administration would offer him a transfer, and gym class requirements were complete. His desire was to continue working within the relationships he had forged at his high school while advocating for change.

At the school board meeting, several local students spoke—describing their experience attending high school in southern Indiana. One talked of bathrooms and cisgender privilege, another of being dismissed as a trouble-making feminist for requesting inclusive language. Carter shared his experience living daily immersed in hateful name-calling. Each of them brought courage and authenticity to the meeting. As Jordan (2013) wrote, they all showed courage through bringing the truth of themselves into the relationship.

The courage of the youth—speaking their truth directly to the source of educational power in our community and the authenticity of their shared stories—created connection with the school board that resulted in one board member openly crying as she thanked them. We were invited for continued problem-solving meetings with the superintendent and board members.

Six months later, the youth who spoke at the board meeting, along with other members of the Prism Youth Community, an inclusive social group for youth celebrating all sexual orientations and gender identities and expressions, conducted training for over 600 teachers and administrators of our local school district on cultural competency.

Standing Still, Listening to Invite Connection

Being available to listen to those who disagree is a form of disruptive empathy—what Walker described in the June Transforming Community conference as joining while remaining grounded; an engagement with paradox. She further stated that listening is a radical form of social justice advocacy that has the potential to transform.

Our local Unitarian Universalist congregation, where I serve as the chair of the LGBTQA+ social justice committee, wanted to advocate for LGBTQA+ youth in a way that reached a broader audience. We decided to host a booth at the county fair.

Ours is a liberal city nestled within a fiercely conservative county and state. With the exception of the high schools and possibly the Fourth of July parade, the two spheres remain separate. There were congregants who had never attended our county fair. There were congregants who were surprised to learn that LGBTQA+ kids faced harassment at school.

Prism members created displays for us that outlined their wishes for culturally-competent public education and arranged this material in front of a giant rainbow flag. We stated goals of building relationships and creating a safe space for conversation, being present and available, plus modeling love and celebratory inclusivity. The first night was quiet.

The next morning Carter came with me to the fair. As we entered the almost empty barn, it became apparent that our booth had been vandalized. Carter saw it first. I experienced the damage through my son's sudden stillness, his slump into the chair, and his pointing at the table. I was less inclined to bring Carter with me after that.

Daily, a group of adolescent boys stalked our booth, shoving each other into our space and calling each other fag, joking about getting gay cooties. They threw wads of paper with anti-gay slogans on it at us and threatened us with water balloons. My mentor in this advocacy, who had spent a lot of time conversing with strangers in southern Indiana about marriage equality, set a tone of equanimity. He was unconditionally friendly, kind, and firm with the teenage boys; and he responded with welcoming questions to all visitors of our booth.

One family visited the adjacent booth frequently with the father doing most of the talking, the mother standing behind him, and their three daughters exploring our displays. The two older daughters spent their time writing bible quotes on our comment boards while the youngest—a four year old named Lily—chatted with me.

Lily came back the next day, after her sisters lost interest in quoting scripture. She told me stories of carnival rides, visiting animals at the fair, and her favorite booths. We drew rainbows together and talked about Wonder Woman, since the shirt I was wearing had that superhero emblazoned across the front.

"I like Wonder Woman," she whispered, leaning in toward me. "I just wish you were modest." It took me a while to realize she referring to my exposed shoulders. I have no idea what I said in return—perhaps something about it being my favorite shirt. I wrestled with whether to choose a different shirt the next day. I wanted to be present for this little girl and for any others like her in order to show that there are adults out there who may love differently than their parents but who love just as deeply. I wanted to offer a refuge, a safe place where they could draw rainbows and be who they are, free of judgment. I would not change my clothes to conform to beliefs that were not mine, but changing into a shirt with sleeves to help Lily be comfortable felt authentic and relational.

Coming Back for More

We can compensate for difficult encounters by bolstering our well-being with healthy relationships. Mutual, authentic relationships can soothe the reactive brain and mitigate harm in challenging interactions (Banks & Hirshman, 2015). In preparation for our second year at the county fair, our training focused on the Five Good Things—zest, desire for connection, increased self-knowledge, self-worth, and motivation to act—to inoculate booth volunteers (Miller, 1986).

Courage to take action and advocate according to moral values emerges in the context of relationship (Jordan, 2009). In the year between county fairs, members of our committee were invited to form relationships with youth in Prism—including an intergenerational tea and weekly opportunities to provide space for their meetings.

Listening to the LGBTQA+ youth in Prism share their definitions, theories, and the reality of being a queer youth in southern Indiana created a relational bridge to this social justice work. The connection between volunteers and the youth they were representing strengthened their relational resilience. We also provided training that included an introduction to RCT, the neuroscience of relationships, and the importance of finding our strength in connection. This was followed by opportunities for participants to share their own stories, to listen, and be heard. Throughout the training, we nurtured our growth-fostering relationships, leading to increased motivation to take action as Jordan (2009) proposed.

During these trainings we agreed on a few guidelines for volunteers. No one should be alone at the fair. Our goal would be to listen first, not to argue or persuade. To discourage vandalism we created a "Question Box" (left out with notecards and a pen) to offer a container for the discomfort experienced by visitors to our booth. Next to it was a bulletin board with the text, "Your questions answered here!" on it. As part of the daily set up, we would pull out any questions, send them to the youth group for answers, and then post answers on the bulletin board.

At the fair, I watched for Lily but didn't see her. Several familiar visitors appeared, some friendly, some not. One youth, who had visited us several times the previous year, stopped by to tell us they had spent the year without any relationships safe enough for them to share their gender identity, since they hadn't come out to their family or friends. Our booth was their one safe place.

On the last day of the fair a young man stopped, furtively looking at our literature, backing away, and then returning. "You can take anything on the table," I offered, but he shook his head and left. A few minutes later, I finally spotted Lily, standing with her mother. The young man was with them. My stomach sank. Here was someone who really needed our information, our welcome, but who might not be able to access it. Before I could finish my thought, the mother strode over to my booth. I braced myself. "These are for anyone?" she asked.

"Yes." I smiled. She shared my smile, took one of everything, and marched back to the young man. She put the brochures in his hands, patted him on the back, and they walked away, calling "thank you" over her shoulder. Lily waved at me, following her mother out of the barn.

Collaborative Conflict

RCT differs from other theories of development by explicitly addressing the impact of power on relationships (Jordan, 2009).

One complicating factor of being at the fair is the dichotomy between wanting to empower marginalized populations—specifically LGBTQA+ people—and remaining cognizant of the fact that most of our harassment comes from a population that has traditionally been in a power-over position: white, straight cisgender males.

In contrasting the strategies of collaborative conflict with those of traditional power-over conflict, Walker (2008) writes:

> To engage in collaborative conflict is to relinquish any claim on the illusion of victory or power over another being. When the focus remains on mutual empowerment, there is little room for the instant gratification of tit-for-tat interactions. In other words, engaging in relational conflict requires relearning how to breathe, to reflect, and to connect with feeling-thoughts before attempting to influence the other person. It also means—and this is crucial—allowing oneself to be moved or influenced by another. (p. 129)

While doing social advocacy work with an RCT perspective, we try to leave our arguments at home and present ourselves as authentically vulnerable, plus available for understanding and listening. If and when a connection is built, injustice will have less space to thrive.

A lot of what we do at the fair is laying relational groundwork for future connection. We offer rainbow beads, rainbow stickers, and friendly smiles. Our table is covered with fliers for local LGBTQA+ support, and displays about gender identity and sexual orientation. Information and deeper engagement is available; but it is built on the platform of connection, without which more in-depth conversation is impossible. When faced with risky connection to a population that may include hatred and hostility, this welcoming behavior creates a common ground from which richer connection may grow.

The first year we were at the fair, we could have engaged in debate with the family who wrote bible verses on our boards and called me immodest. We could have pushed them into a position of defending their family values and worldview. Instead, we stayed present, vulnerable and authentic. As Walker (2008) suggests with her concept of collaborative conflict, we opened a channel and reminded people we were available. Later, that channel was available as an agent of change and support for those who needed it.

Authenticity, Cultural Pain, and Courage in Connection

Walker (2002) notes, "authenticity heals cultural pain when there is a commitment to empathic attunement, and relational accountability". The fact that our booth is even needed at the fair is evidence of the cultural pain and disconnection we carry in our society.

Following the second year at the fair, we scheduled another gathering of the volunteers to debrief our experiences and to hold space for healing. To honor the difficult emotional work of the volunteers, our ministers were also present. We started by sharing our hopes, our reasons for participating, and the passions that brought us together. Following that, volunteers were invited to share challenges and moments of joy and connection. In an effort to keep the emotional brain engaged, we discouraged problem solving and planning until later in the conversation. We encouraged participants to practice empathic listening, defined as being willing to be moved by the other (Jordan & Carlson, 2013).

As I facilitated shared stories, Carter stood in the back of my vision, bouncing the infant child of a same-sex couple in our congregation. I watched him dance with the baby in his arms, mindful of his aspirations for a husband and children of his own. The contrast between my son's joyous connection with an infant and the challenges at the fair was a reminder that in the last decade several bills prohibiting adoption or foster parenting by same sex couples had been proposed in our state. Even now, this infant's parents were required to complete a complicated and expensive legal petition to afford both parents full parental status. I struggled to stay present. The social justice work carried such intensity and immediacy.

After most of the volunteers had space to share their stories, one of them asked if it was time to make suggestions for improving the booth. Listening to the others, I considered what to share. There were concrete challenges I could have shared, like hostile looks from passers-by, or someone sticking their chewed gum in my drink. I refrained from sharing though, because my most challenging moment, the part that could benefit from relational healing, involved me ignoring two of our basic guidelines: don't be alone and don't argue. I was embarrassed.

"Not yet," my minister locked eyes with me. "Amy, we haven't heard from you."

I considered shaking off the offer. It is difficult for me to keep the cognitive and emotional online while processing this work. It was unlikely that I would have shared anything without the explicit invitation of my minister. I took a deep breath and shared my story.

Daily I arrived alone before any volunteers in order to do the set-up—including opening the question box. Our fair almost always happens during the hottest week of the year, usually complete with a heat advisory. It is a hard sell to ask people to sit in a barn with no shade or breeze, let alone air-conditioning, to be present for people who may or may not be hostile. I wanted the experience of working at the fair to be pleasant enough that the volunteers would return the following year, despite the discomfort. Under no circumstances did I want to revisit the experience of watching my son encounter vandalism and hate. I took that responsibility, and it was during one of these times that I faced my biggest challenge. I arrived one morning to find two messages drawn on our rainbow banner. One said, "Hi there, keep on doing amazing stuff, we love you." The other said, "fag." From across the barn, one of the other booth workers called out to me. "Those teenage boys were here, but some lady chased them off," he offered.

The night before some teenage boys had spotted me walking outside the barn in my rainbow shirt and yelled "queers suck" repeatedly at me, but they dispersed once I re-entered the barn. I had told the other booth workers about it in an effort to feel safer. I thanked the booth worker and cleaned up the rainbow banner, checked the question box—empty, they had written their piece on the rainbow banner instead—and put out the beads, stickers and displays.

I had just finished setting up when the teens returned. They elbowed each other and moved up against my chair, effectively blocking me from leaving the booth, while reading the displays to each other and laughing. I couldn't take my eyes off their t-shirts, emblazoned with my son's high school mascot. I imagined them bumping into Carter in the hallways at school, and my heart broke.

With feigned courage, I attempted to banter. I suggested they didn't need to stay in this booth if it made them uncomfortable. They insisted they liked being there, asking, "Why? Don't you like us?"

"Do you have any questions?" I asked, in my least friendly voice. I could barely see them because my vision was flooded with images of them harassing kids like Carter at school—kids without the privilege afforded me by my cisgender, teacher-like appearance. They laughed. "We don't want to talk with you," and continued reading to each other in exaggerated feminine voices.

"Time for you to leave." I used my best authoritarian voice. They didn't leave. When they began their imitations of what a transgender woman would look like using the restroom, and asking if they could go with me to the restroom, I slid right out of speaking my truth and listening, and straight into defensive sarcasm with fear and shaming put-downs. I was hoping to somehow win the conversation, and thus safety for my son. Revisiting that morning was difficult. Twice I stopped sharing to start talking safety tips, only to be drawn back in by my minister's call to pull me back into connection, back into sharing my story.

RCT—like social justice work, like life, and like relationships—is imperfect. There are failures. The most organic beauty in RCT is the reconnection after empathic failure, an opportunity—a calling—for resilience and healing. The moment of sharing my story was an example of supported vulnerability, defined by Jordan (2013) as the kind of sharing that allows one's "full range of being in a safe and mutual context" (p. 207). Sharing in this held space provided an opportunity to reconnect with hope, with the conviction that love matters more than winning arguments, that social progress cannot be accomplished in isolation. Jordan (2013) further wrote that holding space for this type of mutual sharing bolsters our courage in connection, and allows us to grow and affect change.

The Social Justice Work Ahead with RCT

Hartling and Sparks (2010) emphasized the importance of taking small steps toward progress within supportive relationships, adding that the ripple effect of such steps could impact the entire community. They write:

> Most importantly, we must not take these small steps alone!... Participating in a supportive community helps us formulate new and more effective ways to bring about change....Participating in a supportive community strengthens our resilience in the face of daunting institutionalized practices that glorify or reward individual achievement, competitive individualism, power-over tactics, stratification, disconnection and/or separation. (p. 185)

These small steps, whether found in instances of speaking One True Thing, sharing stories in a moment of supported vulnerability, mutual empowerment emerging from growth-fostering relationships, or using the Five Good Things to step outside the power-over paradigm in order to reduce shame and isolation, all create space for movement towards a more just society. Jordan (2009) writes that being willing to fully engage across difference empowers all participants, and ultimately creates systemic transformation.

In the upcoming years, our church task force will continue to host a booth at the county fair. Every year we have stronger relational ties with Prism, our volunteers, the congregation and with the visitors to our booth that support us. The volatile political climate can make this work riskier now, but we are committed both to social justice and to the connections we have nurtured over the course of this outreach. The number of volunteers participating in RCT training for the fair has already more than tripled, and the fair is still several months away.

When we take an RCT approach to social justice work, we become willing to risk transforming the power systems that have surrounded us since birth—the systems that fuel isolation and inequality. RCT encourages us to let go of certainty, of binary thinking, of the fear-based rhetoric fueling our society's polarization, and to lean into openness. Jordan (2008) summarizes this shift:

> We risk the hope of becoming part of something larger, transcending the illusion of the separate self. We can enjoy the spaciousness of real humility or we can become paralyzed with shame, a sense of personal inadequacy. The need for certainty can lead to imposition of simplistic categorizations, whether they be diagnoses or social categories which distort the experience of both the namer and the named. To be present in life…we must dwell in uncertainty. In order to do this, we must tolerate our own and the other person's vulnerability and we must create safe contexts and systems in which this can happen. (p. 205)

We can create these systems through the basic, transformational act of listening. As Walker stated in her keynote at the Transforming Community conference, we listen as if the other person's truth holds as much value as our own, as if we might be wrong, and most importantly, as if love matters. RCT moves us toward reducing strategies of disconnection and isolation through love, listening, and risking exposing our own authentic selves with the knowledge that, as Jordan pointed out in the Transforming Community conference, together in mutuality, we are better.

References

Banks, A. E., & Hirschman, L. A. (2015). *Four ways to click: Rewire your brain for stronger, more rewarding relationships*. New York: Penguin Group.

Cozolino, L. J. (2006). *The neuroscience of human relationships: Attachment and the developing social brain*. New York: Norton.

Hartling, L. M. (2009). Strengthening resilience in a risky world: It's all about relationships. In J. V. Jordan (Ed.), *The power of connection: Recent developments in Relational-Cultural theory*. New York: Routledge.

Hartling, L., & Sparks, E. (2010). Relational-Cultural practice: Working in a nonrelational world. In J. V. Jordan (Ed.), *The power of connection: Recent developments in Relational-Cultural theory* (pp. 167-185). New York: Routledge.

Jean Baker Miller Training Institute (2016). Glossary of Relational-Cultural theory Key Terms. Retrieved from http://www.jbmti.org/Our-Work/glossary-relational-cultural-therapy#relational images

Jordan, J. V. (2008). Valuing vulnerability: New definitions of courage. *Women & Therapy, 31*(2-4), 209-233. doi:10.1080/02703140802146399

Jordan, J. V. (2009). *Relational-Cultural Therapy*. Washington, D.C.: American Psychological Association.

Jordan, J. V. (2013). *The power of connection: Recent developments in Relational-Cultural theory*. New York: Routledge.

Jordan, J. V., & Carlson, J. (2013). *Creating connection: A Relational-Cultural approach with couples*. New York: Routledge.

Jordan, J. V., Hartling, L. M., & Walker, M. (2004). *The complexity of connection: Writings from the Stone Center's Jean Baker Miller Training Institute*. New York: Guilford Press.

Keck, M. (May 16, 2015). Attempt to Start Straight Pride Club at North Raises Concerns. *The Herald-Times*. Retrieved from http://www.heraldtimesonline.com/news/schools/attempt-to-start-straight-pride-club-at-north-raises-concerns/article_cfd7ffbc-1cb9-57f5-bb2e-d98a0b94d7c6.html?mode=story

Miller, J. B. (1986). *Toward a new psychology of women*. Boston: Beacon Press.

Miller, J. B., & Stiver, I. P. (1997). *The healing Connection: How women form relationships in therapy and in life*. Boston: Beacon Press.

Sadowski, M., Chow, S., & Scanlon, C. P. (2009). Meeting the needs of LGBTQ youth: A "Relational Assets" approach. *Journal of LGBT Youth*, 6(2-3), 174-198. doi:10.1080/19361650903013493

Walker, M. (1999). Race, self and society: Relational challenges in a culture of disconnection. (Work in Progress, No. 85, p. 1-7). Wellesley, MA: Stone Center Working Paper Series.

Walker, M. (2002). How therapy helps when the culture hurts. (Work in Progress, No. 95). Wellesley, MA: Stone Center Working Paper Series.

Walker, M. (2008). Power and effectiveness: Envisioning an alternate paradigm. *Women & Therapy*, 31(2-4), 129-144. doi:10.1080/02703140802146266

Ward, J. V. (2000). *The skin we're in: Teaching our children to be emotionally strong, socially smart, spiritually connected*. New York: Free Press.

Traffic Jam

────── · · · ■ ■ ■ · · · ──────

ASPEN ABRAHAMSON-TAYLOR and OLIVIA VINNES

This spoken word piece presented by Aspen (age 15) and Olivia (age 15) at the Transforming Community Conference was created as part of their tenth grade Honors World Literature class taught by Nathan Shaw at the Harbor City International School in Duluth, Minnesota. As an activity highlighting the oppression of women and girls in support of the Malala Fund, they selected sex trafficking as their topic and chose to work together to create this piece of spoken word poetry.

You've all read about it in the papers.

Or maybe you haven't.

You've all passed a victim in the store.

Or maybe you haven't.

You've all bowed your heads in memory of the lost.

Or maybe you haven't.

You've all had to take these things seriously.

Or maybe you haven't.

You all have sons, daughters, brothers, sisters.

Or maybe you don't.

But let's pretend you do.

Let's pretend you have someone.

Just in case you don't have anyone anymore.

Now that you all have someone,

think.

Our children, our innocent children, our brothers,
     sisters, sons, daughters.

They're being taken from us.

Kept just out of our grasp.

And what can we do about it?

Nothing.

It all began with a girl.

She was smart, got good grades.

But, if truth be told, a little too trusting.

Not usually a flaw.

But sometimes a chink in the armor.

But she can't be expected to realize that.

She's supposed to trust others.

She's only fourteen, thirteen, maybe younger,

biking to her friend's house on a warm Sunday night.

She isn't scared.

She isn't nervous.

She's done this before.

She lives in a nice neighborhood.

Her mother knows where she's going.

Her dad does too.

They aren't worried.

What could go wrong?

What her parents don't know is that there are people hunting,

and not for wild game.

They prefer meals of a different kind.

They sit in their perches.

Well concealed.

That wouldn't be a problem, usually.

Because usually the girl takes the long way to her friend's house.

But not this time.

This time, she's late.

So she takes the short cut.

Not bothering to tell her parents.

What they don't know can't hurt them right?

On her way down the street she meets a couple, a nice one.

They can be trusted.

They need her help finding a lost puppy.

She can't say no.

That puppy could be hurt.

Before she realizes what's happening, some strange men
    drive up in a van.

They grab her and shove her into the back seat. She can't fight.

There's five of them, and one of her.

She realizes her mistake.

Little Krissy doesn't trust people anymore.

They take her to a hotel.

And have their way with her.

They dye her hair.

Change her name.

Put her up for sale.

Just like that.

She's a victim.

Looks like Krissy's the lost puppy now.

Her parents wished they said they loved her before she left,

because they don't see her for five years.

Know what we're talking about yet?

We'll sum it up.

What?

Sex trafficking.

Who?

Children.

Why?

How?

We don't know either.

All we know is six of ten girls are victims, two of ten boys.

Stolen.

Broken.

Broken: a lovely term used by sex traffickers that refers
    to when a victim

277

no longer fights against the horrific things a "buyer" does to them.

I'm Lilly Thompson, broken at age twelve.

I'm Regina Mills, raped at age ten. Was my nightgown too short?

I'm Sara Brookes. Stolen at age fifteen.

Hi. I'm Maria. I was thirteen when I came to America
for a better life.

I got across the border and was kidnapped, brought to a trailer
and forced into prostitution.

When the police found me, I was arrested with my traffickers.

What did I do wrong?

I'm Gayan. I'm a fifteen year old boy

I was sold to over 300,000 men and women.

I called the police for help—twenty-two times.

No one listened.

I'm Camila. I'm 14. I was forced into prostitution,
bribed with freedom.

All I had to do was recruit my best friend.

Sandra.

December twenty-third. Merry Christmas, Sandra.

I was fifteen when Camila was freed.

I had to stay behind.

I escaped at seventeen and went to the police.

Instead of rescuing me they brought me to a
    juvenile offender's facility.

Where I was raped over 100 times by the workers there.

It's not like I didn't want to say no.

It's not like I said yes.

But they wouldn't have listened anyways.

They never have before.

Hi. My name is Ashley.

I was eleven years old when I got into a fight with my mom
    and ran away from home.

I stayed with my best friend's older brother, Jason.

Jason, who I had known since birth.

Jason, who was like a brother to me.

I wanted to go home the next day.

But he stopped me.

Telling me,

you're mine now.

They called her Rosie, Rosie the Riveter.

Tough as they came, oozed confidence and fierce determination

wherever she chose to plant her feet, her roots,

as if she was placed on this earth simply to whip
    the rest of us into shape.

You didn't want to get on her bad side.

Keep in mind my use of the word didn't.

Hell, I get it.

I've made some mistakes in my time.

Maybe drank too much.

Smoked a bit much weed.

Partied too hard.

But don't they understand?

Drunk means no.

High means no.

Silence means no.

Just because I couldn't answer,

it didn't mean yes.

When I was wasted out of my mind

on punch I didn't know was spiked

and brownies I didn't know weren't safe,

that meant no too.

No means no.

Only yes means yes.

And we mean sober yes.

Not the drunk kind.

Not the high kind.

Not the so I'm drunk I can't stand up kind.

And yes can change to no.

Oh and if you were wondering

Screaming and struggling means no too.

It all means no.

No matter how many lives those pigs take away.

No matter how many people they lock up in jail.

It can't replace the life I lost.

The hours, the days, the months,

the years

all gone.

All gone because I thought it would be fun

to play a game of 'Button, Button Who's Got the Button?'

Except it wasn't buttons in those cups,

it was LSD.

How was I supposed to know I'd be the lucky one?

Unlucky one.

But it's not like it matters anyway.

I'm just the slut who deserved what she got.

No one deserved what I got.

These children, these innocent children.

Taken, stolen.

Are they scared?

Are they alright?

Are they alive?

Does it hurt when you're kept in a cage that long?

Well, we may never know, because there's no one around them
that cares enough to ask.

Or maybe they are just looking the other way.

These people are not storybooks.

Why would anyone want to write a story about this?

These people are not news articles.

In fact, nine out of ten cases are never reported.

These people are not statistics.

But maybe that's all they are to you.

These are real boys.

These are real girls.

These are real children.

These are real lives.

Reflecting on Marginalization: An Undergraduate Perspective

··· ■ ■ ■ ···

NATALIA SOLER

Natalia Soler is an undergraduate student from Chicago, Illinois majoring in social work and psychology with a concentration in women's and gender studies at St. Olaf College in Northfield, Minnesota. Natalia aspires to cultivate a positive impact in a career that embraces community outreach and work that involves the empowerment of diversity. If you wish you to contact the author please email ncsoler28@gmail.com.

I heard about the *Transforming Community: The Radical Reality of Relationship* conference from my social work professor. Since I knew so little about the conference, I did not know what to expect. I walked into the room and was met by enthusiastic individuals who brought their own powerful narratives and experiences with Relational-Cultural theory. They were excited to make new relationships with people and strengthen the old relationships they had made in past conferences. My background was quite different than the other attendees at the conference, as a Latina undergraduate social work student from Chicago, I had little experience in the workforce. This lack of experience made me all the more eager to hear everyone's stories about working with clients, tackling big issues, and making connections that would help them get through the rough patches.

I felt like a sponge ready to absorb the knowledge from others' stories. At the forefront of my mind was my upcoming social work practicum experience at a nursing home and my general desire to work in geriatric social work. I thought about the challenges that were to come and how important it was going to be for me to create strong relationships with residents and their families to build a sense of trust. My small social work cohort at St. Olaf College is a great support system, but the situations in our conversations are often hypothetical as we anticipate future ups and downs plus the best methods for self-care. This was different. This was the opportunity to hear people's real experiences. The emotion showed through their voices as they talked about their clients, the boundaries presented by their system, and their own feelings of wrestling with ongoing struggles.

Through our breakout sessions after every presentation, I noticed a consistent level of high emotions. After experiencing this throughout multiple conversations, I began to notice the level of support each person had for each other. Being able to talk to people who had a range of experiences may be viewed as a privilege to some, yet it is an essential concept of Relational-Cultural theory. Mutual empathy and empowerment are at the core of growth-fostering relationships; through the contributions of others, we as individuals are able to grow and benefit (Jordan, 2005).

One thing I contemplated as I experienced the high level of support was how, within the undergraduate experience, everyone who surrounds us is working towards attaining their bachelor's degree. The tests, papers, and pressures put students under a high level of stress; but everywhere we look, we can find other students going through similar struggles. Knowing that the students around me are all working towards the same goal somehow alleviates the stress a bit as I feel part of something bigger. It becomes easy to forget that the level of empathy undergraduate students can have for each other may be difficult to come by later in life. The Transforming Community conference brought people together to support and listen to one another; and, in this way, exemplified the importance of relationships. Individuals were able to learn and apply what they learned to their individual lives.

Karen Craddock's and Amy Banks's presentation, STOP the Pain of Marginalization and Social Exclusion, during the second day of the conference occurred after we had both an introduction to RCT and to other attendees at the conference. Within this presentation, they explained the striking neurological similarities between social rejection and physical pain. They stated that the combination of humans being social creatures and our Western culture focusing on hyper-competitiveness creates a cycle of isolation and pain. They proposed that the best type of resistance to the social pain tended to be purposeful, collective, and often times spiritually based. They then demonstrated the STOP the Pain model—with STOP standing for See Stratification, Talk and Tell, Open Outreach, and Partnered Protests.

When everyone broke into small groups discussions, I joined the education group in hopes of discovering forms in which preventing marginalization and oppression within the classroom could be applied outside of the classroom. As a current undergraduate student, surrounded by professionals in the work force, I realized I was simultaneously in a unique and common role. Everyone in the room had at one point been a student, but many were now educators themselves. Their perspective on education was more in the form of what was in their control, asking themselves how they can create a safe place for students. I represented the other piece of that puzzle by conjuring up memories of when we as a group of students in class were able to talk safely about marginalization and oppression.

The STOP the Pain model as the discussion topic seemed straightforward and simple enough at face value; but upon dissecting it, we began to realize the complexities that come with it. There were some of us who felt the model presented high expectations for ourselves. Both Craddock and Banks mentioned that everyone has a role in the model, for when we ourselves find our voice, it takes away from others' ability to define us.

With the word STOP being the very essence of the model, it becomes easy for individuals to feel as if they should be the ones

287

to in fact stop marginalization in its tracks. Now, why is this a great deal to expect of ourselves? Should not we as individuals who care about social justice be able to look out for our friends, neighbors, classmates and ourselves? The simple answer we probably all want to hear is yes. Unfortunately this is not the case; both as a spectator to marginalization and a victim of it, we risk re-injury. The second step of the model, Talk and Tell, is an action that can open the person to feeling vulnerable. To Talk and Tell is to allow other people into your innermost thoughts and feelings; it is the sharing of your personal experiences and stories, exposing your true self to others.

So what, if any, is the solution?

Within the education group, we began discussing these personal struggles we had with the model and possible solutions to avoid re-injuring individuals who were subject to marginalization. A common reflection emerged that we had to be patient with ourselves, so as not to rush through the steps of the model in hopes of quickly reaching the final step of Partnered Protests. To be patient with ourselves means to slow down enough to spend time talking, telling and having open outreach. When we were patient within the small group discussion itself, something powerful happened. During the STOP presentation there was a commercial from China displayed as a visual to the many ways in which racism exists. The commercial was for laundry detergent and displayed a Black man flirting with a Chinese woman. She calls him over only to put him in the washing machine and when the machine finishes the cycle the person who comes out is no longer the Black man but a Chinese man. While I was astounded by the overt racism expressed in the commercial, I admit I did not think much about where the commercial came from. It was not until a person within the small discussion group spoke out that I began to consider the importance of context. Hesitantly a young woman shared her feelings of hurt by watching the video; she saw the stratification and put a name to it ultimately completing the first step of the STOP model. She was from China and perhaps the only

288

Chinese person in attendance at the conference. She was brave enough to speak out about her feelings about an incident to which many people did not give a second thought. She eloquently stated, "Who names the trauma matters."

The presentation was in the context of and presented in the United States of America, a country where it would be an understatement to say racism exists as examples are tragically too easy to find. For the sole visual example of racism to be a commercial from China to display marginalization in a way seems to shift the attention away from the United States. While this example may provide a larger context of how racism and marginalization occurs across the globe, I believe it is crucial for us to be willing to examine the effects of racism and marginalization in our own context first. At the moment, I did not recognize this and would have not stopped to see the potential hurt if she was not courageous enough to speak up—Talk and Tell.

This situation that unfolded at the conference demonstrated the importance of both the See Stratification and Talk and Tell parts of the STOP the pain model. In this case we again were experiencing the all too common scenario in which the person who had experienced the marginalization had to be the one to speak up, leaving the potential for re-injury. The important distinction to note is that through our conversation we were able to address the woman's feelings; and we, as individuals in the group, were able to recognize a situation that created those feelings that personally I would have easily ignored if she did not speak up. I believe this conversation was able to unfold in a positive and productive way because the group created a safe space. There was recognition of vulnerability, and all the group members allowed the space for the vulnerability to be expressed with respect to each person as an individual with their own distinct perspectives. One thought that crossed my mind as the conversation began to unfold that day was how does one help create these safe spaces so that the Talk and Tell piece of the model is more likely to occur?

Because I had come to the conversation as an undergraduate student, I had my recent experiences of speaking about marginalization within the classroom in mind. In one of my social work classes, we were asked to focus on a specific moment where we were either the direct recipient of or a bystander to marginalization and then to reflect on what we wanted to say in that moment. A couple months before I had been discussing education with a White woman, and she stated her belief that Latino parents did not care about education to the same extent as White parents because White parents had a better understanding of the system and therefore encouraged their children to study more. These words went against everything my Latino parents, Latino grandparents, and entire Latino family had taught me. It went against my very being as I pursued higher education. It went against my people. Yet instead of standing up against marginalization, I found myself making excuses for the woman inside my head. She could not have meant it that way, I told myself; she is just framing her beliefs badly. These thoughts and excuses consumed me, and I found myself silenced.

I was the one who was troubled by this conversation long after it occurred — not her. She did not even know she had caused me pain; I felt cowardly for not speaking up. The topic of conversation during the conference surrounding marginalization and social pain brought me back to this moment of helplessness and shame; but more importantly, it brought me back to my assignment. It was through the assignment that I revisited all those negative emotions and began to write ferociously about the things I felt; the words I wish I said; the way I wish I had felt walking away from that conversation.

As could be appropriate in the beginning of the Open Outreach phase, we were expected to bring these reflections back to a small group discussion the next class period; and, from these conversations, choose someone's situation in our small group to act out in a way in which we were stopping marginalization and oppression. Through the small group discussion I had with my classmates, I realized that each and every one of us had either experienced or been a bystander to a form of marginalization during some point in our lives. Through the sharing of experiences and acting out, I witnessed micro-aggressions that would not be evident to me if I were in that particular situation. I heard people struggle to articulate their hurt and explain why what was said or done felt so wrong. This was a situation in which we all wanted to stop these micro-aggressions, yet even we were still struggling. This exemplified just how difficult it is to speak up in the face of marginalization. If you want students to master math, you give them practice problems. If you want them to learn how to write, you give them the tools of peer editing and writing prompts. If you want to foster students that are agents of change, you give them the opportunity to Talk and Tell as well as facilitate Open Outreach to promote healing interaction.

Some students were able to become more comfortable with utilizing humor to ease tense situations, while less assertive students practiced speaking up in general. The approach on stopping marginalization and speaking up was different with each student. The point was not to be right or wrong, but to have an open discussion with our peers. This assignment was important because it provided both the opportunity for us to reflect upon our personal experiences and to practice articulating our response. It gave us back our voice.

If, through our education, and not simply higher education, we can begin to create spaces to have conversations surrounding oppression and marginalization then young students can begin to recognize the importance of these issues and start the dialogue. The confidence to speak up in the face of oppression needs to move beyond the classroom, but it can start there. Individuals may feel less intimidated in that relatively safe classroom environment so that they can speak up, have tough conversations, and then perhaps integrate that learning experience into their daily lives whether they are the direct recipient of, a friend of a recipient, or simply a bystander to such marginalization. This creates a new social space where people can address and discuss these issues.

Through this process we can build and grow in our relationships with each other because we do not feel alone. A core way of reaching connections with each other is embedded in the steps of the STOP the Pain model. We need to foster the ability to See Stratification in order to recognize when marginalization is happening around us so that we can begin the conversation. To Talk and Tell can sometimes mean having difficult, awkward, or uncomfortable conversations. These conversations can resemble the one I had in the classroom that stemmed from the assignment; the honest ones I had during the *Transforming Community* conference. Open Outreach is the willingness to continue the conversation, as individuals in the conference and as the students in my class displayed it. It takes vulnerability, yet this does not take away from the importance of going out into your community and continuing the conversation.

The final piece of the model is Partnered Protest—the beautiful consequences of the conversations; a way for the silenced voices to be heard and individuals to join together. Community organizing may represent Partner Protest at its highest level with numbers of people coming together to reach a common goal, to pinpoint ways in which change is possible, and then to focus on those ways together. Action can be in various forms—a peaceful protest, a panel of resources, or creating a new community resource—that are developed through the steps of the STOP model.

I believe my feeling of being overwhelmed when first introduced to the model, that feeling so many of my small group members shared during the Transforming Community conference, is common. For this reason that last piece of Partnered Protests in the STOP model is not presented as a goal standing on its own with no plan of how to get there. The process needs to begin with developing the awareness to See Stratification, to find a safe place to Talk and Tell, to work towards Open Outreach in order to be able to act in Partnered Protest. Continue this conversation, for it could make all the difference.

Reference

Jordan, J.V. (2010). *Relational-Cultural Therapy*. Washington, DC: American Psychological Association.

Unpacking White Privilege: An Experiment in "Going There" with White Relational-Cultural Practitioners

••• ∎ ∎ ∎ •••

Lisa Eible, DSW, MSW, LCSW

We were an informal group of educators, social workers, and therapists who felt deeply moved by ongoing race-related violence, and the difficulty in talking about race-related topics, even among RCT practitioners. We formed an informal group to examine our own white privilege and to address race-related issues and have been meeting for the past year and a half. As the poster describes, we are focused on further development of our personal and professional lenses in the application of RCT to racism (interpersonal and systemic). We seek to understand our individual and collective journeys and to further develop Relational-Cultural theoretical constructs related to racism. We expect and plan further work on this topic, as our group work continues. Lisa Eible may be contacted at lmeible@yahoo.com.

From its inception and early beginnings, Relational-Cultural theory (RCT) has been characterized by co-creation. Jean Baker Miller strongly held to the notion that the work itself was "in relation"—that is, ever changing in a context of mutual learning and impact (Miller, 1976). In this rich collaborative tradition, a group of Relational-Cultural practitioners began working together on a personal, professional, and theoretical journey related to

295

racism and white privilege after the 2015 Jean Baker Miller Institute (JBMTI) in response to yet another national race related tragedy—the Charleston, South Carolina church shooting. A call to action developed there for further RCT work specific to issues of racism and white privilege. Miller (1976) cited the importance of a "good conflict"; and authors such as Ayvazian and Daniel Tatum (1994), Daniel Tatum (2004), Jordan (1997), Tatum and Garrick Knaplund (2004), and Walker (2002) addressed racial issues. Our group thought there was another layer of "unpacking the knapsack " of white privilege which needed to be done (McIntosh, 1989).

A call was made for conference attendees and other RCT practitioners who were interested in working on issues of racism. It was decided that the group would be composed, at least to start, of those who identified as "white". We observed, in the group's conception, a need for "us to work on our own issues" and not place additional stress and expectations on our sisters and brothers of color to help us "get it". This was a decision made in love and protection, not with the purpose of exclusion. It was also a place to start, not a forever decision.

Initially, two groups of social workers, therapists and educators from across the United States and Canada were established and began meeting in Fall, 2015, via on line meeting forums. While all group members identified as "white" and "female", there was cultural, religious, and sexual orientation differences among group members. The initial goals were to raise each person's individual awareness of their own privilege and to name how it impacted the lens through which they experienced the world. The longer-term goals of the group are to contribute to the Relational-Cultural theory literature as it relates to issues of race, diversity, and white privilege, as well as to develop some sort of individual or collective social action agenda. The two groups combined to form one group after the first series of meetings due to a smaller number of participants at that point, and has continued as such through April 2017.

A closed Facebook group was set up to share information that included materials such as worksheets, journaling, readings and videos (ex. *Race — The Power of an Illusion, Wealth: America's Other Racial Divide*). Survey Monkey was used to gather data from the nine participants in the final group. In response to the question, Have you changed as a result of your participation in this group, participants answered:

- I feel more empowered to speak up on issues of privilege and racism...this group has provided connection and a safe learning place for my continued growth.
- I am angrier. In a good way.
- I am more knowledgeable about the history of racism and institutional privilege in the United States and more aware of how it has affected my habitual perceptions.
- I have become more conscious of my white privilege and have initiated numerous conversations with other white people about white privilege.
- I speak up in uncomfortable situations, whereas before I would be silent. Even if I don't think I will change anyone's viewpoint, I make it known that there are other perspectives.
- My self-awareness has increased though I know I have to keep learning. I also appreciate the access to resources.... I use and will continue to use these resources to expose others in my community. I see it as my responsibility to educate other white people.

In response to the question, What was your biggest learning/ takeaway from this experience/group dialogue, they replied:

- I still have a long way to go with my understanding of privilege. This process is a marathon not a sprint.
- I was once again struck by the importance of taking time for the growth process to unfold, & to continue to hold the responsibility for learning rather than looking outward to people of color to educate me.

- How helpful it is to have an ongoing white affinity group to learn with.
- That I have the option to deal or not deal with racism and privilege, whereas others are confronted with it daily.
- We are all uncomfortable and will all make mistakes (embrace and acknowledge the mistakes).
- I would say becoming sensitized to the pervasiveness of my privilege. Once your eyes are open, it's impossible to "unsee" things. And the group has given me courage to act.
- Hearing the complexity with which some of my colleagues describe their own growth in this area has helped me grow too.

When asked about their experiences and observations, they cited scheduling and technology issues as well as the emotional nature of the interactions. One participant seemed to summarize the emotional impact by writing: Several group members noted that the group provided support in tolerating the shame about unacknowledged privilege, opening participants up to greater consciousness and action.

Since the initial series of meetings, the group has continued to meet, and further published work is anticipated and planned. Our group members include: Christina Borel (christina.borel@ gmail.com), Denise Dojka (dmdojka@comcast.net), Lisa Eible (lmeible@yahoo.com), Shannon Finn (finnshannon@ hotmail.com), Lisa Frey (Melissa.Frey-1@ou.edu), Catie Green (cagreene@email.wm.edu), Lynne Lieberman (llieberman@ comcast.com), Betsy Nordell (bnordell@wellesley.edu), Audra Sbarra (as455@nyu.edu), Harriet Schwartz (harrietschwartz14@ gmail.com), Erica Seidel (drericaseidel@gmail.com), and Gail Walker (GW8215724@aol.com).

References

Ayvazian, A. & Daniel Tatum, B. (1994). *Women, race and racism: A dialogue in black and white*. Boston: Wellesley Centers for Women Publications.

Daniel Tatum, B. (2004). *Racial identity development and Relational Theory: The case of black women in white communities*. Boston: Wellesley Centers for Women Publications.

Jordan, J.V. (1997). *Women's growth in diversity: More writings from the Stone Center*. New York: Guilford Press.

McIntosh, P. (1989, July/August). White privilege: Unpacking the invisible knapsack. In *Peace and Freedom Magazine* (10-12).

Miller, J. B. (1976). Toward a new psychology of women. Boston: Beacon Press.

Tatum, B. & Garrick Knaplund, E. (2004). Outside the circle? The relational implication for white women working against racism. Boston: Wellesley Centers for Women Publications.

Walker, M. (2002). How therapy helps when culture hurts. Boston: Wellesley Centers for Women Publications.

Part IV

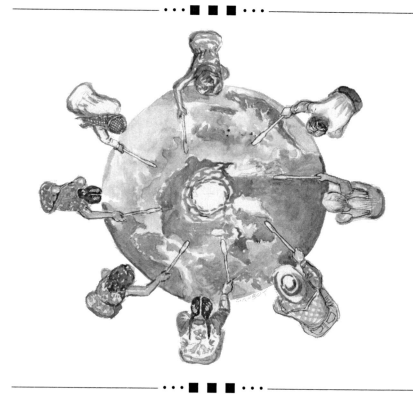

Transforming Community:
The Environment

A Natural Connection: Relational-Cultural Theory and the Environment

—————— · · · ■ ■ ■ · · · ——————

LEAH PRUSSIA, MSW, LICSW

This reflection is a culmination of teachings from Elders, Western education, and personal/professional life experience. My parents can attest that from early on I had what some perceive as an unnatural connection to the trees, water, four-leggeds, fliers.... I later learned that my sensitivity to and for all that lives is innate; what is not natural is humanity's disconnection from the environment. This past year I have watched some from our species threaten Nibi's (Water's) livelihood with the black snake (oil pipeline), while at the same time others joined internationally to stand for Her with our relatives at Standing Rock. I was born from Nibi. She gives me life. The least I can do is try speak for Her and share Elders' wisdom in hopes that all of humankind awakens to this essential connection. Leah Prussia may be contacted at lprussia@css.edu.

"We need relationships like we need air and water..."

Over the last half century, Relational-Cultural theory (RCT) has articulated the worth of human connection in the healing process through a Western lens. Founding RCT scholars have provided an alternative to the separate-self model of assessing and working with the human condition. Though the idea of *relationship* as primary to personal well-being (Miller, 1976) is novel to the social sciences (50 years young), it is an age-old (thousands of years) traditional practice of Indigenous people worldwide. Indigenous teachings not only recognize the import of human relationships, but also the value of connection with all that lives (Peacock, 2011): the four-leggeds, swimmers, crawlers, fliers, rooted relatives, *Nibi* (water), and *Maamaa Aki* (the earth). Within the last few decades western science has slowly awakened to the vast reality that nature is nurturing and necessary for human health and wellness. This reflection will explore the potential for RCT to embrace the natural environment as a collaborator in the relational movement by applying The Five Good Things to humans' relationship with water (Miller & Stiver, 1997). By illuminating the synthesis of nature and RCT, humanity may re-embrace what has been missing from the formula for necessary personal and planetary healing.

Andrew Favorite, *Gaawaabaabiganikaag* (White Earth) Elder, once said, "We are all indigenous to somewhere." History has shown that at one time, all of humanity was one with creation. Humans have learned from the environment for millennia through sensory engagement, mindful curiosity, prayer, and practicing the basic principles of *give* and *take*. Mutuality was inherent to the daily interaction between humans and the environment. According to Gerhard Lenski's Critical Theory (Kennedy, 2004) as humans gained greater power over *other* life forms (domestication of animals, genetic modification of the plant world, harnessing water through the use of dams, aerial chemical trails to shift weather patterns) through technological "advances", our mutual appreciation and relationship with all that lives began to diminish. Humans gradually made the shift from eco-mindfulness to ego-mindedness. What Western society embraced as evolution and advancement, the natural world experienced as loss (extinction of winged, crawlers, four-legged, and swimming relatives, polluted waterways, deforestation).

Western ways of knowing and interacting followed a similar devolutionary trajectory of disconnection and ego until the mid-70s. The conception of *another* way of knowing – a way of knowing similar to Indigenous teachings had germinated to recognize the healing capacity of connection. RCT was birthed from ideas generated by Jean Baker Miller's work (1976) and further nurtured through collaboration with Judith Jordan, Irene Stiver, and Janet Surrey. The founding *mothers* of RCT provided an alternative to the dominant paradigm in psychology that espoused "power-over" dynamics and emphasized autonomy in the therapeutic process. Upon maturation, RCT embraced feminist ideals that challenged the separate-self model by positing that through affiliation (connection), mutuality (power with), and authenticity, individuals thrive. Miller and Stiver (1997) broadened awareness regarding the impact of growth fostering relationships by further delineating the benefits of affiliation via The Five Good Things (zest, sense of worth, clarity, productivity, and a desire for more connection). Later, Banks (2011) augmented RCTs psychosocial model by including "the science of connection" through summarizing research in the neurosciences and concluding that humans truly are hard-wired to connect.

Humans are also mentally, emotionally, physically, and spiritually hard-wired to connect to the natural world. Ecopsychology and contemporary research have become cognizant of the ancient knowledge that was once deemed as lore, truly is (Besthorn & Saleebey, 2003; Burls, 2007, Clinebell, 1996; Miller & Hayward, 2014; Roszak, Gomes, & Kanner, 1995). This begs the question, how does one capture teachings that have been orally passed down for thousands of years and cite in the *language* of Western ways of knowing? How does one "legitimize" Indigenous knowledge received in lodge, fasts, and stories shared by Elders that are a truth and recognize the inherent worth as equally valid as Western truth?

Indigenous peoples have and continue to recognize the sacred relationship with water and honor "Her" with feasts, prayers, and ceremony. In 1994, when Masaru Emoto (2005) published *Hado no Shinri* (The Truth of Wave Fluctuation), the Western academic world began to wake from its slumber and recognize that water responds to words and intentions. Emoto's research in the mid-1990s (that water is relational) supported the traditional Indigenous way of knowing in the Western language of science (Akena, 2012; Barnhardt & Kawagley, 2005). Due to the fact that an adult body is composed of 70% water, Emoto (2005) concludes, "We are Water", which is synonymous with Indigenous teachings that *Water is Life*. The following section will explore the many ways that Water is understood as living, interactional, and essential to all life.

There are a number of intersecting reasons why Water should be thoughtfully integrated and understood to illustrate the natural connection of RCT and the environment. Water shares in acknowledging the essence of the feminine, as well as nurtures The Five Good Things in relationship with humankind. According to *Anishinaabe* teachings, women are caretakers of Water based on their relationship with and role as life-givers, birthing spirits through the sacred maternal waters from the unseen to the physical world. Josephine Mandamin, *Anishinaabekwe*, has said:

> The water of Mother Earth, she carries life to us,
> and as women we carry life through our bodies. We
> as women are life-givers, protectors of the water,
> and that's why we are very inclined to give mother
> earth the respect that she needs for the water.
> (Gursoz, 2014, para. 5)

The role of women is also celebrated and shared through RCT, which recognizes the unique qualities of the sacred feminine.

RCT's feminist perspective holds space for qualitative ways of knowing, which is inherently relational and descriptive in its process (Jordan, 2001). RCT's premise posits that health is incumbent upon "growth fostering relationships". The essence of Water is in and of itself relational, as it is comprised of two elements that need affiliation with one another to *be*. Without Hydrogen, Water does not exist. In the absence of Oxygen, Water cannot take on its full essence. For survival of the lifeblood fundamental to all that lives (Water), relationship is essential. The Five Good Things described by Miller and Stiver (1997), hallmarks of RCT, describe the yield of healthy relationship. Each of The Five Good Things or relational *gifts* (zest, sense of worth, clarity, productivity, and the desire for more connection) will be considered in the context of humans' connection with Water to provide the foundational support for inclusion of the natural world in the relational movement.

Zest is described as the vitality and energy one feels in a mutually growth fostering relationship (Miller, 1986). Humans' connection with Water is invigorating and restorative. One can observe zestful interactions by going to the lakes, oceans, or rivers where adults and children congregate year round to play and renew. Zest is manifest and is the cumulative content of positive exchange between humans and Water. Not only are humans energized by the connection, Water mirrors the zest-filled response (Emoto, 2005).

According to Miller (1986), a sense of worth is developed through an interchange where attention and recognition are conveyed. Water, is non-judgmental and offers unconditional regard and literal absorption of the human exchange through its very presence (Emoto, 2005). Berry (1998), aptly describes the attentiveness and silent recognition of Water:

> When despair for the world grows in me... I come into the presence of still water. And I feel above me the day- blind stars waiting with their light. For a time I rest in the grace of the world, and am free. (p. 30)

Clarity or fuller knowledge of one's self transpires through relationship (Miller, 1986). As Indigenous knowledge has shared and Western ways of knowing are documenting, *Water is Life – We are Water.* As humans take time for reflection with Water, greater awareness of the I and We float to the surface of consciousness and lead to increased understanding of the whole.

Action or productivity is another gift of relationship (Miller, 1986). As one hydrates with the basic nourishment that Water provides, the liquid supplement energizes the physical organs and increases mental sharpness of the human vessel improving engagement in life. The same is realized each Spring, as the lifeblood (water, sap) moves through trees from the earth bound root systems forging up the trunk into the branches creating the conditions for further growth and reproduction. A byproduct of the trees' sap is sustenance in the form of maple/birch syrup once Water is boiled down. The process of gathering sap to produce syrup requires energy, which leads to another cyclical relational exchange between water, trees, and humans.

Miller (1986) concludes that "increased 'zest', empowerment, knowledge and worth...leads to the desire for more and fuller connection...." (p. 7). Water is central to human mental, emotional, physical, and spiritual well-being and is actively sought by way of springs, rivers, lakes, and oceans. The significance that Water holds in the most sacred of ceremonies worldwide (e.g. Japanese Shinto practices, Indigenous Sweat Lodges, Christianity) is indicative of the relational magnitude it holds for humans. Emoto (2005) writes:

> ...the more you know about water, the more clearly
> you will see yourself. As you become clearer, you
> will see the society, the nation, the world, the earth,
> the universe, and eventually the divine being.

The collective *We* is not currently in relationship nor does it recognize mutuality with Water. LaDuke (2016) outlines the effects of the war waged on water by citing the decimation of the Rio Doco (Brazil), Animas River (Colorado), and the Frazier River (British Columbia) along with the collateral effects to systems reliant on this source of life. The Dakota Access Pipeline (DAPL) presently threatens the health of the Missouri River, the *lifeblood* for the Lakota at Standing Rock, along with 8 million people and plant/animal life downstream. Lakota relatives have brought awareness to the world stage about the dire need for humans to acknowledge and engage in relationship with Water—*Mni Wiconi* (Water is Life). It is imperative that the relational movement expand to include the natural environment, similar to way the Maori Tribe recently gained legal human rights for their relative, the Whanganui River in New Zealand. According to the new legal status of the Whanganui River, there is "no differentiation between harming the tribe or harming the river because they are one and the same" (The Guardian, 2017).

Norton (2009) broached the intersection of RCT and the environment through weaving ecopsychology and social work principles. This essay has taken the proposed connection one step further by demonstrating the synthesis and applicability of The Five Good Things between humans and water. The author also encourages RCT theorists to recognize the natural connection of RCT and the environment, and thereby the importance of including this connection in the relational movement. Acknowledging and including this connection may also serve as a potential bridge between Western and Indigenous ways of knowing.

In closing, Day (n.d.) cites Emoto as saying that it is important to start each day speaking to the water:

> Water, we love you.
> We thank you.
> We respect you. (The Water Song, para. 5).

Day translates this into Ojibwemowin as:

> Ne-be Gee Zah-gay-e-goo
> Gee Me-gwetch–wayn ne-me—goo
> Gee Zah Wayn ne-me-goo (The Water Song, para. 10)

This meditation is a beautiful joining of both traditional Indigenous and Western ways of knowing. A product that emerged by uniting two world-views that acknowledge the benefit of quantitative and qualitative processes, as well as the significance of valuing and *hearing* both the female and male voice. These words have been shared with and by many through song and prayer to aid in the healing of *Nibi* (Water), who has fallen ill over the last century due to humanity's nearly forgotten connection to Her. It is time for *all* to remember the original teachings related to humans' sacred bond to Water. It is *Our* obligation to work toward a growth fostering relationship with *Nibi* and all that inhabits the natural world. It is time humanity embraced its relational role toward truly transforming community and advocate and assist with personal and planetary healing.

References

Akena, F. A. (2012). Critical analysis of the production of western knowledge and its implications for indigenous knowledge and decolonization. *Journal of Black Studies,* 43(6), 599-619. doi:10.1177/0021934712440448

Banks, A. (2011). The mythic reality of the autonomous individual: Developing the capacity to connect. *Zygon Journal* 46(1), 168–182.

Barnhardt, R., and Kawagley, A. O. (2005). Indigenous knowledge systems and Alaska native ways of knowing. *Anthropology & Education Quarterly,* 36(1), 8-23

Berry W. (1998). The selected poems of Wendell Berry. Berkeley, CA: Counterpoint Press

Besthorn, F. H., & Saleebey, D. (2003). Nature, genetics, and the biophilia connection: Exploring linkages with social work values and practice. *Advances in Social Work,* 4(1), 1-18.

Burls, A. (2007). People and green spaces: Promoting public health and mental well-being through ecotherapy. *Journal Of Public Mental Health,* 6(3), 24-39.

Clinebell, H. (1996). *Ecotherapy: Healing ourselves, healing the earth.* New York: Haworth Press.

Day, D., (n.d.). Nibi walk. Retrieved from: http://www.nibiwalk.org/nibi-songs/

Emoto, M. (2005). *The true power of water: Healing and discovering ourselves.* Hillsboro, OR: Beyond Words Publishing, Inc.

Gursoz, A. (2014). Meet Josephine Mandamin (*Anishinaabekwe*): The water walker. *Indigenous Rising.* Retrieved from: http://indigenousrising.org/josephine-mandamin/.

Jordan, J. V. (2001). A relational-cultural model: Healing through mutual empathy. *Bulletin of the Menninger Clinic,* 65(1), 92-103.

Kennedy, M. D. (2004). Evolution and event in history and social change: Gerhard Lenski's critical theory. *Sociological Theory,* 2, 315-327.

LaDuke, W. (2016). How do we grieve the death of a river? *The Circle: Native American News and Arts*. Retrieved from: http://thecirclenews.org/index.php?option=com_content&task=view&id=1313&Itemid=63.

Miller, J. B. (1976). *Toward a new psychology of women*. Boston: Beacon Press.

Miller, J. B. (1986). What do we mean by relationships. *Work in Progress, No. 22*, Wellesley, MA: Stone Center Working Papers Series.

Miller, J. B., & Stiver, I. P. (1997). *The healing connection: How women form relationships for therapy and in life*. Boston: Beacon Press.

Miller, S. E., & Hayward, R. A. (2014). Social work education's role in addressing people and a planet at risk. *Social Work Education, 33*(3), 280-295. doi:10.1080/02615479.2013.805192

Norton, C. L. (2009). Ecopsychology and social work: Creating an interdisciplinary framework for redefining person-in-environment. *Ecopsychology, 1*(3), 138-145. doi:10.1089/eco.2009.0046

Peacock, T., & Wisuri, M. (2011). *The four hills of life: Ojibwe wisdom*. Afton, MN: Afton Historical Society Press.

Roszak, T., Gomes, M. E., & Kanner, A. D. (1995). *Ecopsychology: Restoring the earth, healing the mind*. Berkeley, CA: Sierra Club Books.

The Guardian (2017). New Zealand river granted same legal rights as human being. Retrieved from: https://www.theguardian.com/world/2017/mar/16/new-zealand-river-granted-same- legal-rights-as-human-being

Sa Kawanangan:
In the Cosmos

··· ■ ■ ■ ···

MARY A. HERNANDEZ

Sa Kawanangan—In the Cosmos is a visualization exercise that was used by the environment dialogue group during the conference on Transforming Community: The Radical Reality of Relationship, held in June 2016 by the JBMTI, co-sponsored by Wellesley College and College of St. Scholastica. The exercise was used to help participants reach a meditative state steeped in connection and to facilitate an increased awareness of interdependence with each other and within the universe, in celebration of the notion of a "shared self" or kapwa. The exercise is shared in this submission with the hope that it will strengthen feelings of connection with our non-human siblings and with nature at large. Mary Hernandez may be contacted at Maryahnatural@gmail.com.

Sa Kawanangan literally means "in the cosmos" or "in the universe", as stated in the Cebuano language native to the Visayas and Northern Mindanao regions of the Philippines. The languages chosen for the title—Cebuano and English—represent the connection between the author's roots and her current sense of place; from the lands of her ancestors to the lands of her present residence. This title seems apt in consideration of the cosmic journey intended for the participants to embark upon using this exercise.

The exercise is intended to help people experience the notion of a shared self, or *kapwa,* as an indicator of profound

313

interdependence extended into our natural world. The exercise offers an opportunity to gain a deeper understanding of the need for a deep connection; a connection that demonstrates the relationship between the cosmos and people in a way that melds boundaries.

Kapwa is a Filipino philosophical and psychological concept which implies a shared identity through "the unity of the self and others" (Enriquez, 1988), or as De Guia (2005) shared: "the self in the other". *Kapwa* stands in contrast to the notion of the "other" as separate, and can be readily used as an extension to the concepts of Relational-Cultural theory in regard to connection, mutuality, and the relational self.

The *Sa Kawanangan* visualization exercise was first used as an introductory meditation for an ecotherapy class (Hernandez, 2015). The author received feedback from the participants about their affective state during and after the exercise. This helped to refine the exercise. During the 2016 conference, *Transforming Community: The Radical Reality of Relationship,* the revised version of the visualization was used by the environment dialogue group as an introduction to an afternoon proceeding.

Preparing For the Exercise

Before starting, the facilitator should inform the participants that the exercise will ask them to expand their notions of self and physical space. Thus, preparing the participants prior to the exercise is important.

Prime For Readiness

The facilitator must inform the participants that this "cosmic journey" may take them to places where they may not be prepared to go. Reassure the participants that they do not have to "travel" to the full extent of the exercise. Participants have full control over how far they wish to go and can opt to stop at any time.

Respect Boundaries

During the exercise, participants may choose to stay at certain levels of the journey while the exercise continues to travel. Some may decide to linger at preferred places, to take a bit longer in some spots, or to hurry forward and backward. These are all possible actions and do not tend to disrupt the exercise.

Readjustments

It is normal for participants to be in various stages of the exercise. Each person applies her/his own notion of time even though the facilitator speaks each level out loud. Participants may find themselves going ahead, staying behind, or finding that they may linger longer at a certain place. Each participant will naturally readjust as the facilitator continues to move through the levels of the exercise.

Pace and Tone

Proceed with a calm pace and soothing tone. The facilitator should aim to take the same amount of time going into the cosmos as it would take to return from the cosmos. The facilitator is encouraged to practice the timing of the exercise before using it in a therapeutic setting. The facilitator has full capacity, in the moment of the exercise, to add more words or to take away words as she or he deems fit to the group and to the pace they have established.

Sa Kawanangan: In the Cosmos

Please find a comfortable, restful place to sit. Close your eyes. Close your eyes and feel your body slump into your chair. Feel your body's contact with the chair. Scan your body. Feel your shoulders and your back against the chair, your upper thighs on the seat, and your feet on the ground.

Slowly, slowly, feel your self gathering; gathering into the center of your body, your mass concentrating into the center, into a ball, and turning, turning faster, turning faster into a ball of light. Feel yourself, that ball of light, slowly rotating in that space; rotating.

Feel yourself, the golden ball of light, slowly separating into two orbs, joined in the center but slowly stretching, stretching; becoming golden strands—like golden fingers—reaching out in two opposite directions over this space; getting wider.

Wider and wider; the golden strands of your light spread their luminescence; expanding over this room, this building, then over the land, then over rivers, the lakes, the islands, the oceans.

Enveloping the earth from the top and the bottom, from side to side, continuing to reach out into space, into the black expanse of the universe. Reaching out: Your golden strands of light reaching for the other lights you see in the expanse.

And then, suddenly, you, your golden strands of light, burst into a million sparkling pieces and scatter among the lights in the universe. And then, it is and it feels silent. Your millions of particles are there floating, sharing the space with other particles in the universe, lying there in the silence of space, floating amongst matter as old as time.

Floating amongst the stars, each of your particles feeling the energy from other atoms, remnants of the big bang, and you lying there amongst them, as one of them. Interspersed between them, feeling one with all that there was and all that is; not knowing where one particle ends and where you begin.

And then you feel the slow and gentle tug of gravity on every piece of you. You feel your particles slowly coming together, together into two streams of light coming from opposite directions— gathering, gathering.

Slowly, slowly feel yourself becoming golden strands of light reaching out in two opposite directions over the earth; getting smaller, thinner and thinner. The golden strings of your light have spread their luminescence around the world.

Feel yourself, those strands of light, gathering over the continents coming back together over the oceans, over the islands, over lakes, then over rivers, over land, over rainforests, over towns and cities, over this building and back into illuminating the walls of this room. Coming back energized from feeling the atoms in space.

Bringing it all back as your lights converge. Your golden strands joined in the center now, gathering into a mass, concentrating, and gradually turning into an orb that turns just above your seat.

And you start feeling your body rebuilding. Your ball of light keeps turning slowly as your body continues to build. Your feet appear, then your calves, your thighs, your pelvis, then stomach, chest, and your head. And all the while the golden orb continues to turn in your center.

Your light starts fading as your consciousness returns into this room. And, just like the moonlight fades as the sun appears on the horizon, the light fades completely as you slowly awaken your consciousness in this room and start to take a deep breath. And whenever you're ready open your eyes.

After the Exercise

Given the type of expansion that this exercise required of the participants, the facilitator should debrief with the group after people have opened their eyes and completed the exercise.

Check In

The facilitator may wish to ask participants how they felt both going through the exercise and coming back from it. Each person should have the opportunity to respond. It is possible that effects of trauma may surface during the exercise, and the facilitator is advised to conduct a risk assessment, and any related actions, where appropriate.

Check for Speed

The facilitator may wish to ask how the pace felt for the participants. Some may find it appropriate, others may find it too fast or too slow. Adjust as needed the next time.

Apply Information for a Therapeutic Session

The facilitator may choose to use data from the participants' experiences to inform therapeutic sessions in which the participants are engaged.

References

De Guia, K. (2005). *Kapwa: the self in the other.* Manila: Anvil Publishing.

Enriquez, V. E. (1988). Kapwa: A core concept in filipino social psychology. *Philippine Studies.* 36, pp. 118-126.

Hernandez, M. A. (2015). *Sa Kawanangan: In the Cosmos.* Unpublished manuscript.

The Beaver Story:
Life on Amikwiish Lake

··· ■ ■ ■ ···

CONNIE GUNDERSON, "AUNTIE" AND
TAYLOR GUNDERSON, "NIECE"
ARTWORK BY CARL GAWBOY

This poem is based on a true story. On the shores of a beautiful northern Minnesota lake, I live in community with beavers, otters, turtles, fishes, birds, and many other wildlife. To know and understand that we, as people, are not separate from nature affects how we interact with our environment. The beavers are near and dear to my heart. Their gentle nature and diligent, task oriented care-taking offer many learnings about the interconnectedness of life and the unquestionable importance of all our relations. My niece, Taylor, and I decided to write this story after vandals attempted to destroy the lake's only beaver lodge; a lodge that has been home for generations of beaver families. We hope to educate others on the intricacies of relationship. Connie Gunderson, may be contacted at cgundersoncss.edu. Taylor Gunderson may be contacted at tgunders@wellesley.edu.

Carl Gawboy, a member of the Bois Forte Band of the Minnesota Ojibwe, was born to a Finnish mother and an Ojibwe father. in Cloquet, MN. He was raised in Ely, MN. He has lived in the Duluth area for the past twenty years. Carl taught courses in American Indian Studies and Watercolor Painting at UMD and The College of St. Scholastica for many years. Now retired, he devotes his time to painting and writing.

Carl's work is primarily concerned with defining the Ojibwe culture between 1850 and 1950. He focuses on the spirit of

321

*everyday life as depicted in rituals such as harvesting, ricing,
canoeing, and story telling. His work celebrates healthy, peaceful,
and sustainable living. Carl has created artwork for well over
75 exhibits that are in permanent collections at the Minnesota
Historical Society, the Department of Interior, the Indian Arts and
Crafts Board, and the Fond du Lac Reservation.*

Our story began on one day last spring.
Bears woke from their slumber. Fawns blinked their eyes.
Bees busily buzzed. Loons began to sing.
Frogs croaked. The blue sky danced with dragonflies.

Then, three newborn beaver kits waddled out
from their sheltered home on Amikwiish Lake.
At their parents' nudge, they explored about,
gaining courage with each step they would take.

Each morning, we worked and nurtured the land.
I dug in the dirt, giving seeds a home.
An elder came by to give us a hand.
We built nature trails to wander and roam.

Each day, the beavers worked with the earth.
They helped to build canals, marshes, and bogs.
The kits quickly learned how to mend their hearth,
cleverly using bark, branches, and logs.

Auntie and I walked in the autumn wood
Beneath falling leaves of browns, golds, and reds.
We gathered twigs and logs for firewood,
so we could stay warm in our winter beds.

Across the lake, beavers, too, gathered trees.
And as the days grew short they worked harder.
They chewed and dragged fresh branches with leaves,
then they pulled the wood into their larder.

Outside, the wind blew. The lake was snow-swept.
In the cabin, we were warm with our quilt.
We spoke of the beavers before we slept.
Auntie said, "Remember the lodge they built?

They are safe, snuggling under the ground.
And, the beaver family isn't alone.
Beavers are gracious. They share what they found.
They welcome mice, bugs, and frogs in their home."

The frigid winter thawed to good weather.
"Let's wash the windows!" I said with a grin.
Auntie and I sang and scrubbed together,
cleaning the cabin outside and within.

At the winter's end, out came the beavers.
Like us, they fixed up their home on the lake.
They also worked as waterway builders,
making dams with the branches they would take.

I happ'ly splashed in the water all day.
A dragonfly landed on my wet nose.
"Hey, look how me and Miss Dragonfly play!"
Auntie laughed, as we quickly struck a pose.

The kits swam and dove under the water.
They laid on their backs and looked at the sky.
They rolled around and played with an otter,
then rubbed noses before saying goodbye.

One night, we heard a loud and scary sound.
The next morning, we saw a horrid sight.
The lodge was destroyed, no life to be found.
The beavers were gone. We felt shock and fright.

We sat in silence with sad falling tears.
We searched for words, but our voices were lost.
Our hearts were broken, minds clouding with fears.
The vandals were wrong, yet who paid the cost?

In my worried dreams, I heard beavers cry.
I tossed and turned in the dark of the night.
Could the beavers rebuild? They had to try.
In my dream, I stepped out into moonlight.

I saw the beavers from the sandy shore,
and as I watched them work, my eyes went wide.
Where there had once been five, now there were four
One small beaver was gone. One kit had died.

When she saw the lodge's ruins after she woke,
the elder felt and shared in our distress.
As she folded her aging hands, she spoke.
Our grieved hearts calmed at her voice's caress

For us, the beavers are central to life.
Their hard work gives us water we need.
In the past, beavers have overcome strife.
Only time will tell how their lives proceed.

A blizzard hit. We were safe from the cold.
But, would the beavers' marred lodge keep them warm?
Across the lake's frozen surface we strode,
seeking to know if they survived the storm.

On the lodge a beaver stood 'neath the sky.
As he watched us, I saw how he had thinned.
Our eyes met. He breathed deeply, as did I,
our breath turned into ice mist in the wind.

As nature's flowers took breaths of fresh air,
the elder visited, bearing a gift:
A freshly gnawed birch stick, handled with care.
She had found it as it floated adrift.

We saw beavers toil in falling spring rain.
They gathered food as the flora regrew.
They worked together and lived through the pain,
knowing that nature would bring life anew.

We are connected, all life big and small.
We walk and swim and fly beneath the sun,
sharing this earth, which belongs to us all.
We can't erase the marks of past harms done,

but, like the beavers, from loss may we rise,
and venture forth to live another day
with resilience and love in our eyes.
As we paddled back, I heard myself say, …

"I think we should tell the beavers' story."
We nodded: "Yes, it's something we should share."
As we glided on the lake peacefully,
we hoped people would pause, listen, and care.

Unattended

··· ■ ■ ■ ···

ZARYN PRUSSIA

Zaryn Prussia is a member of the White Earth Band of Ojibwa and a sophomore at Harbor City International School, in Duluth, Minnesota. He attended the Transforming Community Conference in June 2016. While participating in the Environmental discussion group, Zaryn was inspired to write the following poem.

The world has little hope.
Apes ravage all that is green,
So here we meet and cope.
Now the "concerned" condole
And dolefully we mourn for fallen flora,
Ignoring their ineffable cries.
For the plants fail to realize
That we lamenters are busy
Discussing our disgust over industry
In our structures of concrete
Made from stolen minerals and ore
Extracted from far beneath our feet.
In our stone halls we scream, "no more"!
These plants yet still wail.
Do they not understand
That we are more frail?
And though their problem is grand,
Can't they see we are important too?
Our society in the west;
That is the crux, the priority issue.

Willow

■ ■ ■

NICOLE LELAND

This poem represents the life-changing, growth-fostering, and beautiful process I personally experienced while having the honor of working with Dr. Connie Gunderson, the amazing members of the Conference Council, and all of the wonderful people I came across during the conference itself. I saw and felt The Five Good Things come to life and am forever changed. Nicole Leland may be contacted at nleland@css.edu.

Weeping willow swaying in the wind;
    always looking towards the ground.
She reaches down to find her roots,
    but they never can truly be found.
Choices made without her consent;
    she's stuck in this lonely place.
Wishing she had someone of her own,
    a true connection with a soul and a face.

Without her knowledge, the sun so bright,
    nourishes her with endless love.
Dark clouds give up their wondrous flight,
    to rain down delectable droplets from up above.
Children play hide and seek;
    they rest under her green boughs.
Blind to all of these amazing gifts,
    she forgets her earthly vows.

Her every breath is exchanged with another's;
    providing sustenance for life.
Yet, how could she feel so alone,
    filled with such immense sadness and strife.
One day she realized soil connects her to others;
    roots alive or buried deep down.
Each leading to a beautiful relationship
    with incredible souls all around.

Part V

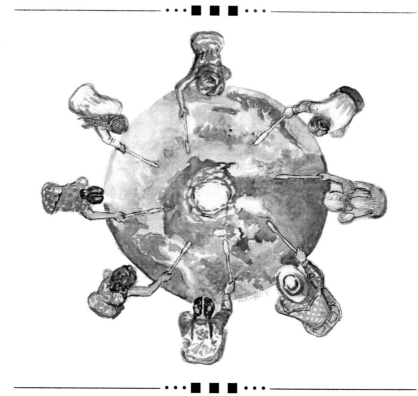

Final Summary

Taking Action to Transform Community with the Radical Reality of Relationship

· · · ■ ■ ■ · · ·

TAYLOR GUNDERSON

Taylor Gunderson is a native Minnesotan and an undergraduate student at Wellesley College. She participated at the Transforming Community Conference as a scribe during discussion groups and undertook the vital role of summarizing the work of the four discussion groups that focused on areas of health/mental health, education, social justice, and environment to present their ideas here for ongoing action to transform communities. Taylor Gunderson may be contacted at tgunders@ wellesley.edu.

In June of 2016, 172 individuals from across the United States and several other countries gathered together in Duluth, Minnesota, to form a new community at the *Transforming Communities: The Radical Reality of Relationship* conference. We explored the transformative nature of Relational-Cultural theory (RCT) within the power of shared stories to address oppression, trauma, human violence, and environmental destruction within our communities and communities across the world. This was a conference of connection. Hands reached out to clasp those of former strangers, smiles were shared, tears were shed, and a better understanding was forged between humans. In our desire to experience the interconnection of all life and to integrate RCT to radically transform community through the power of relationship, we discovered in our discussions that we need to create spaces in which people feel safe to be vulnerable; we need to have empathic listening where all voices can be heard—especially previously silenced or quieted voices; and we need to acknowledge the diversity of language that is necessary for us to understand one another. Furthermore, we agreed on the need to continue the work of this conference by supporting each other and building a network of growth-fostering alliances.

In order to address the continuation of this work, the participants created action plans to build safe spaces within their own communities. Without safe spaces to discuss topics such as race, gender, sexuality, and economic inequality, power dynamics go unaddressed; and the voices of the marginalized are often repressed, silenced, ignored, or not put forth at all for fear of backlash. Vulnerability would be a lot to ask of anybody in that situation; and without vulnerability, it is difficult for positive, productive dialogue to take place. By actively and consciously practicing the principles of RCT in engagements with other people, the conference participants plan to continue to create a wide variety of platforms for discussion, from the local to the digital.

Establishing Safe Places

What do we need to keep in mind when establishing safe spaces? Initially, we need to breathe, pause, and acknowledge power—including our own. Because of the nature of our society, power will always be in play, and the times that we most desire to speak and have the power to do so are often the best times to step back and allow others to speak. We must be proactive in this in order to fairly share the finite amount of space in any productive and focused discourse. Whether we are connecting face-to-face or through an online platform, we need to provide space for people to find and be their authentic selves—including coping in whatever way is most healing, soothing, and helpful for them. With that in mind, we need to help people honor their strategies of disconnection as a survival mechanism—rather than something they should feel shame for—so they can move on towards future healing and growth.

Mutual Empathy

Honoring each person's truth is essential for respectful communication and mutual empathy. Mutual empathy means being supportive and meeting people where they are at while remaining open to possibly very different—and potentially conflicting—beliefs. In order to have productive dialogues, we can model vulnerability by taking healthy risks in empathetically exploring differences and commonalities within shared stories. Without witnessing others' stories, we remain ignorant of them. Ignorance can beget fear, which in turn can fester hatred that may move our society towards further polarization. We need to overcome our fear of the unknown and learn to tolerate difference to promote respectful dialogue in the effort to foster mutual empathy. Instead of balking when we encounter seemingly stratifying difference, we need to be willing to examine and question our own dearly held beliefs to try to see issues from multiple perspectives. When it appears that the parties in a dialogue come from different worlds or completely different walks of life with different vocabularies and different methods of storytelling, we must work towards establishing mutual languages that are accessible to all and transcend cultural, political, and academic boundaries.

Action Plans for Creating Safe Places

With the aforementioned group consensus pertaining to the establishment of safe spaces in mind, the conference participants put forth the following action plans that they would strive to complete, either as an individual or supported by their communities. Among many excellent ideas, the set below involves bringing RCT to specific physical spaces within their communities.

Community actions.

Specific plans included:

- Create and sponsor dialogue sessions in the Duluth community.
- Become involved in an inter-religious forum of Duluth and attend the fall conference on cultural differences in healthcare delivery.
- Seek to develop compassionate housing in Duluth.
- Attend the Future of Chicago Conference next week and be a social work anti-gun, anti-racism voice.
- Attend an anti-racist action group in Seattle.
- Challenge the local church community to break with the status quo and be more accepting towards the LGBTQIA+ community.
- Continue the actions on white privilege that were started at last year's conference, as well as publish and share the work with others.

Broader actions.

Upon recognizing how important space is, the participants discussed various scales of spaces affected by power dynamics. An example of small scale space: public transportation, upon which women often hold their limbs close as their personal space is invaded, in contrast to men, who often sit with their legs splayed to claim space. An observation about larger-scale space: the media, in which white cis-gender men greatly outnumber women, especially women of color, both behind the scenes and onscreen. An observation on an even broader scale: the United States government, in which white heterosexual cis-male Christians dominate political seats of power both on state and national congressional levels. This disparity of space and representation needs to be addressed so that marginalized voices can express their power and share their stories in order to promote constructive, community-transformative, mutually empathetic dialogue.

Implementing their action plans, conference participants seek to claim physical space within their professional and community circles in an effort to expand awareness of different voices long-silenced or ignored by current powerful groups—claiming their right to exist and be heard.

Ways to Connect as People

Face-to-Face and Digital Connection

Conference participants emphasized the importance of face-to-face conversations. When humans see each other and take in the emotional expression on another person's face, they share a new level of empathy through the firing of mirror neurons. This experience is poignant and invaluable. However, face-to-face conversations in the same physical space are not always possible, and they are not the only form of valuable and productive communication. Emailing, texting, tweeting, blogging, Tumblr groups, Facebook pages, and Internet resources in general can promote the sharing of stories, information, and opinions with those at a distance. Today's and tomorrow's technology provide an opportunity to expand current communities, build new communities, and share stories in new and more accessible ways. That is why participants proposed to also bring RCT to virtual platforms to establish safe spaces in the digital realm. They suggested:

- Practice empathetic listening and engaging in dialogue on social media.
- Create intentional communities to support each other in learning, accountability, and practice by establishing regular face-to-face online/teleconference, and/or RCT satellite groups that focus on specific areas of interest or practice.

Workplace Connection

More and more, effective computer skills and digital communication are required in the workplace—another area that can feel the strain of a lack of healthy communication and the unhealthy implementation of power structures. RCT can be utilized to create healthier, more efficient workplaces, specifically in the field of social work. With the stress of everyday life, we sometimes forget to take time to breathe, listen to our co-workers, and see them as humans with skills and needs. Those who proposed the following action plans seek to create healthier professional communities in which employees can thrive, and thus better provide for those they serve.

- Form with colleagues an RCT consultation group for supervisors.
- Propose that staff have an understanding of RCT.
- Show coworkers and clients that they and their stories matter.
- Establish a college/university social work club.

Education Connection

Along with creating a positive professional social work community, conference participants heavily focused on another vocation—that of education. They discussed how school years are the formative years of young citizens' lives. What children experience during childhood can potentially affect their mental health and standard of living for the rest of their lives. Just like vulnerability can be modeled, so can healthy relationship. The education of youth is the foundation upon which our society's future will be built, so it is essential that children learn not only a breadth of academic knowledge, but that they also are nurtured with demonstrated healthy relationships that will encourage them to pursue similarly healthy relationships as their lives unfold.

While it has been traditional for the teacher to dominate classroom discussion with one-way lectures, allowing children the space to speak and move promotes healthy dialogue as well as healthier bodies. When their creative ideas are heard and acknowledged in a positive way, children feel that they matter. Such early experiences may encourage them to share their stories more confidently as they grow and mature. Participants agreed that children are, quite literally, our future; they need to be respected and provided with safe spaces that promote healthy relationships that impact their families, communities, and future generations. Educators in the discussion groups proposed the following action plans:

- Intentionally integrate RCT into the overarching framework and structure of the teacher education courses.
- Use the framework of RCT to hold space and facilitate dialogue between the two approaches to deaf education to better take student needs into account.
- Teach "mattering" to teachers since all children need to know they matter.
- Use RCT principles to help create ways for students to discover their own realities of who they are.

Personal Connection

Conference participants spoke of bringing RCT to other conferences across the country, into the vast online world, into their hometowns, into their churches, into their workplaces, and into their classrooms—all goals that will affect a large number of people. Beyond this, though, they did not forget that the smallest interaction— whether it is a smile between friends, an offered hand to strangers, and act of ally-ship, or a simple kind word—can also make a little difference with a potentially big effect. They reported plans to:

- Make a connection with an elderly neighbor at home.
- Say hello to and bring a gift to neighbors.
- Share the knowledge gained here with family at home.
- Create RCT dialogue sessions at home and with family.

Summarizing Suggestion for Connection

One conference participant who seemed to understand and encompass the core values of RCT proposed the following—something that we might all strive towards as we live our lives to the fullest, work to tear down walls that divide us, and build bridges that have never before been forged. She stated:

> I will continue to live and teach Relational-Cultural theory as a way of life—a foundation of who I am in relation to the world around me—with others, within myself, at work, home, in the community, embracing and acknowledging the power of love, connection, mutuality, empathy, and vulnerability.

WholePerson

Whole Person Associates is the leading publisher of training resources for professionals who empower people to create and maintain healthy lifestyles. Our creative resources will help you work effectively with your clients in the areas of stress management, wellness promotion, mental health, and life skills.

Please visit us at our web site: **WholePerson.com**. You can check out our entire line of products, place an order, request our print catalog, and sign up for our monthly special notifications.

Whole Person Associates
800-247-6789
Books@WholePerson.com

CPSIA information can be obtained
at www.ICGtesting.com
Printed in the USA
FFOW02n0652131017
41070FF